Theories and Methods of an Integrative Transactional Analysis

Theories and Methods
of an Integrative
Transactional Analysis

A Volume of Selected Articles

By Richard G. Erskine

TA Press
San Francisco

Printed in the United States of America

09 08 07 06 05 04 03 02 01 00   5 4 3 2

ISBN 0-89489-004-2

Published by TA Press
436 14th St., Suite 1301
Oakland, California 94612-2710, U.S.A.
Phone: 510-625-7720
Fax: 510-625-7725
email: itaa@itaa-net.org

Contents

TRANSACTIONAL ANALYSIS IN ACTION

―――――――――

Introduction

These articles on theory, commentary, clinical observations, and psychotherapy methods represent years of thinking about both Eric Berne's writings and the contributions of other transactional analysts to the theory and practice of psychotherapy. Based on an avid interest in comparative philosophy and theory and my training in other schools of psychotherapy, these articles offer an integrative contribution to the literature on transactional analysis in psychotherapy. The collection in this volume spans the publication years 1974-1997. I am honored that you, the reader, are interested in these ideas, some of which were published many years ago.

In this collection you will read my attempts to solve theoretical confusions or inconsistencies and my ever-evolving understanding of human functioning and therapeutic involvement. In each article I grapple with a theoretical or pragmatic question and attempt to define what the psychotherapy profession knows, what the client needs, and what we as therapists provide. I invite you to share in my professional journey and to expand on the therapeutic experiences and methods presented here so that together we may evolve an even more effective psychotherapy.

The articles are organized to emphasize a contact-based, developmentally oriented relationship therapy that is the hallmark of an integrative transactional analysis. The term "integrative" as it is used in these articles has several meanings. It refers to the process of integrating the personality: helping the client to become aware of and assimilate the content of his or her ego states, to develop a sense of self that decreases the need for defense mechanisms and a life script, and to reengage the world and relationships with full contact. It also refers to the process of making whole: taking disowned, unaware, unresolved aspects of the ego and making them part of a cohesive self. Through integration, it becomes possible for people to have the courage to face each moment openly and anew, without the protection of a preformed opinion, position, attitude, or expectation.

"Integrative" also refers to the integration of theory, the bringing together of affective, cognitive, behavioral, physiological, and systems approaches to psychotherapy. The concepts are used within a perspective on human development in which each phase of life presents developmental tasks, need sensitivities, crises, and opportunities for new learning. Integrative transactional analysis takes into account many views of human functioning: psychodynamic, client-centered, behavioral, family therapy, Gestalt therapy, Reichian-influenced body psychotherapy, object relations theories, psychoanalytic self psychology, and, primarily, Eric Berne's theoretical concepts and ideas. Each of the theories provides a valid explanation of behavior and each is enhanced when selectively integrated with the others. Psychotherapeutic interventions are based on knowledge of normal development and the theories describing the self-protective defensive processes used when there are interruptions in normal development.

I hope that you, the reader, will gain a new perspective and renewed enthusiasm that will find its way into your practice and somehow enrich your clients' lives and the lives of those with whom they interact. In writing these articles I have grown both personally and professionally. I have gained much through the collegial relationships with coauthors and the people I have trained and supervised. Most importantly, I have learned from my clients about the significance of contact-in-relationship and the importance of repairing the relationship when there have been disruptions in contact.

I owe a great deal to Rebecca L. Trautmann, R.N., M.S.W., my wife and psychotherapy partner. We spend countless hours discussing theory, reviewing our successes and failures with clients, reading and critiquing the psychotherapy literature, and exploring how to practice and teach psychotherapy better. When I first watched Rebecca practice psychotherapy in the early 1970s I was struck by the way in which she continually focused on the therapist-client relationship with a strong emphasis on child development. Over the years it has been her influence more than any other that has shaped the theory and methods of integrative transactional analysis.

I want to express my thanks to Robin Fryer, M.S.W., for many years of careful editing. It was her hard work that saw this project to fruition. Her dedication to the refinement of the transactional analysis literature is appreciated by all of us who write for and read the *Transactional Analysis Journal,* for which she serves as managing editor. I also want to thank Sally Hyatt, M.F.A., who as reference editor for the *TAJ* has corrected citations in many of my *Journal* articles. She also did the index for this volume and redid some of the older figures.

This collection of articles includes most of my transactional analysis publications; it illustrates the ever-changing ideas as well as the continuities in theory and therapeutic approach in our profession of psychotherapy. In fact, if these ideas are still credible and stand up to further learning and professional scrutiny 20 or 30 years from now, I'll be surprised. In the intervening years since writing many of these articles I have also learned a great deal from reading a wide range of literature and from my ongoing training, supervision, and personal therapy. As I review this collection I am embarrassed by some of what I wrote years ago. Yet these articles represent my efforts to express what I understood at the time, to put the ideas in writing, and to address a particular audience.

The writing of each article was an attempt either to solve a theoretical problem or to clarify and refine methods; it was a confrontation with what I did not understand, failed to express, or tended to accept without thinking. Usually by the time an article was in press I had gained another perspective that clarified or refined what I had just written. I invite you to share in my discoveries, mistakes, and attempts to improve clinical practice.

There is no smooth road with regard to professional growth—bumps, holes, and sharp curves confront us at every turn. Yet I am compelled by a continual commitment to learning how to facilitate the welfare of each client. A guiding principle of this contact-oriented, relationship-based psychotherapy is that of honoring the integrity of the client. Through respect, kindness, compassion, and validating contact we establish a personal presence and allow for an interpersonal relationship that provides affirmation of the individual's integrity.

The articles in this volume are organized somewhat in reverse order of publication. The first section, "Processes and Methods of an Integrative Transactional Analysis," begins with "The Therapeutic Relationship: Integrating Motivation and Personality Theories." This article describes the theoretical ground on which the relationship-oriented methods are based. The second article, "Methods of an Integrative Psychotherapy," delineates how Rebecca Trautmann and I practice a psychotherapy of gentle inquiry into the client's experience; attunement to the client's rhythm, affect, and developmental level of functioning; responsiveness to relational needs; and a respectful involvement with another unique and whole person. Importantly, this article describes eight relational needs that require a reciprocal response from others. These needs are present throughout the life cycle, at every developmental age.

These methods are further illustrated in an essay entitled "Inquiry, Attunement, and Involvement in the Psychotherapy of Dissociation" and in "Shame and Self-Righteousness: Transactional Analysis Perspectives and Clinical Interventions." These are followed by "The Dynamics of Shame: A Roundtable Discussion" and "A Relationship Therapy: Developmental Perspectives." The first section concludes with "The Process of Integrative Psychotherapy," an article that was begun in 1987 and that summarizes our analysis, transaction-by-transaction, of the transcripts of recorded therapy sessions. The terms "inquiry," "attunement," and "involvement" were used to describe the methods of an integrative transactional analysis.

"The Structure of the Ego" is the theme of section two, which begins with an article entitled "Ego State Analysis: A Comparative View." Coauthored with Rebecca Trautmann, this article takes a comparative view of ego state analysis. This section continues with a definitive article, "Ego Structure, Intrapsychic Function, and Defense Mechanisms: A Commentary on Eric Berne's Original Theoretical Concepts," which elaborates Berne's original theoretical concepts of the ego and states of the ego. This is followed by "Ego State Theory: Definitions, Descriptions, and Points of View," the write-up of a conference panel. Then, "Transference and Transactions: Critique from an Intrapsychic and Integrative Perspective" provides a pragmatic base for applying Berne's conceptual model of ego states in clinical practice. Finally, "Fourth-Degree Impasse" builds on the three types of impasse described by Robert Goulding in 1974 and is a mere outline of what should be a much more elaborate article. The concepts contained in it are the theoretical base for an in-depth psychotherapy of the Parent ego state described in *Integrative Psychotherapy in Action*, coauthored with Janet Moursund, Ph.D. (originally published in 1988 by Sage Publications; republished in 1997 by The Gestalt Journal Press, Highland, NY).

"Life Scripts" is the overall theme of section three. The first article, "Script Cure: Behavioral, Intrapsychic, and Physiological," lays the theoretical foundation for intrapsychic analysis and is the basis for "The Racket System: A Model for Racket Analysis," written with Marilyn Zalcman. It was for this article that Marilyn Zalcman and I received the Eric Berne Memorial Scientific Award in 1982 for adding intrapsychic analysis as a major concept in transactional analysis theory. My award speech, "The Ultimate Psychological Concern: Nuclear War," follows. "Identification and Cure of Stroke Rip-Off" and "Transactional Analysis and Family Therapy" elaborate the use of the interlocking racket system with couples and families. The other articles in this section are examples of specific perspectives in script analysis.

The last section, "Transactional Analysis in Action," includes a potpourri of articles on supervision, treatment, and education. Many of these articles reflect the excitement of the growing theory and use of transactional analysis in a variety of settings during the 1970s. The initial article, "Supervision of Psychotherapy: Models for Professional Development," ties together the theme that runs through the first three sections of this collection on integrative transactional analysis: "Healing is in the relationship."

Each evening for a week, after a training workshop, I have been rereading the articles in this volume while sitting outdoors watching the midnight sunset over northern Sweden. I have traveled for many years teaching and refining the concepts outlined in these articles. Yet as I read them once again I realize that the written words do not adequately express the aliveness and vitality of these concepts and methods; that is done much better when they are presented in a workshop or applied in clinical practice. I can only hope that you, the reader, will sense the emotions that accompany what is written here.

When at home in Kent, Connecticut, I am an avid gardener. I've surrounded the pond and woodland paths with a multitude of flowers, both hybrid and wild. I love to mix wild flowers with horticultural hybrids to create a muted transition from the more formal gardens to the natural landscape. I aim to create an uninterrupted visual experience that integrates the woodlands, open fields, lawns, and flower beds. So, too, with my teaching and writing about psychotherapy. I have attempted to integrate my own ideas, perspectives, and understandings—the wild flowers—with the hybrid theories borrowed from a long succession of teachers and writers. A perusal of the reference lists will identify many authors whose "flowers" are growing in my garden. Many individuals have stimulated my thinking and challenged my assumptions. Yet, what seems most important in retrospect is that the cited authors have often provided the words and concepts that verified my "wild flowers." Ideas that I thought were uniquely my own I frequently find "growing" in the words of others. Their "hybrid" theories often grow in harmony when selectively planted with my flowering weeds. I transplant the "hybrid" theories and methods, experiment with growing conditions, and occasionally generate a cross-pollinated species.

Although many of the ideas presented in these pages may be familiar in another "garden," it is the unique arrangement here that makes these articles original. In the practice and teaching of psychotherapy, as with my garden, I am awed by which plants flower each year, how each year the growth and flowering patterns change, and by the continual challenge to create an integrated sense of beauty.

I welcome you to stroll with me through this garden of ideas, to take some seeds or cuttings to plant in your own unique way, and while you are here, to pick some flowers to take to your clients and loved ones.

Richard Erskine
June 1997

Part 1

Processes and Methods of an Integrative Transactional Analysis

The Therapeutic Relationship:
Integrating Motivation and Personality Theories

Richard G. Erskine

Eric Berne's writings have provided psychotherapists with a rich and thorough understanding of human behavior, psychological functioning, and communication. The concepts of ego states and intrapsychic processes, transactions and transference, and psychological games and life scripts are each a subset of a comprehensive transactional analysis theory of personality. These theoretical concepts dominate and shape an orientation to the clinical practice of transactional analysis by affecting our understanding of behavior and determining the method of intervention. Inherent in the integration of transactional analysis theories of personality and theory of motivation is a theory of method that emphasizes the importance of relationship.

Berne (1961, 1963, 1966, 1970, 1972) identified a transactional analysis theory of motivation when he wrote about human drives that he termed stimulus hunger, structure hunger, and recognition hunger. However, in spite of articulating these motivational factors, he based his methods of psychotherapy and communication exclusively on his personality theories, originally on ego states and emanating transactions (Berne, 1961, 1966) and later on the theory of life script (Berne, 1972). In fact, overall the transactional analysis literature has underemphasized the importance of a theory of motivation and the application of such a theory to forming both theories of personality and theories of method.

Berne (1966) applied his theory of ego states and transferential transactions in clinical practice when he asserted that the client will present his or her "past experiences in coded form to the therapist, and the therapist's task is to decode and detoxify them, rectify distortions, and help the patient regroup the experience" (pp. 242-243). This statement regarding the therapist's task is an organizing principle that serves to guide therapeutic interventions. Berne's eight therapeutic operations—interrogation, specification, explanation, confrontation, confirmation, interpretation, illustration, and crystallization—are the specific methods he used to decontaminate ego states, deconfuse a fixated Child ego state, and decommission an influencing Parent ego state (Berne, 1966, pp. 233-247).

This set of methods or therapeutic operations is a direct outgrowth of Berne's psychoanalytic background and original theory of ego states (1961) as derived from Federn's (1953) concept of the ego and states of the ego. Although Berne did not directly relate these methods to a theory of motivation, his personality theory of the structuring or fragmenting of the ego into separate states is consistent with the idea that there is a dynamic interplay between structure hunger and relationship (recognition) hunger. Berne's eight therapeutic operations apply to the original application of his conceptual model of ego states (Erskine, 1988). Other descriptions of ego states, such as second-order, functional, and structural

(Trautmann & Erskine, 1981) lack a theory of methods and are not related to a theory of motivation.

The transactional analysis literature pertaining to script theory contains much that is concerned with the historical origin of an individual's personality (Berne, 1972; Steiner, 1974) with a focus on parental programming (Steiner, 1971), decisions (Goulding & Goulding, 1979), conclusions (English, 1977), and survival reactions (Erskine, 1980). Writings about the elements of scripts, that is, games and miniscripts (Berne, 1964; Kahler with Capers, 1974), are also descriptions of a theory of personality. Berne's methods for the treatment of script consisted of the confrontation of the programmed script, cognitive explanation, interpreting the function, contracting for change, and permission to change (Berne, 1972).

Additionally, the transactional analysis literature is rich with an eclectic variety of psychotherapy methods, such as reparenting and self-reparenting (James, 1974; Osnes, 1974; Schiff, 1969); behavioral options (Dusay, 1972; Karpman, 1971); redecision, rubberbands, and disconnecting rubberbands (Erskine, 1974; Goulding & Goulding, 1979; Kupfer & Haimowitz, 1971); permission and protection (Allen & Allen, 1972; Crossman, 1966; Holloway, 1974); and the treatment of introjected Parent ego states (Dashiell, 1978; Erskine & Moursund, 1988). Erskine (1975, 1980, 1982; Erskine & Moursund, 1988) proposed a methodological orientation to script cure that integrates affective, behavioral, cognitive, and physiological therapeutic interventions, with specific interventions determined by where the client is open or closed to contact. Ware (1983) and Joines (1988) applied this orientation to selecting methods suitable for clients with disorders falling into specific diagnostic categories.

A review of articles in the *Transactional Analysis Journal* from 1971 to the present reveals that most writers followed Berne's emphasis on theories that categorize or describe behavior and that explain personality dynamics. Their contributions to the transactional analysis literature are a clarification, elaboration, and enrichment of descriptions, classifications, personality theories, and specific therapeutic interventions. Reading the literature just cited shows that most of the writing on the practice of transactional analysis in psychotherapy bases a specific method on personality theory: There is a need for a theory of methods that emerges from the integration of personality and motivation theories. The thesis of this article is that the practice of transactional analysis will be enhanced by a consistent and unified theoretical link between motivation and personality theories, from which methods are directly derived (Trautmann & Erskine, 1995).

Integrating Motivation, Personality, and Method

Theories of motivation provide a metaperspective that encompasses theories of personality. A theory of motivation determines which theories of personality can be integrated and which are conceptually inconsistent and do not integrate into a unified, comprehensive theory of human functioning. When theories of motivation and personality have an internal validity and consistency, they work together as a conceptual organization for a unified theory of method.

To be consistent, a theory of method must emerge from corresponding theories of human motivation and personality. The integration of Berne's theories of personality (ego states and life scripts) and his theory of drives or hungers (stimulus, structure, and recognition) provides such a unified understanding of human functioning. This integration of personality and motivation theories explains individuals' intrapsychic and interpersonal dynamics and leads to a theory of method that is consistent with both a theory of motivation and theories of personality.

Methods are the actual interventions that are used in psychotherapy practice. They are reproducible; that is, a therapist can model a specific intervention and another therapist can learn to create a somewhat similar intervention. A theory of method provides an understanding of how methods may be designed. It provides an orientation to the practice of psychotherapy, a therapeutic stance: supportive, analytic, relational, or replacement (Trautmann, 1981). One such methodological orientation is the premise that *healing occurs through the use of a therapeutic relationship that focuses on enhancing internal and external contact*. This provides both an overall framework from which specific methods are designed and a conceptual beacon that serves as a guide to the therapist in the continual monitoring of observations, theories, hypotheses, and specific interventions (Erskine, 1982).

Overview of Motivation, Personality, and Method in Other Schools of Psychotherapy

In classical psychoanalytic theory, motivation consists of the drives referred to as libido, aggression, and morbido. Id, ego, and superego comprise the structural theory. Conscious, preconscious, and subconscious are the strata of the topographic theory, the divisions of the human mind defined by Freud. Together these elements constitute the personality theory. The theory of method is composed of nongratification, neutrality, and interpretation in response to free association.

Beginning with Fairbairn's (1952), Guntrip's (1961, 1968, 1971), and Bowlby's (1969, 1973, 1980) writings on object relations theory, the psychoanalytic understanding of human motivation shifted from Freud's drive theory to an understanding that humans are motivated to seek attachment and relationship. Internalized object representations, split objects, and true and false selves are constructs of this updated psychoanalytic theory of personality. The playful use of free association, encouraging the client's expression of true self, and the therapist's countertransferential process are elements of its therapeutic methods (Bollas, 1987; Tustin, 1986; Winnicott, 1965).

In the concepts of psychoanalytic self psychology people are thought to be motivated by self experience to form selfobjects whose function is to provide continuity, stability, and nurturance to the self. The personality theory of self psychology centers on the effects of the adequacy or failure of selfobject functions. Its methods have centered on empathy and interpretation (Kohut, 1977) and recently on the intersubjective experience of both client and therapist (Stolorow, Brandchaft, & Atwood, 1987).

In client-centered therapy the central organizing construct is Rogers's (1951) premise that people require unconditional positive regard. When the core conditions of unconditional positive regard, accurate empathy, and congruence are provided, people express themselves and grow. Rogers's ideas emerged from Sullivan's (1953) interpersonal therapy, which emphasized the importance of person-to-person communication, rather than being based on a theory of personality.

The behaviorist theory of motivation revolves around the cycle of stimulus-response. Personality is considered to be the result of learned behavioral patterns, and therapy methods consist of arranging operants and contingencies (Bandura, 1969; Dollard & Miller, 1950).

In Gestalt therapy theory humans are motivated by both the urge for organism-environment contact and the drive to organize experience, that is, to form gestalten (Perls, 1944). Personality theory emerges out of an understanding of interruptions to contact and fixed gestalten. The theory of methods emphasizes experimentation that produces excitation and growth at the contact boundary of the organism-environment field (Perls, Hefferline, & Goodman, 1951).

Within transactional analysis, English (1977, 1987, 1988) introduced a unique perspective on personality theory related to motivation that she refers to as "existential patterns." Her personality theory emerges from three primary drives: survival, expressive, and quiescence. English (1987) equates Berne's stimulus hunger to the expressive drive and recognition hunger to the survival drive. She does not refer to Berne's ideas on structure hunger, although she does see individual personality or character as formed by a "defensive existential position, which develops around age three" (p. 93). English does not propose a theory of psychotherapy method; her approach is informative and concerned with how "drive[s] interact, to what extent one inhibits the other, [and]. . . what support or interference the third offers" (1988, p. 296).

Steiner (1974) emphasized a method of psychotherapy that focused on the importance of strokes and permission. Scripts were seen as the outgrowth of the drive or hunger for strokes. His theory emphasized the deprivation and manipulation of strokes as a method of social control that produced individuals with mindless, loveless, and joyless scripts.

Berne's Theory of Motivation

As described earlier, the foundation for a theory of motivation was laid by Berne (1966) when he wrote about psychological hunger as that which "drives an individual to social action" (p. 230). He categorized drives as the hunger for stimulus, structure, and relationship. These hungers or drives of the human organism operate nonconsciously. The hungers are the motivations determining physiological, affective, cognitive, and behavioral responses.

Berne (1961, 1963, 1964, 1966, 1970, 1972) was consistent in his description of *stimulus hunger* as the basic need or drive of the human organism. He described stimulus hunger as originating in the reticular activating system of the brain stem and how such "hunger" requires constant stimulation. Berne (1964) cited Spitz's writing on hospitalism and related "emotional deprivation" to the lack of sufficient stimulation.

Structure hunger, according to Berne, is a "psychological need" (1963, p. 221) involved in the organization of "perceptual experiences" (1972, p. 22). He identified the derivatives of structure hunger as leadership hunger (1963, 1966) and incident hunger, which are respectively the driving force in games and scripts (1970). Berne (1966) elaborated the concept of structure hunger into a six-order taxonomy of time structuring: withdrawal, ritual, pastimes, activities, games, and intimacy.

Throughout his writings Berne referred to the urge for interpersonal relationships or *relationship hunger* as "a hunger for human contact" (1970, p. 208). He variously referred to the drive for relationships as tactile hunger (1966), recognition hunger (1970, 1972), and the need for verbal recognition (1970). Since relationships emerge from "the quest for special kinds of sensations that can only be supplied by another human being" (1972, p. 21), each of these various descriptions of human motivation may be generalized as a hunger or drive for relationship.

Berne often interwove the concepts of stimulus, structure, and relationship hungers. He described the interactive influence of stimulus, structure, and relationship hungers, yet inadvertently clouded the distinction between them. Berne (1961) initially described stimulus hunger as "represented by physical relationship" (p. 84). He explained the merged concepts of stimulus hunger and recognition hunger as the "original craving for physical contact" (1964, p. 14) with "a partial transformation of infantile stimulus-hunger into something that may be termed *recognition hunger*" (p. 14). Recognition hunger is referred to as "the first order sublimation" of stimulus hunger (Berne, 1961, p. 84). The satisfying stimuli in Berne's examples are provided by another person who makes physical contact or recognizes an individual, as when he describes "tactile hunger" as emerging from the physical intimacy, tactile recognition, and stimulation given by the mother to a young child (1966, p. 282). Berne also referred to an adult's version of the infant's need to be touched as "recognition hunger" (1966, p. 230).

In Berne's (1964) words, "structure-hunger has the same survival value as stimulus-hunger" and yet it is unique in that its function is to establish equilibrium (p. 18). He (1966) later wrote, "Structure hunger expresses the antipathy to monotony, stereotyping, and boredom" (p. 230); "The everyday problem of the human being is the structure of his waking hours" (1961, p. 85). Berne (1970) also defined structure hunger as the reason people play games. In the *Hello* book he (1972) stated, "The need to structure time is based on three drives or hungers. . . . Stimulus or sensation hunger, . . . recognition hunger, the quest for special kinds of sensations which can only be supplied by another human being . . . [and] structure hunger," a hunger for "perceptual experience" (pp. 21-22). He (1966) called these hungers "particular needs" (p. 230) and described them as the basis for a taxonomy of time structuring. Intimacy, he asserted, is the "only completely satisfying answer to stimulus-hunger, recognition-hunger, and structure-hunger" (1964, p. 18).

Unfortunately, by writing about hungers as an introduction to his concepts of time structure Berne did not emphasize how the concept of stimulus, structure, and relationship hungers form a significant theory of motivation. He did not fully develop how these drives are related to ego states, intrapsychic processes, transactions, and life scripts. It is ironic that this theory of motivation, for which Berne did not claim (nor was he given) particular credit, can now be shown to encompass and give organization to his overall understanding of personality.

An Integrative Theory of Motivation

The human drive or hunger for stimulus is necessary for survival. Stimuli operate both internally and externally and provide the informational feedback system that leads to the satisfaction of basic needs. The survival needs for oxygen, water, food—as well as psychological and relational needs—all begin with awareness of a discomfort or a deficit. As biological and psychological processes come to awareness a person must also become aware of the environment that can supply the resources for survival.

To satisfy that which is needed, the organism must make contact not only with its internal sensations and needs but also with the external environment. Survival and quality of life are ensured through the continual moment-by-moment interplay between internal and external stimuli and the capacity to make full contact both internally and externally. Stimulus hunger is satisfied through the interaction of the central nervous system and the proprioceptive organs. Our *sensory system provides us with an orientation* (Perls, 1973, p. 17) that makes external and internal contact possible. Full contact is essential for life—it satisfies the biological drive for stimuli that influences and regulates the drives for structure and relationship.

Structure hunger is the drive to organize experience, to form perceptual configurations—visually, auditorily, tactilely, and kinesthetically. The experimental Gestalt psychologists demonstrated that there is an innate drive to form perceptual patterns and configurations (Kohler, 1938; Lewin, 1938). The drive to structure perceptual configurations and the inevitability of figure-ground formation create and organize pattern, meaning, and predictability in our lives. This, in turn, makes concept formation, categorization, and language possible.

The formation of perceptual configurations refers not only to auditory or visual patterns—such as the recognition of a familiar sound or the meaning in these written words—but also to tactile and kinesthetic patterns such as the habitual tightening of muscles in response to fear or anger. Stern (1985) referred to the three-day-old infant's capacity to form an olfactory configuration that allows the baby to turn his or her head toward the smell of breast milk from his or her own mother rather than in the direction of milk from another woman.

This innate tendency to structure configurations that create meaning and predictability and to organize the continuity of experience over time also provides the possibility for perceptual variability and the creation of new organization and meaning. It is only because we form perceptual patterns that it is also possible to perceive novelty, variation, and contrast (Perls, Hefferline, & Goodman, 1951).

Both continuity and variability in perception are necessary for stimulus hunger and relational hunger to be satisfied. If there is a disruption in the structuring (figure-ground formation) of sensations or perceptions then there will also be a disruption in the full processing of internal and external stimuli and/or the satisfaction of relationship hunger. Thus, the drive to organize and generalize patterns of experience (structure hunger) regulates the satisfaction of both stimulus and relationship hungers.

A growing body of literature supports the premise that people are born relationship-seeking and continue patterns of bonding and attachment throughout life (see Erskine, 1989 for a review of the literature). Stern's (1985) compilation of research on infant development supports the idea that the infant's and young child's sense of self emerges through interpersonal relationships. In addition, authors writing from a feminist perspective on psychotherapy emphasize the centrality of interpersonal connection and relationship in the formation of a healthy sense of self in both females and males (Bergman, 1991; Miller, 1986; Surrey, 1985). Sullivan's (1953) interpersonal theory also places central importance on establishing and maintaining relationships. Recent writings in Gestalt therapy have emphasized the importance of a dialogical, healing relationship (Hycner & Jacobs, 1995; Yontef, 1993). Each of these theorists described a developmental thrust for relationship.

Relationship hunger is the drive for intimacy. Berne's "recognition hunger" (1964, p. 14), "tactile hunger" (1966, p. 282), and "contact hunger" (1970, p. 210) all describe an aspect of the motivation for person-to-person connection. As he wrote, "A striving for intimacy underlies the most intense and important operations" (Berne, 1963, p. 217).

Relationships are built on interpersonal contact that includes the stimulus of physical touch and a valuing recognition by another person of an individual's being and attributes. Relationships provide the experience from which the configuration of a sense of self, of others, and of the quality of life emerge. Although relationships are built on the stimulus of moment-by-moment verbal and nonverbal transactions, they also reflect the drive to structure pattern and meaning from an individual's whole history of interpersonal experiences. Satisfaction of relationship hunger depends on the awareness of relational needs (internal stimulus), what the individual believes about self and others in the interpersonal relationships (structure), and the behavior of the other person in the relationship (external stimulus).

Relationship hunger is affected by and influences the drives for stimulus and structure. When an individual's hunger for relationship is repeatedly not met by a reciprocal response from another person, the individual may overgeneralize and rigidify the conclusions drawn from this experience. The conclusions and decisions are an attempt to make sense of the cumulative rupture in relationship and thus make it (temporarily) bearable. From a perspective of transactional analysis theories of personality, the compensating structure can be viewed as splitting the ego into various Child or Parent states, making script decisions, or fantasizing and collecting selective evidence that reinforces script beliefs.

If the drive to structure experience does not compensate for a lack of need-fulfilling relationship, the drive for stimulus may be employed in its place. The compensating drive for stimulus may be manifested as emotional escalation or physical agitation or, conversely, as disavowal of affect, desensitization, or dissociation. Anxious obsessing is one of many examples of psychological phenomena in which stimulus hunger and structure hunger are both used as overcompensation for a lack of fulfillment of relationship hunger. As already described, the three hungers or drives are in dynamic balance: Any disruption in one of the hungers causes an overcompensation in at least one of the others. More specifically, the drives for stimulus and for structure, on the one hand, and relationship hunger on the other, are interactive: The satisfaction of one hunger or drive is affected by the satisfaction—or nonsatisfaction—of another.

A Theory of Methods

Transactional analysis has lacked an explicit and comprehensive theory of method emerging from the integration of motivation and personality theories with a focus on relationship. Its clinical application has been influenced primarily by its theories of personality, particularly the theory of ego states and life scripts. These theories describe the excessive reliance on structuring (scripts, ego states, etc.) to compensate for relationship hunger and the loss of awareness of internal stimuli. The overstructuring results from an individual's loss of internal contact in an attempt to cope with repeated disruptions of relationships. For example, the development of an unconscious life plan composed of fixated core beliefs about self, others, and the quality of life is a defensive organization of experience: It impedes awareness of both relational needs and the affect resulting from the absence of satisfaction of those needs (Erskine & Zalcman, 1979). It results in inhibiting spontaneity and limiting flexibility in problem solving and relating to people (Erskine, 1980). The theory of ego states also depicts a person's fragmentation or splitting off of a sense of "I" in an attempt to cope with either specific disruptions in significant relationships or the cumulative lack of fulfillment of relational needs (Lourie, 1996). Each of the subtheories within transactional analysis, such as games or miniscript, is a further explanation of psychological overstructuring and resulting behavior.

When the psychotherapist emphasizes only cognitive or behavioral change—such as confronting games or rackets, programming a redecision or OK miniscript, or determining how a person should behave or think—then the process of psychotherapy emphasizes replacing one overused and rigid structure with another. Instead, the use of methods that enhance increased awareness of internal stimuli (needs, sensations, memory, etc.) and the significance of interpersonal relationships increases the possibility of new meanings and understandings that may not be rigid or overstructured. The use of methods that integrate the affective, cognitive, and physiological domains of human functioning with the behavioral domain significantly lessens the likelihood that the client will merely replace one psychological structure with another. When the psychotherapist focuses on the integration of affect, bodily experiences, and thought processes there is a greater possibility of responding to all these aspects of motivation—stimulus, structure, and relationship.

Much of the transactional analysis literature has emphasized structure. In developing a theory of therapeutic method there is a need to place equal emphasis on internal and external contact, relational needs, and the function of relationship. To be useful, a theory of method must be influenced by a balanced perspective that includes stimulus, structure, and relationship-motivated drives. By putting relationship at the center of our theory of methods, we create such a balanced perspective. The premise that "healing is in the relationship" is the basis for a theory of method that emphasizes the significance of the therapeutic relationship in enhancing internal and external contact, dissolving fixated compensating structures, and responding to relational needs (Erskine, 1982, p. 316). A theory of method that emphasizes the significance of the therapeutic relationship shifts the psychotherapist's focus from methods geared toward rebuilding structures to those that dissolve interruptions to contact. Rather than a therapy aimed at creating structure to replace structure, this theory of method centers on the dynamic relationships that underlie the structure-making process. A psychotherapy such as this will take into account where the client is open or closed to contact—affectively, cognitively, behaviorally, or physiologically.

The transactional analysis view of motivation and of the balance among stimulus, structure, and relationship hungers allows for such a shift in therapeutic focus. With my understanding that *life script and ego states are compensating attempts to manage relationship hunger and a loss of internal contact, the therapeutic focus can be placed on relationship itself* (Erskine, 1980, 1988). From this perspective the purpose of analyzing ego states or a life script is not to erect a new, more useful structure, but rather to gather information about which relational needs were not met, how the individual coped, and even more importantly, how the satisfaction of today's relational needs can be achieved (Erskine & Trautmann, 1996). These therapeutic tasks are accomplished through contact-oriented, relationship-focused methods:
   - *inquiry* into the client's phenomenological experience, transferential process, system of coping, and vulnerability;
   - *attunement* to the client's affect, rhythm, developmental level of functioning, and relational needs; and
   - *involvement* that acknowledges and values the client's uniqueness.
These three components together validate the existence and significance of the client's psychological functioning, normalize his or her defensive strategies, and provide a therapeutic presence that centers on the client's intrapsychic process (Erskine, 1991, 1993, 1994; Erskine & Moursund, 1988; Erskine & Trautmann, 1993, 1996).

Consistency in the practice of transactional analysis in psychotherapy is enhanced when clinical interventions are based on a comprehensive theory of method that emphasizes the therapeutic relationship (see Figure 1). The application of such a theory must:
   - respond to the unique experience of each client;
   - emerge from knowledge of human motivation and the compensating balance in stimulus, structure, and relationship hungers;

Theory of Motivation	stimulus, structure, relationship hungers
Theory of Personality	ego states, life script, intrapsychic processes
Theory of Method	healing through a contactful relationship
Methods	inquiry, attunement, involvement
Subsets of Methods	acknowledgment, validation, normalization, presence
Therapeutic Transaction	"Does it seem to you that when you need to feel secure you begin to worry about whether you have offended me?"

Figure 1
Theories of Motivation, Personality, and Method

- use the theories of personality (ego states and life scripts);
- account for where the client is open or closed to contact—affectively, cognitively, behaviorally, or physiologically;
- enhance internal and external contact;
- acknowledge and respond to relational needs; and
- facilitate the recovery of spontaneity and flexibility in problem solving and in relating to people.

In a contactful, relationship-oriented psychotherapy the therapeutic interventions shift from an emphasis on the structure of ego states or life scripts to focusing on the client's phenomenological experience, psychological vulnerabilities, and relational needs. To paraphrase the earlier quotation from Berne, the psychotherapist's task is to create a contactful therapeutic relationship that facilitates decoding of the client's transferential expression of past experiences, detoxifying introjections and rectifying fixated script beliefs and defensive structures, and helping the client identify relational needs and opportunities for need fulfillment through enhancing the client's capacity for internal and external contact.

Summary

The hungers for stimulus, structure, and relationship (recognition) are interwoven, interactive, and interdependent. They form the foundation for a transactional analysis theory of motivation. These three hungers operate as a dynamic motivational system. The satisfaction or lack of satisfaction of one of the hungers systemically affects the other two, either satisfying or potentiating the deficits in one or both of the others. When there is a deprivation of stimulus or relationship hunger, compensating structures of fragmented ego states, life scripts, and fixated patterns of defense emerge. A psychotherapy of contact-in-relationship responds to each of the client's hungers. It is through a respectful, attuned, and healing relationship that people gain autonomy, spontaneity, and intimacy.

REFERENCES
Allen, J. R., & Allen, B. A. (1972). Scripts: The role of permission. *Transactional Analysis Journal, 2*(2), 72-74.

Bandura, A. (1969). *Principles of behavior modification.* New York: Holt, Rinehart & Winston.

Bergman, S. J. (1991). Men's psychological development: A relationship perspective. In *Works in progress* (No. 48). Wellesley, MA: The Stone Center, Wellesley College.

Berne, E. (1961). *Transactional analysis in psychotherapy: A systematic individual and social psychiatry.* New York: Grove Press.

Berne, E. (1963). *The structure and dynamics of organizations and groups.* New York: Grove Press.

Berne, E. (1964). *Games people play: The psychology of human relationships.* New York: Grove Press.

Berne, E. (1966). *Principles of group treatment.* New York: Grove Press.

Berne, E. (1970). *Sex in human loving.* New York: Simon & Schuster.

Berne, E. (1972). *What do you say after you say hello? The psychology of human destiny.* New York: Grove Press.

Bollas, C. (1987). *The shadow of the object: Psychoanalysis of the unthought known.* New York: Columbia University Press.

Bowlby, J. (1969). *Attachment. Volume I of Attachment and loss.* New York: Basic Books.

Bowlby, J. (1973). *Separation: Anxiety and anger. Volume II of Attachment and loss.* New York: Basic Books.

Bowlby, J. (1980). *Loss: Sadness and depression. Volume III of Attachment and loss.* New York: Basic Books.

Crossman, P. (1966). Permission and protection. *Transactional Analysis Bulletin, 5*(19), 152-154.

Dashiell, S. (1978). The parent resolution process. *Transactional Analysis Journal, 8,* 289-294.

Dollard, J., & Miller, N. (1950). *Personality and psychotherapy.* New York: McGraw-Hill.

Dusay, J. (1972). Egograms and the "constancy hypothesis." *Transactional Analysis Journal, 2*(3), 37-41.

English, F. (1977). What shall I do tomorrow? Reconceptualizing transactional analysis. In G. Barnes (Ed.), *Transactional analysis after Eric Berne: Teachings and practices of three TA schools* (pp. 287-347). New York: Harper's College Press.

English, F. (1987). Power, mental energy and inertia. *Transactional Analysis Journal, 17,* 91-98.

English, F. (1988). Whither scripts? *Transactional Analysis Journal, 18,* 294-303.

Erskine, R. G. (1974). Therapeutic interventions: Disconnecting rubberbands. *Transactional Analysis Journal, 4*(1), 7-8.

Erskine, R. G. (1975). The ABC's of effective psychotherapy. *Transactional Analysis Journal, 5*(4), 163-165.

Erskine, R. G. (1980). Script cure: Behavioral, intrapsychic and physiological. *Transactional Analysis Journal, 10,* 102-106.

Erskine, R. G. (1982). Supervision of psychotherapy: Models for professional development. *Transactional Analysis Journal, 12,* 314-321.

Erskine, R. G. (1988). Ego structure, intrapsychic function, and defense mechanisms: A commentary on Eric Berne's original theoretical concepts. *Transactional Analysis Journal, 18,* 15-19.

Erskine, R. G. (1989). A relationship therapy: Developmental perspectives. In B. R. Loria (Ed.), *Developmental theories and the clinical process: Conference proceedings of the Eastern Regional Transactional Analysis Conference* (pp. 123-135). Madison, WI: Omnipress.

Erskine, R. G. (1991). The psychotherapy of dissociation: Inquiry, attunement and involvement. In B. R. Loria (Ed.), *The Stamford papers: Selections from the 29th annual International Transactional Analysis Association conference.* Madison, WI: Omnipress.

Erskine, R. G. (1993). Inquiry, attunement, and involvement in the psychotherapy of dissociation. *Transactional Analysis Journal, 23,* 184-190.

Erskine, R. G. (1994). Shame and self-righteousness: Transactional analysis perspectives and clinical interventions. *Transactional Analysis Journal, 24,* 86-102.

Erskine, R. G. (1995, August). A transactional analysis theory of methods. Keynote speech presented at the 33rd annual conference of the International Transactional Analysis Association, San Francisco, CA. (Cassette Recording KN-2). Hobart, IN: Repeat Performance.

Erskine, R. G., & Moursund, J. P. (1988). *Integrative psychotherapy in action.* Newbury Park, CA: Sage Publications.

Erskine, R. G., & Trautmann, R. L. (1993). The process of integrative psychotherapy. In B. R. Loria (Ed.), *The boardwalk papers: Selections from the 1993 Eastern Regional Transactional Analysis Association conference* (pp. 1-26). Madison WI: Omnipress.

Erskine, R. G., & Trautmann, R. L. (1996). Methods of an integrative psychotherapy. *Transactional Analysis Journal, 26,* 316-328.

Erskine, R. G., & Zalcman, M. J. (1979). The racket system: A model for racket analysis. *Transactional Analysis Journal, 9,* 51-59.

Fairbairn, W. R. D. (1952). *An object-relations theory of the personality.* New York: Basic Books.

Federn, P. (1953). *Ego psychology and the psychoses.* London: Imago Publishing.

Goulding, M. M., & Goulding, R. L. (1979). *Changing lives through redecision therapy.* New York: Brunner/Mazel.

Guntrip, H. (1961). *Personality structure and human interaction.* London: Hogarth.

Guntrip, H. (1968). *Schizoid phenomena, object relations and the self.* London: Hogarth.

Guntrip, H. (1971). *Psychoanalytic theory, therapy and the self.* New York: Basic Books.

Holloway, W. H. (1974). Beyond permission. *Transactional Analysis Journal, 4*(2), 15-17.

Hycner, R., & Jacobs, L. (1995). *The healing relationship in Gestalt therapy.* Highland, NY: The Gestalt Journal Press.

James, M. (1974). Self-reparenting: Theory and process. *Transactional Analysis Journal, 4*(3), 32-39.

Joines, V. (1988). Diagnosis and treatment planning using a transactional analysis framework. *Transactional Analysis Journal, 18,* 185-190.

Kahler, T., with Capers, H. (1974) The miniscript. *Transactional Analysis Journal, 4*(1), 26-42.

Karpman, S. (1971). Options. *Transactional Analysis Journal, 1*(1), 79-87.

Kohler, W. (1938). Physical gestalten. In W. Ellis (Ed.), *A source book of Gestalt psychology* (pp. 17-54). London: Routledge & Kegan Paul.

Kohut, H. (1977). *The restoration of the self: A systematic approach to the psychoanalytic treatment of narcissistic personality disorder.* New York: International Universities Press.

Kupfer, D., & Haimowitz, M. (1971). Therapeutic interventions, Part I: Rubberbands now. *Transactional Analysis Journal, 1*(2), 10-16.

Lewin, K. (1938). Will and needs. In W. Ellis (Ed.), *A source book of Gestalt psychology* (pp. 283-299). London: Routledge & Kegan Paul.

Lourie, J. (1996). The non-problem problem. *Transactional Analysis Journal, 26,* 276-283.

Miller, J. B. (1986). What do we mean by relationships? In *Works in progress* (No. 22). Wellesley, MA: The Stone Center, Wellesley College.

Osnes, R. E. (1974). Spot reparenting. *Transactional Analysis Journal, 4*(3), 40-46.

Perls, F. S. (1944). *Ego, hunger and aggression: A revision of Freud's theory and method.* Durban, RSA: Knox Publishing.

Perls, F. (1973). *The Gestalt approach and eye witness to therapy.* Palo Alto, CA: Science & Behavior Books.

Perls, F. S., Hefferline, R. F., & Goodman, P. (1951). *Gestalt therapy: Excitement and growth in the human personality.* New York: Julian Press.

Rogers, C. R. (1951). *Client-centered therapy: Its current practice, implications, and theory.* Boston: Houghton Mifflin.

Schiff, J. L. (1969). Reparenting schizophrenics. *Transactional Analysis Bulletin, 8*(32), 47-63.

Steiner, C. (1971). *Games alcoholics play: The analysis of life scripts.* New York: Grove Press.

Steiner, C. (1974). *Scripts people live: Transactional analysis of life scripts.* New York: Grove Press.

Stern, D. N. (1985). *The interpersonal world of the infant: A view from psychoanalysis and developmental psychology.* New York: Basic Books.

Stolorow, R. D., Brandchaft, B., & Atwood, G. E. (1987). *Psychoanalytic treatment: An intersubjective approach.* Hillsdale, NJ: The Analytic Press.

Sullivan, H. S. (1953). *The interpersonal theory of psychiatry* (H. S. Perry & M. L. Gawel, Eds.). New York: Norton.

Surrey, J. L. (1985). The "self-in-relation": A theory of women's development. In *Works in Progress* (No. 13). Wellesley, MA: The Stone Center, Wellesley College.

Trautmann, R. L. (Speaker). (1981). *Treatment planning.* (Cassette Recordings #81196-511 and #81196-512). Columbia, MD: Eastern Audio Associates.

Trautmann, R. L., & Erskine, R. G. (1981). Ego state analysis: A comparative view. *Transactional Analysis Journal, 11,* 178-185.

Trautmann, R. L., & Erskine, R. G. (Speakers). (1995). *Inquiry, attunement, and involvement: The application of TA theory.* (Cassette Recording No. F-19AB). Hobart, IN: Repeat Performances. (2 tapes)

Tustin, F. (1986). *Autistic barriers in neurotic patients.* London: Karnac Books.

Ware, P. (1983). Personality adaptations. *Transactional Analysis Journal, 13,* 11-19.

Winnicott, D. W. (1965). *The maturational processes and the facilitating environment: Studies in the theory of emotional development.* New York: International Universities Press.

Yontef, G. M. (1993). *Awareness, dialogue and process.* Highland, NY: The Gestalt Journal Press.

———————

Portions of this article were presented as a keynote speech, "A Transactional Analysis Theory of Methods," and also as a workshop with Rebecca Trautmann, R.N., M.S.W., entitled "Inquiry, Attunement, and Involvement: The Application of Transactional Analysis Theory" at the 33rd Annual Conference of the International Transactional Analysis Association, San Francisco, California, August 11, 1995. The author gratefully acknowledges the members of the Professional Development Seminars of the Institute for Integrative Psychotherapy, New York, New York; Kent, Connecticut; Dayton, Ohio; Chicago, Illinois; and Indianapolis, Indiana, for their contributions in formulating the ideas in this article.

Methods of an Integrative Psychotherapy

Richard G. Erskine and Rebecca L. Trautmann

The term "integrative" as it is used in our approach to integrative psychotherapy has a number of meanings. Primarily it refers to the process of integrating the personality, which includes helping clients to become aware of and assimilate the contents of their fragmented and fixated ego states into an integrated neopsychic ego, to develop a sense of self that decreases the need for defense mechanisms and a life script, and to reengage the world and relationships with full contact. It is the process of making whole: taking disowned, unaware, unresolved aspects of the ego and making them part of a cohesive self (Erskine & Trautmann, 1993).

"Integrative" also refers to the integration of theory—the bringing together of affective, cognitive, behavioral, physiological, and systems approaches to psychotherapy. A central focus of an integrative psychotherapy is assessing whether each of these domains—affective, behavioral, cognitive, and physiological—is open or closed to contact (internally and externally) and applying methods that enhance contact (Erskine, 1975, 1980, 1982a). The concept of internal and external contact is used within a perspective of human development in which each phase of life presents heightened developmental tasks, unique sensitivities in relationship with other people, and opportunities for new learning. The term integrative psychotherapy, as used in this article, includes both meanings.

Integrative psychotherapy takes into account many views of human functioning: psycho-dynamic, client-centered, behaviorist, family therapy, Gestalt therapy, Reichian-influenced body psychotherapy, object relations theories, and psychoanalytic self psychology in addition to transactional analysis, which forms the main basis of our theory and method. Each provides a valid explanation of psychological function and behavior, and each is enhanced when *selectively integrated* with the others (Erskine & Moursund, 1988).

Contact and Relationships

A major premise of integrative psychotherapy is that the need for relationship constitutes a primary motivating experience of human behavior, and contact is the means by which the need is met. We especially emphasize the importance of contact in using the range of modalities just mentioned. Contact occurs internally and externally: It involves the full awareness of sensations, feelings, needs, sensorimotor activity, thoughts, and memories that occur within the individual and a shift to full awareness of external events as registered by each of the sensory organs. With internal and external contact, experiences are continually integrated. When contact is disrupted, however, needs are not satisfied. If the experience of need arousal is not satisfied or closed naturally, it must find an artificial closure that distracts from the discomfort of the unmet need. These artificial closures are the substance of survival reactions and script decisions that may become fixated. They are evident in the disavowal of affect, habitual behavior patterns, neurological inhibitions within the body, and the beliefs that limit spontaneity and flexibility in problem solving and relating to people. Each defensive interruption to contact impedes awareness (Erskine, 1980; Erskine & Trautmann, 1993).

Contact also refers to the quality of the transactions between two people: the awareness of both one's self and the other, a sensitive meeting of the other, and an authentic acknowledgment of one's self.

Integrative psychotherapy correlates constructs from many different theoretical schools. For a theory to be integrative, as opposed to merely eclectic, it must also separate out those concepts and ideas that are not theoretically consistent to form a cohesive core of constructs that inform and guide the psychotherapeutic process. A review of the psychology and psychotherapy literature reveals that the single most consistent concept is that of relationship (Erskine, 1989). From the inception of a theory of contact by Laura and Frederick Perls (Perls, 1944; Perls, Hefferline, & Goodman, 1951) to Rogers's (1951) focus on client-centered therapy, to Fairbairn's (1952) premise that people are relationship seeking from the beginning of and throughout life, to Sullivan's (1953) emphasis on interpersonal contact, to Winnicott's (1965) and Guntrip's (1971) relationship theories and corresponding clinical applications, to Berne's (1961, 1972) theories of ego states and script, to Kohut (1971, 1977) and his followers' application of "sustained empathic inquiry" (Stolorow, Brandchaft, & Atwood, 1987, p. 10), to the relationship theories developed by the Stone Center (Bergman, 1991; Miller, 1986; Surrey, 1985), to Buber's (1923/1958) philosophy of an I-Thou relationship, there has been a succession of teachers, writers, and therapists who have emphasized that relationships—both in the early stages of life as well as throughout adulthood—are the source of that which gives meaning and validation to the self.

The literature on human development also leads to the understanding that the sense of self and self-esteem emerge out of contact-in-relationship. From a theoretical foundation of contact-in-relationship coupled with Berne's (1961) concept of ego states (particularly fixated Child ego states) (Erskine, 1987, 1988; Trautmann & Erskine, 1981) comes a natural focus on child development. The works of Stern (1985, 1995) and Bowlby (1969, 1973, 1980) are presently influential in informing an integrative perspective, largely because of their emphasis on early attachment and the natural, lifelong need for relationship. Bowlby emphasized the significance of early as well as prolonged physical bonding in the creation of a visceral core from which all experiences of self and other emerge. When such contact does not occur in accordance with the child's relational needs, there is a physiological defense against the loss of contact (Fraiberg, 1982).

Integrative psychotherapy makes use of many perspectives on human functioning, but always from the point of view that the client-therapist relationship is crucial. The concepts of contact-in-relationship, ego states and intrapsychic function, transference and transactions, relational needs and affective reciprocity, and developmental process and life script are central to our integrative theory. The psychotherapist's self is used in a directed way to assist the client's process of developing and integrating contact and satisfying relational needs (Erskine, 1982a). Of central significance is the process called attunement, which involves not just a focus on discrete thoughts, feelings, behaviors, or physical sensations, but also on what Stern (1985) termed "vitality affects" (p. 156). We aim to create an experience of unbroken feeling-connectedness. The client's sense of self and sense of relatedness that develop seem crucial to the process of integration and wholeness, particularly when there have been specific, ego-fragmenting traumas in the client's life and when aspects of the self have been disavowed or denied because of the cumulative failures of contact-in-relationship (Erskine, 1991a, 1993, 1994).

The central premise underlying the practice of integrative psychotherapy is that integration can occur through a variety of modalities—affective, behavioral, cognitive, and physiological (Erskine, 1975, 1980)—but most effectively when there exists a respectful, contactful interpersonal therapeutic relationship (Erskine, 1982a). Inquiry, attunement, and involvement are sets of contact-facilitating, relationship-oriented methods. Previous publications defined and described the methods of inquiry, attunement, and involvement (Erskine & Trautmann, 1993), applied the methods to the treatment of dissociation (Erskine, 1991a, 1993) and shame and self-righteousness (Erskine, 1994), and demon-strated the application through actual therapy transcripts (Erskine, 1982b, 1991b; Erskine & Moursund, 1988). What follows is an outline of some of the methods that foster contact-in-relationship.

Inquiry

Inquiry begins with the assumption that the therapist knows nothing about the client's experience and therefore must continually strive to understand the subjective meaning of the client's behavior and intrapsychic process. The process of inquiry involves the therapist being open to discovering the client's perspective while the client simultaneously discovers his or her sense of self with each of the therapist's awareness-enhancing statements or questions. Through respectful exploration of the client's phenomenological experience, the client becomes increasingly aware of both current and archaic relational needs, feelings, and behavior. Affect, thoughts, fantasy, script beliefs, body movements or tensions, hopes, and memories that have been kept from awareness by lack of dialogue or by repression may come to awareness. With increased awareness and the nonactivation of internal defenses, needs and feelings that may have been fixated and left unresolved due to past experiences are integrated into a more contactful self.

It should be stressed that the *process* of inquiring is as important, if not more so, than the content. The therapist's inquiry must be empathic with the client's subjective experience to be effective in discovering and revealing the internal phenomena and in uncovering the internal and external interruptions to contact.

This type of inquiry requires a genuine interest in the client's subjective experiences and construction of meanings. It proceeds with questions about what the client is feeling, how he or she experiences both self and others (including the psychotherapist), and what meanings and conclusions are made. With sensitive questioning, our experience is that clients will reveal previously repressed fantasies and out-of-awareness intrapsychic dynamics. This provides both the client and the therapist with an ever-increasing understanding of who the client is, the experiences he or she has had, and when and how he or she interrupts contact.

Therapeutic inquiry about the client's fears, anticipations, and expectations often reveals the transferring of historical experiences, archaic defenses, and past relational disruptions into current life, including the therapy relationship. Transference within this integrative perspective can be viewed as:

1. the means whereby the client can describe his or her past, the developmental needs that have been thwarted, and the defenses that were created to compensate;
2. the resistance to remembering and, paradoxically, an unaware enactment of childhood experiences (the repeated relationship);
3. the expression of an intrapsychic conflict and the desire to achieve the satisfaction of relational needs and intimacy in relationships (the therapeutically needed relationship); or
4. the expression of the universal psychological striving to organize experience and create meaning.

This integrative view of transference provides the basis for a continual honoring of the inherent communication in transference of both the repeated and the needed relationship (Stern, 1994), as well as recognition of and respect for the fact that transactions may be nontransferential and may have to do only with the here-and-now relationship between therapist and client (Erskine, 1991c).

Inquiry may include an exploration of intrapsychic conflicts and unaware enactments of childhood experiences and continue with historical questions as to when an experience occurred and the nature of the significant relationships in the person's life. Through inquiry we explore the client's script beliefs and related behaviors, fantasies, and reinforcing experiences (Erskine & Zalcman, 1979). In accordance with the client's welfare, we integrate Gestalt therapy experiments, behavioral change contracts, body psychotherapy, intensive Parent ego state psychotherapy, or developmental regression (Erskine & Moursund, 1988). Through a combination of these techniques for enhancing self-awareness and through our respectful inquiry, experiences that in the past were necessarily excluded from awareness can again be remembered in the context of an involved therapeutic relationship. With memories, fantasies, or dreams coming to awareness, the therapist's inquiry may return to the client's phenomenological experience or proceed to the client's strategies of coping, that is, to an inquiry about the defensive internal and external interruptions to contact.

As we explore defensive processes we make use of observable, external interruptions to contact as representative of internal interruptions to contact. Archaically fixated defensive interruptions to contact—for example, introjections and script beliefs—interfere with the satisfaction of today's relational needs and emerge in the therapeutic relationship.

To be vulnerable is to be highly aware of relational needs and to be open, without defenses, to the other's response to those needs. Inquiring about vulnerabilities both outside of and in the therapeutic relationship uncovers relational needs and the effects within the client of both the satisfaction or nonsatisfaction of those needs. The focus of the therapeutic dialogue may then cycle to phenomenological, transferential, or defensive levels of experience. The process of inquiry is not linear but moves in harmony with the client's ever-increasing internal awareness and awareness of self-in-relationship.

The goal of therapeutic inquiry is for the client and therapist together to discover and distinguish the functions of intrapsychic processes and defensive dynamics. Each defensive dynamic has unique intrapsychic functions of identity, stability, continuity, and integrity that require specific emphasis in psychotherapy. Our thesis is that *attunement and involvement allow the client to effectively transfer these intrapsychic functions to the relationship with the therapist.* In what follows we will refer to the classifications shown in Figure 1.

It is essential that the therapist understand each client's unique need for a stabilizing, validating, and reparative other person to take on some of the relationship functions that the client is attempting to manage alone. A contact-oriented relationship therapy requires that the therapist be attuned to these relationship needs and be involved, through empathic validation of feelings and needs and by providing safety and support.

A contactful inquiry about a client's phenomenological experience enhances the client's sense of self through facilitating the client's awareness of the *existence* of feelings, fantasies, internal sensations, and thought processes as well as the existence of interruptions to contact. A patient, nonhumiliating inquiry into the client's transferential dynamics reveals the *significance* of the internal and external interruptions to contact, how the person organizes experience, and the significance of both the repeated and the therapeutically needed relationship. The needed relationship is the client's call for the reciprocal involvement by an essential other who can respond to relational needs. A respectful inquiry about the client's defensive process—his or her means of coping—reveals the client's integrity and unique style of *resolving* disruptions in relationship. This level of inquiry also brings to the client's awareness other avenues of coping with relational disruptions and new possibilities for resolving interpersonal conflicts. A sensitive inquiry about the client's vulnerabilities and his or her unique combination of relational needs increases the client's *value of self* (see Figure 1). In the presence of an attuned, involved, and self-aware therapist who can respond to those relational needs, the client will feel a stronger, clearer sense of self and self-in-relationship. Psychological well-being is enhanced through full interpersonal and intrapsychic contact.

Attunement

Attunement is a two-part process: It begins with empathy—that is, being sensitive to and identifying with the other person's sensations, needs, or feelings—and the communication of that sensitivity to the other person. More than just understanding or vicarious introspection, attunement is a kinesthetic and emotional sensing of the other—knowing his or her rhythm, affect, and experience by metaphorically being in his or her skin, thus going beyond empathy to provide a reciprocal affect and/or resonating response.

Attunement is more than empathy: It is a process of communion and unity of interpersonal contact. Effective attunement also requires that the therapist simultaneously remain aware of the boundary between client and therapist as well as his or her own internal processes. Attunement is facilitated by the therapist's capacity to anticipate and observe the effects of his or her behavior on the client and to decenter from his or her own experience to extensively focus on the client's process.

METHODS OF PSYCHOTHERAPY

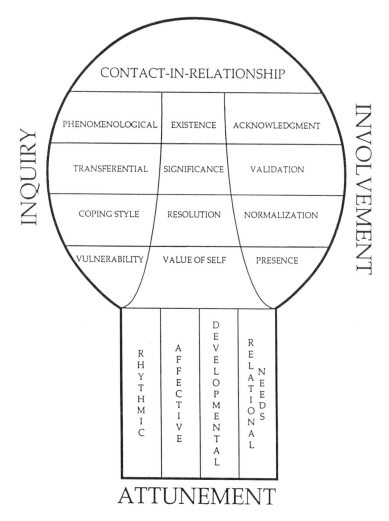

Figure 1
Methods of an Integrative Psychotherapy

The communication of attunement validates the client's needs and feelings and lays the foundation for repairing the failures of previous relationships. Attunement is communicated not only by what the therapist says, but also by facial or body movements that signal to the client that his or her affect and needs are perceived, are significant, and make an impact on the therapist.

Attunement is often experienced by the client as the therapist gently moving through the defenses that have prevented the awareness of relationship failures and the related needs and feelings. Attunement facilitates contact with long-forgotten parts of Child ego states. Over time this results in a lessening of internal interruptions to contact and a corresponding dissolving of external defenses. Needs and feelings can increasingly be expressed with comfort and assurance that they will receive an empathic and caring response. Frequently the process of attunement provides a sense of safety and stability that enables the client to begin to remember and to endure regressing into childhood experiences that may bring a fuller awareness of the pain of past traumas, past failures of relationship(s), and loss of aspects of self. The process of attunement can be categorized according to the resonance and reciprocity required for contact-in-relationship. This attunement may be to rhythm, level of development, nature of affect, or relational need.

Rhythmic attunement is the pacing of the therapeutic inquiry and involvement at a tempo and cadence that best facilitates the client's processing of both external information and internal sensations, feelings, and thoughts. In our experience the mental processing of affect often occurs at a rate different from cognitive processing. In the presence of intense affect the use of perception or cognition may be slower than when affect is not intense. For example, the compounded affective components of shame often make the processing of information and the organizing of behavior occur at a diminished rate. Shame is a complex process involving the disavowal and retroflection of anger, the sadness of not being accepted as one is, the fear of rejection because of who one is, and confluence and compliance with the relationship-interrupting humiliation (Erskine, 1994). The affective, perceptual, cognitive, behavioral, and physiological reactions occur at differing rhythms than would otherwise occur in the absence of shame.

Some clients are quickly aware of visceral and kinesthetic sensations while others process them slowly. Internal interruptions to contact or any of the complex psychological defenses such as desensitization, disavowal, denial, or dissociation disrupt the natural rhythm of processing physical sensations, affects, perceptions, and thoughts.

Affective attunement refers to one person sensing the other's affect and responding with a reciprocal affect. It begins with valuing the other person's affect as an extremely important form of human communication, being willing to be affectively aroused by the other person, and responding with the resonating affect.

"*Affect is transactional-relational in its nature, requiring a corresponding affect in resonance*" (Erskine, 1994, p. 99). The resonance of one person's affect to another's provides affective contact that is essential to human relationships. Symbolically, affective attunement may be pictured as one person's yin to the other's yang, which together form a unity. *Affective attunement is the resonance with the other's affect that provides nonverbal interpersonal contact—a unity in the relationship.*

When a client feels sad, the therapist's reciprocal affect of compassion and his or her acts of compassion complete the interpersonal contact. Relationally, anger requires the reciprocal affects related to attentiveness, seriousness, and responsibility, with possible acts of correction. The client who is afraid requires that the therapist respond with affect and action that conveys security and protection. When clients express joy the response from the therapist that completes the unity of contact is the reciprocal affect of vitality and expression of pleasure.

Affective attunement involves nonverbal communication from the therapist that acknowledges, validates, and normalizes the client's affect. The therapist's affective presence communicates that affect has an important function in relationship and thereby values the client—a communication of unconditional positive regard or "You're OK with me."

Developmental attunement. Attunement to the client's developmental level of psychological functioning and organization of experiences is essential in a contact-oriented, relationship-centered psychotherapy. The purpose of the developmental focus is to respond to the client at the age level at which there was a lack of contact-in-relationship, when fixations occurred in the representational system of self, others, and the quality of life. The script beliefs and related archaic defenses represent attempts of a younger person to cope with life situations.

To attune to a client's developmental needs, the therapist listens with a "third ear" or watches with a "third eye" the words and behaviors of the client in the moment to sense what may be the communication of a child. Often based on the age when a particular trauma occurred or when a script decision or survival reaction was made, the therapist begins to develop a sensitivity for the Child ego states as they are unconsciously manifested in current transactions. Having a sense of this child and its needs, its developmental challenges, ways of thinking and organizing, unique vulnerabilities, and relationship needs guides the therapist in the way he or she may inquire, interpret, or interact with the client.

As an example, in response to a client who was expressing frustration at her inadequacy in finding ways to talk about her feelings, the therapist commented that learning to use language brings a child two different experiences. On the one hand, words allow for increased communication and understanding, which is gratifying and fosters closeness. On the other, as the child experiences that words do not adequately convey feelings or experiences, there is a greater sense of separateness and sometimes aloneness (Stern, 1985). The tears in the client's eyes conveyed that the therapist had understood her developmental frustration and at least one significant aspect of her lifelong difficulty with relationships—that unspoken experience of aloneness.

Attunement to the developmental level is easiest when the client enters a regressed state or is able to describe his or her Child ego state experiences. A subtler and sometimes more powerful experience occurs when the therapist is attuned to the client's developmental needs, level of functioning, and childhood experiences while the client is completely unaware of them. For example, with a client who grew up anxiously trying to please his separated parents and who used compulsive checking to ward off anxiety, it seemed important not to make an issue of his consistent lateness until he was able to identify and express his anger at his parents. Near the end of the therapy he talked about how significant it was to him that the therapist never confronted his lateness, making his therapy a place of safety in which he could be free of his compulsions.

By being attuned to the archaic level of a person's functioning and placing it directly in the context of the therapeutic relationship, the therapist makes it possible for fixed ways of being and relating to be integrated into a more dynamic whole.

Relational needs. The process of attunement also includes responding to relational needs as they emerge in the therapeutic relationship. Relational needs are the needs unique to interpersonal contact (Erskine, 1995). They are not the basic needs of life—such as food, air, or proper temperature—but the essential elements that enhance the quality of life and a sense of self-in-relationship. Relational needs are the component parts of a universal human desire for intimate relationship. Although there may be a large number of relational needs, the eight that we describe in this article represent those needs that our clients most frequently describe as they talk about significant relationships. Some of these relational needs have also been described in the psychotherapy literature as fixated needs of early childhood, indicators of psychopathology, or problematic transference (Bach, 1985; Basch, 1988; Kohut, 1971, 1977; Wolf, 1988), while Clark's (1991) integrative perspective on empathic transactions bridges the concepts of transference and relational needs.

Relational needs are not only needs of childhood or needs that emerge in a developmental hierarchy; they are components of relationship that are present every day of our lives. Each of the eight relational needs may become figure or conscious as a longing or desire while the other seven remain out of consciousness or as background. A satisfying response by another person to an individual's relational need allows the pressing need to recede to ground and another relational need to become figure as a new interest or desire.

Often it is in the absence of need satisfaction that an individual becomes most aware of the presence of relational needs. When relational needs are not satisfied the need becomes more intense and is phenomenologically experienced as longing, emptiness, a nagging loneliness, or an intense urge often accompanied by nervousness. The continued absence of satisfaction of relational needs may be manifested as frustration, aggression, or anger. When disruptions in relationship are prolonged, the lack of need satisfaction is manifested as a loss of energy or hope and shows up in script beliefs such as "No one is there for me" or "What's the use?" These script beliefs are the cognitive defense against the awareness of needs and the feelings that occur when needs do not get a satisfying response from another person (Erskine, 1980).

The satisfaction of relational needs requires the contactful presence of another who is sensitive and attuned to the relational needs and who also provides a reciprocal response to each need. The eight principal relational needs that we observe are the needs for:

1. *Security:* the visceral experience of having our physical and emotional vulnerabilities protected. This involves the experience that our variety of needs and feelings are natural. Security is a sense of simultaneously being vulnerable and in harmony with another. It

includes the absence of both actual or anticipated impingement or danger.

Attunement involves the empathic awareness of the other's need for security within the relationship plus a reciprocal response to that need. The needed response is the provision of physical and affective security in which the individual's vulnerability is honored and preserved. It communicates, often nonverbally, "Your needs and feelings are normal and acceptable to me." Therapeutic attunement to the relational need for security has been described by clients as "total acceptance and protection," a communication of "unconditional positive regard" or "I'm OK in this relationship." Attunement to the need for security involves the therapist being sensitive to the importance of this need and conducting himself or herself both emotionally and behaviorally in a way that provides security in the relationship.

2. *Validation, affirmation, and significance within a relationship:* the need to have the other person validate the significance and function of our intrapsychic processes of affect, fantasy, and constructing of meaning and to validate that our emotions are a significant intrapsychic and interpersonal communication. It includes the need to have all of our relational needs affirmed and accepted as natural. The therapist's affective reciprocity with the client's feelings validates the client's affect and provides affirmation and normalization of the client's relational needs.

3. *Acceptance by a stable, dependable, and protective other person:* the need to look up to and rely on parents, elders, teachers, and mentors. The relational need for acceptance by a consistent, reliable, dependable other person is the search for protection and guidance and may manifest as an idealization of the other. In psychotherapy such idealization is also the search for protection from a controlling, humiliating Parent ego state's intrapsychic effect on the vulnerability of Child ego states. It can also be the search for protection from one's own escalation of affect or exaggeration of fantasies.

The therapist protects and facilitates integration of affect by providing an opportunity to express, contain, and/or understand the function of such dynamics. The degree to which an individual looks to someone and hopes that he or she is reliable, consistent, and dependable is directly proportional to the quest for intrapsychic protection, safe expression, containment, or beneficial insight. Idealizing or depending on someone is not necessarily pathological as implied in the popular psychology term, "codependent," or when misinterpreted as "idealizing transference" (Kohut, 1977), or as Berne's game of "Gee, You're Wonderful, Professor!" (1964). When we refer to some clients' expressions of this need to be accepted and protected as "a Victim looking for a Rescuer," we potentially depreciate or even pathologize an essential human need for relationship that provides a sense of stability, reliability, and dependability.

In psychotherapy, attunement involves the therapist's recognition, often unspoken, of the importance and necessity of idealizing as an unaware request for intrapsychic protection. Such a therapeutic involvement includes both the client's sense of the psychotherapist's interest in the client's welfare and the use of the therapist's integrated sense of self as the most effective therapeutic tool (Erskine, 1982a). This relational need to be accepted by a stable, dependable, and protective other person provides a client-centered reason to conduct our lives and psychotherapy practices ethically and morally.

4. *Confirmation of personal experience:* The need to have experience confirmed is manifested through the desire to be in the presence of someone who is similar, who understands because he or she has had a like experience, and whose shared experience is confirming. Attunement is provided by the therapist valuing the need for confirmation by revealing carefully selected personal experiences—mindfully (i.e., client-focused) sharing vulnerabilities or similar feelings and fantasies—and by being personally present and vital.

For example, affirmation of the client's experience may include the therapist joining in or valuing the client's fantasies. Rather than define a client's internal storytelling as "just a fantasy," it is essential to engage the client in the expression of the needs, hopes, relational conflicts, and protective strategies that may constitute the core of the fantasies. Attunement to the need for affirmation of experience may be achieved by the therapist accepting everything said by the client, even when fantasy and reality are intertwined, much like the telling of a dream reveals the intrapsychic process. Fantasy images or symbols have significant intrapsychic and interpersonal functions that may include stability, continuity, identity, and predictability. When the *function* of the fantasy is acknowledged, appreciated, and valued, the person feels affirmed in his or her experience.

The client who needs confirmation of personal experience requires a uniquely different reciprocal response from the client who needs validation of affect or who needs to be accepted by a dependable and protective other. In neither of the latter two relational needs is the sharing of personal experience or the creating of an atmosphere of mutuality an attuned response to the client's need.

5. *Self-definition:* the relational need to know and express one's own uniqueness and to receive acknowledgment and acceptance by the other. Self-definition is the communication of one's self-chosen identity through the expression of preferences, interests, and ideas without humiliation or rejection.

In the absence of satisfying acknowledgment and acceptance, the expression of self-definition may take unconscious adversarial forms such as the person who begins sentences with "No, ..." even when agreeing, or who constantly engages in arguments or competition. People often compete to define themselves as distinct from others in order to maintain a sense of their own integrity. The more alike people are the greater the thrust for self-defining competition.

Therapeutic attunement occurs in the therapist's consistent support for the client's expression of identity and his or her normalization of the need for self-definition. It requires the therapist's consistent presence, contactfulness, and respect even in the face of disagreement.

6. The need *to have an impact on the other person:* Impact refers to having an influence that affects the other in some desired way. An individual's sense of competency in a

relationship emerges from agency and efficacy—attracting the other's attention and interest, influencing what may be of interest to the other person, and effecting a change of affect or behavior in the other.

Attunement to the client's need to have an impact occurs when the psychotherapist allows himself or herself to be emotionally impacted by the client and to respond with compassion when the client is sad, to provide an affect of security when the client is scared, to take the client seriously when he or she is angry, and to be excited when the client is joyful. Attunement may include soliciting the client's criticism of the therapist's behavior and making the necessary changes so the client has a sense of impact within the therapeutic relationship.

7. *The need to have the other initiate:* Initiation refers to the impetus for making inter-personal contact with another person. It is the reaching out to the other in some way that acknowledges and validates the importance of him or her in the relationship.

The psychotherapist may be subject to a theory-induced countertransference when he or she universally applies the methodological concepts of nongratification, rescuing, or self-responsibility. While waiting for the client to initiate, the psychotherapist may not be accounting for the fact that some behavior that appears passive may actually be an expression of the relational need to have the other initiate.

To respond to the client's need it may be necessary for the therapist to initiate a dialogue, to move out of his or her chair and sit near the client, or to make a phone call to the client between sessions. The therapist's willingness to initiate interpersonal contact or to take responsibility for a major share of the therapeutic work normalizes the client's relational need to have someone else reach out to him or her.

8. The need *to express love:* Love is often expressed through quiet gratitude, thankfulness, giving affection, or doing something for the other person. The importance of the relational need to give love—whether it be from children to parents, sibling, or teacher, or from client to therapist—is often overlooked in the practice of psychotherapy. When the expression of love is stymied, the expression of self-in-relationship is thwarted. Too often psychotherapists have treated clients' expression of affection as manipulation, transference, or a violation of a neutral therapeutic boundary.

Those clients for whom the absence of satisfaction of relational needs is cumulative require a consistent and dependable attunement and involvement by the psychotherapist that acknowledges, validates, and normalizes relational needs and related affect. It is through the psychotherapist's sustained contactful presence that the cumulative trauma (Khan, 1963) of the lack of need satisfaction can be addressed and the needs responded to within the therapeutic relationship.

Involvement

Therapeutic involvement that includes *acknowledgment, validation, normalization,* and *presence* diminishes internal defensive processes. The therapist's *acknowledgment* of the client begins with an attunement to the client's affect, relational needs, rhythm, and developmental level of functioning. Through sensitivity to relational needs or physiological expression of emotions the therapist can guide the client to become aware of and to express needs and feelings or to acknowledge that feelings or physical sensations may be memory—the only way of remembering that may be available. In many cases of relationship failure the person's relational needs or feelings were not acknowledged, and it may be necessary in psychotherapy to help the person gain a vocabulary and learn to voice those feelings and needs. Acknowledgment of physical sensations, relational needs, and affect helps the client claim his or her own phenomenological experience. It includes a receptive other who knows and communicates about the existence of nonverbal movements, tensing of muscles, affect, or even fantasy.

Occasionally, selectively chosen, caring confrontations are also a part of acknowledgment. Confrontation is a statement or question used by the therapist to bring into the client's awareness a discrepancy between his or her perceptions and behaviors or between script beliefs and actual events (Erskine, 1982b, 1991b). The goal of confrontation is for both client and therapist to acknowledge the existence and then the significance of behaviors, interruptions to contact, or script beliefs. The usefulness of the confrontation is related to the client's discovering the *psychological function* (e.g., stability, continuity, identity, and/or predictability) of the behavior or defensive reaction and the therapist's validation of its archaic significance. Confrontations are only effective if done respectfully and without humiliation so that the client experiences his or her welfare being enhanced.

There may have been times in a client's life when feelings or relational needs were acknowledged but not validated. *Validation* communicates to the client that his or her affect, defenses, physical sensations, or behavioral patterns are related to something significant in his or her experience. Validation makes a link between cause and effect; it values the individual's idiosyncrasies and way of being in relationship. It diminishes the possibility of the client internally disavowing or denying the significance of affect, physical sensation, memory, or dreams. And it supports the client in valuing his or her phenomenological experience and transferential communication of the needed relationship, thereby increasing self-esteem.

The intent of *normalization* is to change the way clients or others categorize or define their internal experience or their behavioral attempts at coping from a pathological or "something's-wrong-with-me" perspective to one that respects archaic attempts at resolution of conflicts. It may be essential for the therapist to counter societal or parental messages such as "You're stupid for feeling scared" with "Anyone would be scared in that situation." Many flashbacks, bizarre fantasies, and nightmares as well as much confusion, panic, and defensiveness are normal coping phenomena in abnormal situations. It is imperative that the therapist communicate that the client's experience is a normal defensive reaction—a reaction that many people would have if they encountered similar life experiences.

Presence is provided through the psychotherapist's sustained, attuned responses to both verbal and nonverbal expressions of the client. It occurs when the behavior and communication of the psychotherapist at all times respect and enhance the client's integrity. Presence includes the therapist's receptivity to clients' affect—to be impacted by their emotions, to be moved and yet to stay responsive to the impact of their emotions and not to become anxious, depressed, or angry. Presence is an expression of the psychotherapist's full internal and external contact. It communicates the psychotherapist's responsibility, dependability, and reliability. Through the therapist's full presence, the transformative potential of a relationship-oriented psychotherapy is possible. Presence describes the therapist's providing a safe interpersonal connection. More than just verbal communication, presence is a communion between client and therapist.

Presence is enhanced when the therapist decenters from his or her own needs, feelings, fantasies, or hopes and centers instead on the client's process. Presence also includes the converse of decentering, that is, being fully contactful with his or her own internal process and reactions. The therapist's history, relational needs, sensitivities, theories, professional experience, own psychotherapy, and reading interests all shape unique reactions to the client. Presence involves both bringing the richness of the therapist's experiences to the therapeutic relationship as well as decentering from the self of the therapist and centering on the client's process.

Presence also includes allowing oneself to be manipulated and shaped by the client in a way that provides for the client's self-expression. As effective psychotherapists we are played with and genuinely become the clay that is molded and shaped to fit the client's expression of his or her intrapsychic world toward the creation of a new sense of self and self-in-relationship (Winnicott, 1965).

The therapist's involvement through transactions that acknowledge, validate, and normalize the client's phenomenological experience, system of organization, and integrity is the antidote to the toxicity of discounting the existence, significance, or responsibility for resolving disruptions of contact-in-relationship. The dependable, attuned presence of the therapist counters the client's discounting of his or her self-worth (Erskine, 1994).

Juxtaposition

The psychotherapist who is involved and responsive to the therapeutically needed relationship may stimulate a reaction in the client to the *juxtaposition* between the attuned contact offered by the therapist and the emotional memories of previous misattunements (Erskine, 1991a, 1993). The juxtaposition is in the contrast between what is provided in the therapy, such as the attuned, reciprocal responsiveness of the therapeutic relationship, and what was previously needed, longed for, and not experienced. It represents a challenge to the client's script system and psychological homeostasis (Bary & Hufford, 1990). The juxtaposition stimulates emotional memories that the client may then try to push out of consciousness. Often juxtaposition is manifested by pushing the therapist away after a close encounter, finding fault with the therapist for focusing on the client's "neediness," or coming late or canceling a session following one in which the client allowed himself or herself to depend on the therapist's affective reciprocity or responsiveness to relational needs.

Such a reaction to the juxtaposition between the attuned involvement of the therapist and the client's emotional memories may indicate that the psychotherapist is pacing the therapy faster than the client can integrate the experience. In cases of physical and sexual abuse or cumulative trauma from prolonged misattunements to affect and relational needs, the client's reactions to juxtaposition may also indicate that the intensity of the therapeutic involvement is too great and does not allow for a sense of safety. The reaction to juxtaposition occurs when the client's coping or defensive system is relaxed and the self-protective functions are transferred to the therapeutic relationship faster than the homeostatic process allows. The therapist's sensitive involvement is in the continual adjustment of the rhythmic and affective attunement, the quality of responsiveness to relational needs, and a respect for the homeostatic function of the client's coping style and integrity.

Summary

A contact-oriented relationship psychotherapy that centers on inquiry, attunement, and involvement responds to the client's current needs for an emotionally nurturing relationship that is reparative and sustaining. The aim of this kind of therapy is the integration of affect-laden experiences and fragmented states of the ego and an intrapsychic reorganization of the client's fixated script beliefs about self, others, and the quality of life.

Contact facilitates the dissolving of defenses and the integration of the disowned parts of the personality. Through contact, the disowned, unaware, unresolved experiences are made part of a cohesive self. In integrative psychotherapy the concept of contact is the central focus from which clinical interventions are derived. Transference, ego state regression, activation of the intrapsychic influence of introjection, and the presence of defense mechanisms and script beliefs are all understood as indications of previous contact and relationship deficits. Full intrapsychic and interpersonal contact becomes possible when a client experiences that the therapist (1) stays attuned to the client's rhythm, affect, and needs; (2) is sensitive to the client's psychological functioning at the relevant developmental ages; (3) respects each interruption to contact and self-protective defense; and (4) is interested in understanding the client's way of constructing meaning.

The four dimensions of human functioning—affective, behavioral, cognitive, and physiological—are an important guide in determining where someone is open or closed to contact and therefore to therapeutic support. A major goal of integrative psychotherapy is to use the therapist-client relationship—the ability to create contact in the present—as a stepping-stone to satisfying relationships with other people and a unified, fulfilled sense of self.

A guiding principle of this contact-oriented, interactive psychotherapy is respect for the integrity of the client. Through respect, kindness, compassion, and maintaining contact we establish a personal presence and allow for an interpersonal relationship that provides affirmation of the client's integrity. The methods that ease intrapsychic conflict, facilitate script cure, resolve transference, and promote the integration of a fragmented ego are based on the belief that *healing occurs primarily through the interpersonal contact of a therapeutic relationship.* With integration it becomes possible for the person to face each moment with spontaneity and flexibility in solving life's problems and in relating to people.

REFERENCES

Bach, S. (1985). *Narcissistic states and the therapeutic process.* New York: Jason Aronson.

Bary, B. B., & Hufford, F. M. (1990). The six advantages to games and their use in treatment. *Transactional Analysis Journal, 20,* 214-220.

Basch, M. F. (1988). *Understanding psychotherapy: The science behind the art.* New York: Basic Books.

Bergman, S. J. (1991). *Men's psychological development: A relationship perspective.* Works in progress (No. 48). Wellesley, MA: The Stone Center, Wellesley College.

Berne, E. (1961). *Transactional analysis in psychotherapy: A systematic individual and social psychiatry.* New York: Grove Press.

Berne, E. (1964). *Games people play: The psychology of human relationships.* New York: Grove Press.

Berne, E. (1972). *What do you say after you say hello?: The psychology of human destiny.* New York: Grove Press.

Bowlby, J. (1969). *Attachment. Volume I of Attachment and loss.* New York: Basic Books.

Bowlby, J. (1973). *Separation: Anxiety and anger. Volume II of Attachment and loss.* New York: Basic Books.

Bowlby, J. (1980). *Loss: Sadness and depression. Volume III of Attachment and loss.* New York: Basic Books.

Buber, M. (1958). *I and thou* (R. G. Smith, Trans.). New York: Scribner. (Original work published 1923)

Clark, B. D. (1991). Empathic transactions in the deconfusion of child ego states. *Transactional Analysis Journal, 21,* 92-98.

Erskine, R. G. (1975). The ABC's of effective psychotherapy. *Transactional Analysis Journal, 5,* 163-165.

Erskine, R. G. (1980). Script cure: Behavioral, intrapsychic and physiological. *Transactional Analysis Journal, 10,* 102-106.

Erskine, R. G. (1982a). Supervision of psychotherapy: Models for professional development. *Transactional Analysis Journal 12,* 314-321.

Erskine, R. G. (1982b). Transactional analysis and family therapy. In A. M. Horne & M. M. Ohlsen and contributors, *Family counseling and therapy* (pp. 245-275). Itasca, IL: F. E. Peacock Publishers.

Erskine, R. G. (1987). A structural analysis of ego: Eric Berne's contribution to the theory of psychotherapy. In *Keynote speeches: Delivered at the EATA conference, July, 1986, Noordwikerhout, The Netherlands.* Geneva, Switzerland: European Association for Transactional Analysis.

Erskine, R. G. (1988). Ego structure, intrapsychic function, and defense mechanisms: A commentary on Eric Berne's original theoretical concepts. *Transactional Analysis Journal, 18,* 15-19.

Erskine, R. G. (1989). A relationship therapy: Developmental perspectives. In B. R. Loria (Ed.), *Developmental theories and the clinical process: Conference proceedings of the Eastern Regional Transactional Analysis Conference* (pp. 123-135). Madison, WI: Omnipress.

Erskine, R. G. (1991a). The psychotherapy of dissociation: Inquiry, attunement and involvement. In B. R. Loria (Ed.), *The Stamford papers: Selections from the 29th annual International Transactional Analysis Association conference* (pp. 53-58). Madison, WI: Omnipress.

Erskine, R. G. (1991b). Transactional analysis and family therapy. In A. M. Horne & J. L. Passmore & contributors, *Family counseling and therapy* (2nd ed.) (pp. 498-529). Itasca, IL: F. E. Peacock Publishers.

Erskine, R. G. (1991c). Transference and transactions: Critique from an intrapsychic and integrative perspective. *Transactional Analysis Journal, 21,* 63-76.

Erskine, R. G. (1993). Inquiry, attunement, and involvement in the psychotherapy of dissociation. *Transactional Analysis Journal, 23,* 184-190.

Erskine, R. G. (1994). Shame and self-righteousness: Transactional analysis perspectives and clinical interventions. *Transactional Analysis Journal, 24,* 86-102.

Erskine, R. G. (1995, August). *A transactional analysis theory of methods.* Keynote speech presented at the 33rd annual conference of the International Transactional Analysis Association, San Francisco, CA. (Also available as a cassette recording [KN-2] from Repeat Performance, Hobart, IN.)

Erskine, R. G., & Moursund, J. P. (1988). *Integrative psychotherapy in action.* Newbury Park, CA: Sage Publications.

Erskine, R. G., & Trautmann, R. L. (1993). The process of integrative psychotherapy. In B. R. Loria (Ed.), *The boardwalk papers: Selections from the 1993 Eastern Regional Transactional Analysis Association conference* (pp. 1-26). Madison, WI: Omnipress.

Erskine, R. G., & Zalcman, M. J. (1979). The racket system: A model for racket analysis. *Transactional Analysis Journal, 9*, 51-59.

Fairbairn, W. R. D. (1952). *An object-relations theory of the personality*. New York: Basic Books.

Fraiberg, S. (1982). Pathological defenses in infancy. *Psychoanalytic Quarterly, 51*, 612-635.

Guntrip, H. (1971). *Psychoanalytic theory, therapy and the self*. New York: Basic Books.

Khan, M. M. R. (1963). The concept of cumulative trauma. In R. S. Eissler, A. Freud, H. Hartman, & M. Kris (Eds.), *Psychoanalytic study of the child, XVIII* (pp. 286-306). New York: International Universities Press.

Kohut, H. (1971). *The analysis of the self*. New York: International Universities Press.

Kohut, H. (1977). *The restoration of the self: A systematic approach to the psychoanalytic treatment of narcissistic personality disorder*. New York: International Universities Press.

Miller, J. B. (1986). *What do we mean by relationships?* Works in progress (No. 22). Wellesley, MA: The Stone Center, Wellesley College.

Perls, F. S. (1944). *Ego, hunger and aggression: A revision of Freud's theory and method*. Durban, RSA: Knox Publishing.

Perls, F. S., Hefferline, R. F., & Goodman, P. (1951). *Gestalt therapy: Excitement and growth in the human personality*. New York: Julian Press.

Rogers, C. R. (1951). *Client-centered therapy: Its current practice, implications, and theory*. Boston: Houghton Mifflin.

Stern, D. N. (1985). *The interpersonal world of the infant: A view from psychoanalysis and developmental psychology*. New York: Basic Books.

Stern, D. N. (1995). *The motherhood constellation: A unified view of parent-infant psychotherapy*. New York: Basic Books.

Stern, S. (1994). Needed relationships and repeated relationships: An integrated relational perspective. *Psychoanalytic Dialogues, 4*(3), 317-345.

Stolorow, R. D., Brandchaft, B, & Atwood, G. E. (1987). *Psychoanalytic treatment: An intersubjective approach*. Hillsdale, NJ: The Analytic Press.

Sullivan, H. S. (1953). *The interpersonal theory of psychiatry* (H. S. Perry & M. L. Gawel, Eds.). New York: Norton.

Surrey, J. L. (1985). *The "self-in-relation": A theory of women's development*. Works in progress (No. 13). Wellesley, MA: The Stone Center, Wellesley College.

Trautmann, R. L., & Erskine, R. G. (1981). Ego state analysis: A comparative view. *Transactional Analysis Journal, 11*, 178-185.

Winnicott, D. W. (1965). *The maturational processes and the facilitating environment: Studies in the theory of emotional development*. New York: International Universities Press.

Wolf, E. S. (1988). *Treating the self: Elements of clinical self psychology*. New York: Guilford Press.

This article was originally published in the Transactional Analysis Journal, *Volume 26, Number 4, October 1996, pp. 316-328. The authors gratefully acknowledge the members of the Professional Development Seminars of the Institute for Integrative Psychotherapy, New York, New York; Kent, Connecticut; Dayton, Ohio; Chicago, Illinois; and Vancouver, British Columbia, Canada, for their contributions in forming the ideas in this article. A special thank you to Steven Roberts, M.S.W., and Barbara Clark, Ph.D., for their clarification of ideas. Portions of this article were presented as a keynote speech entitled, "A Transactional Analysis Theory of Methods," and also as a workshop entitled, "Inquiry, Attunement, and Involvement: The Application of Transactional Analysis Theory," at the 33rd Annual Conference of the International Transactional Analysis Association, San Francisco, CA, August 11, 1995.*

Inquiry, Attunement, and Involvement in the Psychotherapy of Dissociation

Richard G. Erskine

This essay distills a quarter century of experience as a psychotherapist with clients who use dissociation as a strategy for coping with traumatic events and stressors. My most challenging professional developments have resulted from my therapeutic errors—errors that demonstrated either ineffectiveness or the reinforcement of defenses that result from the methods of interrogation, confrontation, and explanation and the techniques of behavioral change, redecision, and reparenting. When using these methods and techniques, we as psychotherapists often fail to value the client's sense of vulnerability and perceived need for self-protection; we fail to respect the client's integrity in constructing his or her system of making meaning, and we fail to realize how our interventions may increase the client's sense of shame for having his or her experiences and defenses.

My clinical experience has demonstrated that the defense of dissociation results not only from traumatic experiences but, equally or even more importantly, from the lack of a protective and reparative relationship. Therefore, clients who use dissociation require a relationship-oriented psychotherapy that emphasizes contact through gentle inquiry into the client's experience, attunement to the client's affect and developmental level of functioning, and an interpersonal involvement that provides consistency and dependability through acknowledgment, validation, normalization, and the reliable presence of the therapist. I invite you to share in my professional journey and to expand on the therapeutic experiences and methods I present here so that together we may evolve an even more effective psychotherapy.

Dissociative Defenses

Dissociation is a complex defensive process that maintains mental and physical stability. During a traumatic experience, dissociation allows a person to remove himself or herself cognitively and emotionally from the experience and to physically adapt and behaviorally conform to external demands. Continuing the dissociation after a traumatic event enables a person to disengage from related needs and emotions and to evade the memory and its devastating impact.

Dissociation is the predominant defense present in multiple personality disorder, post-traumatic stress disorder, and schizoid disorder. It is also found in many less pronounced disorders, often masked by anxiety or depression. The presence of dissociation is a highly reliable indicator of previous mental, physical, and/or sexual abuse. In some cases dissociation is a reaction to early abandonment, severe sustained pain, near-death experiences, and/or prolonged neglect. These overwhelming experiences, usually, but not always, in childhood, threaten the cognitive and emotional stability and physical security, if not the life, of the individual.

Psychological defenses protect against the pain of overwhelming stimuli, unmet needs, and unexpressed emotions. In order to get on with life and to adapt as well as possible, many people keep these needs, feelings, and traumatic memories out of awareness. This results in a fixation of defenses—the habitual maintenance today of patterns of coping and psychological defense that were necessary at a previous time. These fixated defenses interrupt an individual's ability to be contactful both internally with self and externally with others. It is because of the fixation of contact-interrupting defenses that traumatic experiences remain dissociated as separate states of the ego or self rather than being integrated into a here-and-now whole—a neopsychic ego.

The neopsychic ego—at every age—is a continually contacting, integrating, and emerging process. If a traumatized person also suffered from a failure of contact in a caretaking relationship, clinical experience indicates that the traumatic experience will most likely not be integrated. The unmet needs for empathy, nurturing, and protection during the trauma are not acknowledged or validated satisfactorily, further compounding the trauma. This initiates the process of isolating the experience from awareness and, in more extreme situations, may lead to isolating aspects of self from awareness as well. The person must engage in a complex set of defenses in order to limit internal contact and to encapsulate the awareness of the traumatizing experience, related feelings, and unmet needs. These needs, feelings, and experiences reside within the ego in a separate state of consciousness, neither contacting nor contactable. Thus the fixated trauma does not become integrated with later experience and learning.

Ego fragmentation and dissociation. Following traumatization there is an intense need for a reliable other to respond empathically to the individual's extreme emotional reactions and unmet needs, to be attuned to the unspeakable, to offer a realistic understanding of what happened, and to provide safety through continued involvement and problem solving. Dissociation begins because those in the person's life fail to provide necessary restorative and nurturing functions. In many incest situations the child was told that he or she "liked it," or the child's withdrawal and depression were ignored by adults. Without attunement, validation, and empathic transactions from a significant person, a child does his or her best to deeply sequester those feelings, needs, and memories, sometimes to the point of no longer even realizing his or her need for relationship. This is the process of ego fragmentation and dissociation.

Contact: Inquiry, Attunement, and Involvement

Contact internally is the full awareness of internal sensations, feelings, needs, sensorimotor activity, thoughts, and memories, and externally it involves the rapid shift to full awareness of external events as registered by each of the sensory organs. With full internal and external contact, experiences are continually integrated. Defenses interrupt full contact and impede awareness internally and/or externally. Contact is thus the medium through which the process of dissociation can be dissolved and the encapsulated traumatic experiences, hidden needs, and feelings can be integrated into a cohesive sense of self (a neopsychic ego). Contact also refers to the quality of the transactions between two people, that is, the full awareness of both one's self and the other as exemplified in an authentic and sensitive encounter.

A guiding principle of contact-oriented psychotherapy is respect for the client's integrity. Through respect, kindness, and compassion, a therapist establishes an interpersonal relationship that provides affirmation of such integrity. This respectfulness may be described best as a consistent invitation to interpersonal contact between client and therapist, with simultaneous support for the client's contacting his or her internal experience and receiving external recognition of that experience. Withdrawing from contact may often be identified and discussed, but the client is never forced, trapped, or tricked into more openness than he or she is ready to handle.

Contact between client and therapist is the therapeutic context in which the client explores his or her feelings, needs, memories, and perceptions. Such contact is possible when the therapist is fully present, that is, attuned to his or her own inner processes and external behaviors, constantly aware of the boundary between self and client, and keenly observant of the client's psychodynamics. Contact within psychotherapy is like the substructure of a building: It cannot be seen, but it undergirds and supports all that is above ground. Contact provides the safety that allows the client to drop defenses, to feel again, and to remember.

Psychotherapy often begins with conversation and engagement in a contracting process. The ongoing negotiation of therapeutic contracts is an important element in establishing a contactful therapeutic relationship. The traumas that produce the defenses comprising dissociation usually occur in situations in which clients could not negotiate with regard to their own needs for physical and mental security. Instead, they were deprived of a sense of impact, valuation, and efficacy. Rather than relying on negotiation as a means of achieving satisfaction of needs, such clients may anticipate either being overwhelmed or having to use strong methods of manipulation or control, including dissociation. Therefore, the use of contracts is an essential part of the initial therapeutic contact with clients who dissociate (perhaps even more than with other clients) because their mental and/or physical being has been violated.

When traumatic experiences are being actively remembered or relived, it is important to have a contract that specifically defines the therapeutic territory in advance. In therapy, vividly remembered experiences may arise that surprise both client and therapist. These spontaneous memories may not be predictable, and responses to them cannot always be specifically negotiated beforehand. Therefore, procedures should be agreed on in advance as to how the client can signal that the experience is becoming overwhelming and how the therapist will stop the intervention. For example, one client used a specific word to indicate an entire set of feelings, needs, and impending defenses; others have used gestures or sounds.

Inquiry. Inquiry is a constant focus in contact-oriented psychotherapy. It begins with the assumption that the therapist knows nothing about the client's experience and thus must continually strive to understand the subjective meaning of the client's behavior and intrapsychic process. As a result of respectful investigation of the client's phenomenological experience, the client becomes increasingly aware of both current and archaic needs, feelings, and behaviors. It is with full awareness and the absence of internal defenses that needs and feelings that were fixated as a result of past traumas are integrated into a fully functioning neopsychic ego.

The *process* of inquiry is as important, if not more so, than the content. The therapist's inquiry must be empathic with the client's subjective experience to be effective in discovering and revealing the internal phenomena (physical sensations, feelings, thoughts, meanings, beliefs, decisions, hopes, and memories) and uncovering the internal and external interruptions to contact. Inquiry involves constantly focusing on the client's experience of affect, motivation, beliefs, or fantasy and not on behavior alone or on a problem to be solved.

Inquiry begins with a genuine interest in a client's subjective experience and construction of meaning. It proceeds with questions from the therapist as to what the client is feeling, how he or she experiences both self and others (including the psychotherapist), and what conclusions are reached. It may continue with historical questions about when an experience occurred and who was significant in the person's life.

In the treatment of dissociation, inquiry is used in the preparatory phase of therapy to increase the client's awareness of when and how he or she dissociates. It involves investigating the client's experience of the component interruptions to contact that constitute the dissociation. What does he or she do? Are self-hypnotic activities being used? Some clients report that they roll their eyes back, get small inside, or wag a finger.

When treating a client who dissociates it may be important to assess the function of the dissociation relevant to the needs of the whole person and to the needs of fragmented ego states. With multiple personalities, one might ask each part, "What is your role?" Each personality may have a specific function to fulfill, such as expressing a particular feeling (only anger or only sadness), engaging in an isolated defense (compulsive cleaning or amnesia), or coping with life's demands (organization or productivity). Frequently a personality serves a protective and/or nurturing function that was missing in the past and that may still be unfulfilled in current relationships, such as validation, attunement to needs and feelings, or providing safety and nurturing.

It is essential to inquire about who failed to provide the developmentally necessary functions that should have been fulfilled by a responsible caretaker. How did they fail? Inquiry is also essential about the client's likely anticipation that others will again fail him or her in a relationship. This anticipation constitutes one of the dimensions of transference—the dread of retraumatization—and the justification for maintaining defenses against contactful relationships.

In the psychotherapy of dissociation it is crucial that the therapist understand each client's unique need for a stabilizing, validating, and reparative other person to take on some of the relationship functions that the client is attempting to manage alone. A contact-oriented relationship therapy requires that the therapist be attuned to these relationship needs and be involved, through empathic validation of feelings and needs and by providing safety and support.

Attunement. Attunement is a two-part process: It involves both being fully aware of another person's sensations, needs, or feelings and communicating that awareness to the other.

Attunement requires understanding the developmentally based needs and related feelings that were fixated in the traumatic experience and that are now requiring expression. More than just understanding, attunement is a kinesthetic and emotional sensing of the other—knowing the other's experience by metaphorically being in his or her skin. Effective attunement also requires that the therapist simultaneously remain aware of the boundary between client and therapist. It is enhanced by focusing on the client at the developmental age of the trauma and knowing what a traumatized person of that age is attempting to express, what he or she requires in the way of experiencing needs, and his or her need for a protective, safe, and validating relationship with a caretaker.

The communication of attunement validates the client's needs and feelings and lays the foundation for repairing the failures of previous relationships. Attunement may be demonstrated by what we say, such as "that hurt," "you seemed frightened," or "you needed someone to be there with you." It is more frequently communicated by the therapist's facial or body movements signaling to the client that his or her affect exists, that it is perceived by the therapist to be significant, and that it makes an impact on the therapist.

Attunement is often experienced by the client as the therapist gently moving past the defenses that protect the client from awareness of trauma and its related needs and feelings and making contact with the long-forgotten parts of the client's Child ego state. Over time, this results in a lessening of external interruptions to contact and a corresponding dissolving of internal defenses. Needs and feelings can then be increasingly expressed with the comfort and assurance that they will be met with an empathic response. Frequently the attunement provides a sense of safety and stability that enables the client to begin to remember and to endure regressing into the traumatic experience, becoming fully aware of the pain of the trauma, the failure of relationship(s), and the loss of a sense of self.

Juxtaposition. The juxtaposition of the therapist's attunement with the memory of the lack of attunement in previous significant relationships produces intense, emotional memories of needs not being met. Rather than experience those feelings, the client may react defensively to the contact offered by the therapist with fear, anger, or even further dissociation. The contrast between the contact available with the therapist and the lack of contact in the original trauma(s) is often more than clients can bear, so they defend against the current contact to avoid the emotional memories.

It is important for the therapist to work sensitively with the process of juxtaposition. The affect and behavior expressed by the client are an attempt to disavow emotional memories. Therapists who do not account for these defensive reactions may mistakenly identify the juxtaposition reaction as negative transference and/or experience intense counter-transference feelings in response to the client's avoidance of interpersonal contact. The concept of juxtaposition helps therapists to understand the intense difficulty the client has in contrasting the current contact offered by the therapist with the awareness that needs for contactful relationship were unfulfilled in the past.

Juxtaposition reactions may signal that the therapist is proceeding faster than the client can assimilate. Frequently it is wise to return to the therapeutic contract and clarify the purpose of the therapy. Explaining the concept of juxtaposition has been beneficial in some situations. Most often a careful inquiry into the phenomenological experience of the current interruption to contact will reveal the emotional memories of disappointment and painful relationships.

Once the interruptions to contact have dissolved, the relationship offered by the therapist provides the client with a sense of validation, care, support, and understanding—"someone is there for me." This involvement is an essential factor in dissolving the defenses that constitute dissociation and in resolving and integrating previous traumas and unrequited relationships.

Involvement. Involvement is best understood via the client's perception; it is a sense that the therapist is contactful. It evolves from the therapist's empathic inquiry into the client's experience and is developed through the therapist's attunement with the client's affect and validation of the client's needs. Involvement is the result of the therapist being fully present, with and for the client, in a way that is appropriate to the client's developmental level. It includes a genuine interest in the client's intrapsychic and interpersonal world and a communication of that interest through attentiveness, inquiry, and patience.

Involvement begins with the therapist's commitment to the client's welfare and a respect for the client's phenomenological experience. Full contact becomes possible when the client experiences that the therapist: (1) respects each defense; (2) stays attuned to his or her affect and needs; (3) is sensitive to the psychological functioning at the developmental age when the trauma(s) occurred; and (4) is interested in understanding the client's way of constructing the meaning of the trauma(s).

The complex set of defenses that constitutes dissociation was erected in the absence of a caring and respectful involvement by a reliable and dependable other. Clients who have relied on dissociation as a protective measure experienced that they had to protect and comfort themselves in the face of impinging and overwhelming stimuli. It is in the absence of reliable and consistent need-fulfilling contact with a dependable other that defenses become fixated.

Therapeutic involvement that emphasizes acknowledgment, validation, normalization, and presence diminishes the internal discounting that is part of dissociation. These engagements allow previously disavowed feelings and denied experiences to come to full awareness. The therapist's *acknowledgment* of the client's feelings begins with attunement to the client's affect, even if the affect is unexpressed. Through sensitivity to the physiological expression of emotions the therapist guides the client to express his or her feelings or to acknowledge that feelings or physical sensations may be the memory—the only memory available. For instance, if the person's eyes were closed during a traumatic event there will be no visual memory. In other situations the child may have been too young to remember cognitively. In many cases of trauma, the person's feelings were not acknowledged, and it may be necessary in psychotherapy to help such individuals develop a vocabulary with which to voice those feelings. Acknowledgment of physical sensations and affect helps the client claim her or his own phenomenological experience. Acknowledgment includes a receptive other who knows and communicates about the existence of nonverbal movements, tensing of muscles, affect, or even fantasy.

There are times in clients' lives when their feelings were acknowledged but not validated. *Validation* communicates to the client that his or her affect or physical sensations are related to something significant. Validation is linking cause and effect. For example: "Based on what you described, you feel sad because no one was there for you," or "Your fantasies and dreams are saying something important." Validation diminishes the possibility of the client internally discounting the significance of affect, physical sensation, memory, or dreams. It enhances for the client the value of his or her phenomenological experience and therefore an increased sense of self-esteem.

Normalization depathologizes the client's or the other's categorization or definition of internal experience or behavioral attempts to cope with the effects of trauma. Under extreme circumstances it is normal to dissociate. It may be essential for the therapist to counter societal or parental messages such as, "You're crazy for feeling scared," with "Anyone would be scared in that situation." Many flashbacks, bizarre fantasies, and nightmares as well as much confusion, panic, and defensiveness are normal coping phenomena in abnormal situations. It is imperative that the therapist communicate that the client's experience is a normal defensive reaction, not pathological.

Presence is provided by the psychotherapist's sustained empathic responses to both the verbal and nonverbal expressions of the client. It occurs when the behavior and communication of the psychotherapist respects and enhances the client's integrity. Presence includes the therapist's receptivity to the client's affect, that is, to being impacted and moved by the client's emotions and yet not to become anxious, depressed, or angry. Presence is an expression of the psychotherapist's availability for full internal and external contact. It communicates the psychotherapist's responsibility, dependability, and reliability.

Remembering traumatic and neglectful experiences may be frightening and painful for the client; therefore, therapeutic involvement is maintained by the therapist's constant vigilance in providing an environment and a relationship that is safe and secure. The therapist, of necessity, must be constantly attuned to the client's ability to tolerate the emerging awareness of the traumatic experience(s) so that he or she is not overwhelmed again in the therapy as he or she was in the original traumatic situation. When inquiry into the client's phenomenological experiences and therapeutic regressions occurs in surroundings that are calming and containing, the fixated defenses are relaxed further, and the needs and feelings that derive from the traumatic experience(s) are integrated.

The psychotherapist's involvement—through transactions that acknowledge, validate, and normalize the client's phenomenological experience and sustain an empathic presence—fosters therapeutic potency that allows the client to safely depend on the relationship. Potency is the result of engagement that communicates that the therapist is fully invested in the client's welfare. Acknowledgment, validation, and normalization provide the client with permission to know his or her own feelings, to value the significance of his or her affects, and to relate them to actual or anticipated events. Such therapeutic permission to diminish defenses, to know his or her physical sensations, feelings, and memories, and to reveal them must come only after the client experiences protection within the therapeutic environment. Such therapeutic protection is adequately provided only after there is a thorough assessment of dynamics related to intrapsychic punishment and the client feels safe.

Intrapsychic punishment involves the child's perceived loss of bonding or attachment, shame, or threat of retribution. Protective interventions may include supporting a regressive dependency, providing a reliable and safe environment in which the client can rediscover what has been dissociated, and pacing the therapy so experiences may be fully integrated. Putting some memories on hold until others are dealt with is a way to ensure that the client will not be flooded with overwhelming anxiety. For example, for one client, traumatic memories first emerged in nightmares. She was often overwhelmed by terror and exhausted by lack of sleep. Periodically she was encouraged to stop dreaming until the material already dreamed had become clear and had been worked through. Once she connected her dreams to memories of childhood events and understood and resolved the ramifications of those events in her adult life, the therapist encouraged her to dream the next episode. The client was also encouraged to draw the dreams on a sketch pad so that she could go back to sleep or concentrate on her job the next day. She brought the sketch pad to therapy sessions as an aid to remembering and deciphering the dreams. Postponing or sketching her dreams served as a protection from overwhelming sensations.

There are times when a client attempts to elicit attunement and understanding by acting out a problem that cannot be expressed in any other way. Such acting out expressions are simultaneously a defensive deflection of the emotional memories and also an attempt to communicate the person's internal conflicts. Confrontations or explanations can intensify the defenses making the awareness of needs and feelings less accessible. Involvement includes a gentle, respectful inquiring into the internal experience connected with the acting out. The therapist's genuine interest in and honoring of the communication, which often may be without language, is an essential aspect of therapeutic involvement.

Involvement may include the therapist actively facilitating the client's undoing repressive retroflections and the inhibition of activating responses, such as screaming for help or fighting back. The therapist's considered revelation of his or her internal reactions or compassion is further expression of involvement. This may also include responding to earlier developmental needs in a way that symbolically represents need fulfillment, but the goal of a contact-oriented therapy is not the satisfaction of archaic needs. Rather, the goal is the dissolution of fixated, contact-interrupting defenses that interfere with the satisfaction of current needs and full contact with self and others. This is often accomplished by working transferentially to allow the intrapsychic conflict to be expressed within the therapeutic relationship and to be responded to with appropriate empathic transactions.

Conclusion

In work with dissociative clients, a contact-oriented psychotherapy using inquiry, attunement, and involvement responds to the individual's current needs for an emotionally nurturing relationship that is reparative and sustaining. The aim of the therapy is the integration of affect-laden experiences and the intrapsychic reorganization of the client's beliefs about self, others, and the quality of life. Contact facilitates the dissolution of defenses and the integration of the dissociated parts of the personality. Through contact, disowned, unconscious, and unresolved experiences are made part of a cohesive self. With integration it becomes possible for a person to face each moment with spontaneity and flexibility in solving life's problems and in relating to people without resorting to the defense of dissociation.

This article was originally published in the Transactional Analysis Journal, *Volume 23, Number 4, October 1993, pp. 184-190. Portions of this paper were also presented at the Symposium on the Treatment of Dissociation held at the 29th Annual International Transactional Analysis Association Conference, October 26, 1991, in Stamford, Connecticut, U.S.A. The author wishes to thank the members of the Professional Development Seminars of the Institute for Integrative Psychotherapy in New York, New York, Kent, Connecticut, Chicago, Illinois, and Dayton, Ohio, for their valuable suggestions in the development of this essay.*

Shame and Self-Righteousness: Transactional Analysis Perspectives and Clinical Interventions

Richard G. Erskine

Shame and self-righteousness are protective mechanisms that help the individual to avoid the vulnerability to humiliation and the loss of contact in relationship. When a relationship is tainted by criticism, ridicule, blaming, defining, ignoring, or other humiliating behaviors, the result is an increased vulnerability in the relationship. The contact or attachment is disrupted. Shame and self-righteousness result from humiliating disgrace or reproach and a loss of self-esteem.

Both shame and self-righteousness reflect the defenses used to avoid experiencing the intensity of how vulnerable and powerless the individual is to the loss of relationship. Simultaneously, shame is an expression of an unaware hope that the other person will take the responsibility for repairing the rupture in the relationship. Self-righteousness involves a denial of the need for relationship.

A Personal Experience

A few years ago a colleague telephoned and criticized my behavior, defining my motivation as pathological. Although I apologized, attempted to explain the situation, and tried to rectify the problem in writing, the previously warm and respectful relationship ended in a lack of communication.

In each subsequent attempt to talk to that person, I tripped over my own words, experienced myself as inept, and avoided talking about both my feelings and our relationship. The experience of being humiliated by a respected colleague left me feeling debilitating shame. I longed for a reconnection. I wished that the person would inquire about my feelings and our lack of contact and recognize and respond empathically and reciprocally to the humiliating experience I had had in the original phone conversation.

The sense of shame and longing compelled me to examine my internal reactions to the humiliation. In my psychotherapy sessions I reexperienced being a little boy in the second and third grades, filled with hurt and fear and adapting to a highly critical teacher. The personal benefit of the psychotherapy was a reclaiming of sensitivity to others and to myself and a personal sense of contentment. The professional benefit of resolving my shame was an evolution in the therapeutic methods and interactions in my clinical practice. I was faced with several questions: How and when do I define people? Do I ascribe motivation rather than facilitate the person's self-understanding of his or her behavior? What is the effect of my inner affect or behavior on the other person? Am I, in my attempt to be therapeutic, implying to the client, "Something is wrong with you?"

The theoretical ideas on shame and defensive self-righteousness and the clinical interventions presented in this article are the result of several years of my investigating my errors as a therapist, the ruptures I have created in the therapeutic relationship with clients, and the methods that may increase a client's sense of shame. A respectful inquiry into each client's phenomenological experience of our therapy process provided a transaction-by-transaction exploration of my empathic failures, misperceptions of developmental levels of functioning, and affective misattunements—the interruptions to contact-in-relationship. When I take responsibility for the ruptures in the therapeutic relationship, my therapy focuses on attuning to the client's affective experience and responding with a reciprocal affect. My therapeutic involvement is in my consistency, responsibility, and dependability. It is in the exploration and resolution of the ruptures in our relationship that I can be most effective in uncovering the core script beliefs that determine the significant interpersonal experiences in my client's life.

Transactional analysis psychotherapy in the 1970s and early 1980s was marked by the defining of clients' behaviors and was skewed by clinical methods that emphasized explanation, confrontation, and behavioral change. Such methods often overshadow underlying issues related to shame and self-righteousness. To define a client's feeling as a racket, or behavior as a game or as scripty, is adverse to resolving psychological problems that originate in the experience of humiliation, neglect, or abuse.

To define someone, even if accurately, may devalue and humiliate them. To genuinely inquire about another's experience, motivation, self-definition, and the meaning of his or her behavior avoids potential humiliation. To respond with empathy and attunement empowers the person to fully express feelings, thoughts, perceptions, and talents. Inquiry, attunement, and involvement invite a revealing of the other's underlying meaning and unconscious motivation.

Clinical practice and theoretical development push and pull each other in the process of evolving. Clinical interventions that make use of respect (Erskine & Moursund, 1988); empathic transactions (Clark, 1991); emotional engagement (Cornell & Olio, 1992); and inquiry, attunement, and involvement (Erskine, 1991a; Erskine, 1993; Erskine & Trautmann, 1993) have revealed that shame and self-protective fantasies are dominant in the lives of many clients. However, these phenomena have not been adequately integrated with a transactional analysis theory of ego states and scripts. Clinical experience helped to evolve a theoretical understanding that views shame and self-righteousness as archaic intrapsychic dynamics designed to protect the individual from reproach, humiliation, and the loss of contact in relationship. Unresolved *archaic shame* increases the pain of any current criticism. Archaic intrapsychic conflict adds a toxicity that floods current humiliation with debilitating shame or defensive self-righteousness.

The Literature

In the transactional analysis literature, shame and self-righteousness have received little attention, either as theoretical topics or as areas of clinical concern. Obliquely, Berne (1972), Ernst (1971), and Erskine and Zalcman (1979) all presented a theoretical basis for understanding the existential position and script beliefs related to shame. Erskine's (1988) description of Child ego state defenses against intrapsychic conflicts, when elaborated to include affect and fantasy, provides an ego state theory for understanding the dynamics of shame and self-righteousness.

English (1975) directly addressed shame and social control, describing shame as "the price of the child's having internalized a specific message of *control* from his family and culture" (p. 26). She went on to say that the effect is the inhibiting, limiting, and controlling of expansive curiosity. English emphasized that the act of shaming children serves "the function of adapting the child to the family's civilization, for better or worse" (p. 26). Recently, Klein (1992) defined righteousness as "the core of the defensive structures of our egos" (p. 76). She indirectly related the defensiveness of self-righteousness to shame when she described righteousness as "the camouflage for our negative self-esteem" (p. 78). Although Berne (1972) and Ernst (1971) did not specifically write about shame or self-righteousness, dynamics related to these feelings are reflected in the existential positions of "I'm not-OK—You're OK" or in the defense "I'm OK—You're not-OK."

The general psychotherapy literature on shame and self-righteousness has also been sparse, although recently the concept of shame has received increased attention. Goldberg began *Understanding Shame* (1991) by tracing the origin of the modern English word "shame" from the Indo-European word "scheme," which means "to hide" or "cover up." He continued with clinical case examples of how individuals hide and cover up their full self-expression following incidents of insult and disgrace. Each of Goldberg's examples about shame reflected a debasing, degrading, or humiliating experience inflicted by the behavior of another person. According to Goldberg, shame is caused by "the loss of loving connection with significant others, who are, or are believed to be, necessary to one's psychological and physical survival" (p. 59). The result is the loss of self-esteem and the protective hiding of the degraded sense of self both from others and any possible future reproach and insult. Shame represents a special fear—"like an instinct for self-preservation" (p. 18), like "a silencing vehicle that keeps the misery a secret" (p. 22). In essence, shame is a lonely yet self-protective experience. However, Goldberg (1990) also views shame as "the crucible of human freedom," with a constructive potential (p. 591).

Lynd (1958), one of the earliest writers on shame, defined shame as a sense of injury to the trust of oneself and of others. Lewis (1971) described shame as a reduction in self-esteem and in the esteem of others resulting in fury or anger that functions to regain a sense of being valued. Wilson (1990), writing for a lay audience, said, "Shame is a strong sense of being uniquely and hopelessly different and less than other human beings" (p. 25).

Kaufman, in *The Psychology of Shame* (1989), wrote:
Phenomenologically, to feel shame is to feel *seen* in a painfully diminished sense. (p. 17)
Shame is the source of what has been referred to as narcissistic wounds or injuries [with] low self-esteem, poor self-concept, or diminished self-image. (p. 25)

Shame becomes activated whenever fundamental expectations of a significant other (imagined scenes of interpersonal need) or those equally fundamental expectations of oneself (imagined scenes of accomplishment or purpose) are suddenly exposed as wrong or are thwarted. (p. 35)

Silvan Tomkins (1963) described shame as one of the nine human affects: as "the affect of indignity, of defeat, of transgression and alienation" (p. 118). As one of the first psychologists to seriously investigate emotions, Tomkins (1962, 1963, 1991) pioneered an elaborate theory that gave voice to many psychotherapists' clinical observations of the interplay between affect, perception, cognition, bodily reactions, and behavior. Tomkins was particularly interested in facial, respiratory, and body gestures as an expression of various affects and how emotions serve as the primary motivational system for human beings. He described shame as an affect on a continuum with humiliation, shame being of lesser intensity and humiliation related to much greater affect arousal. Although Tomkins theorized that shame was among the nine primary affects that motivated cognition and behavior, he described shame as always occurring in the presence of other emotions. Shame serves as an alternator or impediment to the expression of interest, excitement, or joy, and it interferes with the pleasure of an experience.

Nathanson (1992) applied Tomkins's affect theory—specifically as it relates to shame and pride—to descriptions of daily life and to psychotherapy and psychoanalysis. The psychoanalytic writers have generally ignored the topic of shame. From a psychoanalytic perspective shame is a resistance—a reaction formation that intends the converse of what is phenomenologically experienced. Shame is seen as inhibiting exhibitionist impulses by disguising forbidden drives and wishes from awareness (Goldberg, 1991).

Erikson (1950, 1959, 1968) was one of the first psychoanalytic developmental theorists to dispense with Freud's instinctual drive theory and the central importance of guilt in that paradigm. Instead, he wrote about the ontological development of identity throughout the life cycle. He described eight developmental stages or crises through which individuals form and refine their identity—a personal approach to viewing self and the world. Erikson's second stage centered on a sense of autonomy versus shame and doubt. He (1968) wrote that just as autonomy and pride emanate from a sense of inner goodness, so doubt and shame derive from the sense of badness: "A sense of self-control without loss of self-esteem is the ontogenetic source of a sense of *free will*. From an unavoidable sense of loss of self-control and of parental overcontrol comes a lasting propensity for *doubt* and *shame*" (p. 109). The quality of the relationship between a child and parent is the primary factor in whether the child develops a sense of self-worth and competency or a feeling of being powerless, inhibited, and shamed. "The quality of autonomy which children develop depends on their parents' ability to grant autonomy with dignity and a sense of personal independence which they derive from their own lives" (Erskine, 1971, p. 60). Shame results when parents resort to belittling or teasing, which impels the child to abandon desires and interests; doubt results from external overcontrol which robs the child of the sense of efficacy—that he or she is capable of controlling himself or herself (Wolf, 1988).

Lewis (1971, 1987), following Erikson's ideas, seemed to be one of the first psychoanalytic writers to relate the phenomenon of shame to clinical practice. She emphasized the struggle to regain a sense of being valued following a loss of value or esteem in the eyes of others or one's self. Wurmser (1981) described shame as related to beliefs about something being wrong with the self, that is, "I am weak," "I am dirty," "I am defective" (pp. 27-28). Basch (1988) gave shame a significant place within psychoanalytic self psychology theory. He described shame as "a painful emotion . . . a basically protective maneuver" (p. 136) that puts an end to self-expression or expectations. Both Kohut (1977, 1984) and Morrison (1987) related the origin of shame to experiences of empathic failure in current life and also, importantly, to feelings of insecurity resulting from early childhood parental empathic failure.

Sullivan (1954) described the dynamics of shame with the term anxiety:

> As I use the term, anxiety is a sign that one's self-esteem, one's self-regard is endangered. . . . Anxiety is a signal of danger to self-respect, to one's standing in the eyes of significant persons present, even if they are only ideal figures from childhood. (p. 207)

Sullivan also described how people use anger and "misunderstanding" to avoid the anxiety of "*foreseen* lowering of self-esteem" (p. 207).

Self-righteousness has received even less attention in the psychotherapy literature than has shame. The literature on the treatment of narcissistic disorders is one area in which writers have implied a direct connection between humiliation, shame, low self-evaluation, rageful anger, and self-righteousness (Kohut, 1978; Lewis, 1987; Modell, 1986; Morrison, 1986; Reich, 1986; Wurmser, 1987). Bursten (1973) described the adoption of a stance of arrogance, self-glorification, and aggressiveness as the repair of shame. Bach (1985) defined the narcissistic grandiose fantasy as a defense against an "experienced defect in the sense of self which requires some unusual overcompensation" (p. 93). Overcompensation is accomplished through self-righteous fantasies, a defense against shame and low self-esteem caused by humiliating experiences with others. Horowitz (1981) related self-righteous rage and the attribution of blame to others as a defense against insult and shame. Basch (1988) provided a clinical example of the reversal of insult and shame in the case of a woman who was dreadfully humiliated and fantasized revenge as a disavowal of her sense of shame. Goldberg (1991) related such self-righteous fantasies to an attempt at gaining control over powerlessness. Wallace and Nosko (1993) described how rage and violence serve as a means of avoiding the sense of abandonment linked to shame in men who batter their wives. Although self-righteousness has not received adequate attention in the clinical or theoretical literature, the authors who do describe the phenomenon imply that self-righteousness is a defensive process used to ward off a sense of shame and the memories or anticipation of humiliation and reproach.

The clinical methods for the treatment of shame and self-righteousness that emphasize respect, attunement, and a contactful relationship are more fully developed than is a defined theoretical perspective in this area. The distinction between shame and humiliation needs to be clarified. Is shame an innate human affect or a combination of intrapsychic processes that include emotions, belief systems, and defense processes? Is shame a reaction to the current behavior of others, the result of archaic introjections and compliance, or an existential position? Further, how can these phenomena be explained within the framework of transactional analysis theory?

Shame: A Theoretical Clarification

Shame is a self-protective process used to avoid the affects that result from humiliation and vulnerability to loss of contact-in-relationship with another person. When children, and even adults, are criticized, devalued, or humiliated by significant others, the need for contact and the vulnerability in maintaining the relationship may produce a self-protective defensive affect and compliance with the imposed diminishing definitions. Shame is a complex process involving:

1. a diminished self-concept, a lowering of one's self-worth in *compliance* with the external humiliation and/or introjected criticism;
2. *a defensive transposition of sadness and fear*; and
3. *a disavowal of anger.*

Shame involves a disavowal of anger in order to maintain the semblance of a connected relationship with the person who engaged in humiliating transactions. *When anger is disavowed, a valuable aspect of the self is lost*: the need to be taken seriously and respectfully, and the need to make an impact on the other person. One's self-worth is diminished.

Shame also involves a transposition of the affects of sadness and fear: sadness at not being accepted *as one is*—with one's own urges, desires, needs, feelings, and behaviors—and fear of abandonment in the relationship because of *who one is*. The fear and the loss of an aspect of self (disavowal of anger) fuel the pull toward compliance—a lowering of one's self-esteem in order to establish confluence with the criticism and/or humiliation.

Compliance with the humiliation, the transposition of fear and sadness, and the disavowal of anger produce the sense of shame and doubt described by Erikson (1950). Writing from a feminist perspective on relationship therapy, both Miller (1987) and Jordan (1989) validate this explanation by relating shame to the loss of human connection.

> Shame is most importantly a felt sense of unworthiness to be in connection, a deep sense of unlovability, with the ongoing awareness of how very much one wants to connect with others. While shame involves extreme self-consciousness, it also signals powerful relationship longings. (Jordan, 1989, p. 6)

Kaufman (1989) similarly expressed that shame reflects the need for contact in relationship: "In the midst of shame, there is an ambivalent longing for reunion with whomever shamed us" (p. 19). *Shame is an expression of an unaware hope that the other will take responsibility for repairing the rupture in the relationship.*

Tomkins (1963) wrote that shame is the affect present when there has been a loss of dignity, defeat, transgression, and alienation. He implied that shame is an affect different in nature and function from the other eight affects in his theoretical schema. The affect of shame, according to Tomkins (see Nathanson, 1992), serves as an alternator or impediment to other affects—a defensive cover for interest and joy. Tomkins's ideas parallel Fraiberg's (1982/1983) observations about the formation of psychological defenses in children. She described the process of "transformation of affect" (p. 71), in which one affect is substituted or transposed for another when the original affect fails to bring about the necessary contact between the child and the caretaking adult, sometimes as early as nine months of age. When the child is humiliated, the fear of a loss of relationship and the sadness of not being accepted are transposed into the affect of shame. Shame is composed of sadness and fear, the disavowal of anger, and a lowered self-concept—compliance with the humiliation.

This compliance with humiliation ensures a continuing relationship and, paradoxically, is a defense as well. This self-protective lowering of worth is observable among wild animals when one animal crouches in the presence of another to avoid attack and to guarantee acceptance. It is self-protective to lower one's status in order to hold off aggression when a fight for dominance might occur. The lowered self-concept or self-criticism that is a part of shame lessens the pain of the rupture in relationship while at the same time maintaining a semblance of relationship. The often quoted boxing coach's phrase, "Beat 'em to the punch," describes the function of lowered self-esteem and self-criticism used as a defense against possible humiliation from others. However, the punch is delivered to one's self in the form of diminished self-worth.

Shame and Self-Righteousness:
A Transactional Analysis Perspective

The formulations of a transactional analysis theory of shame and self-righteousness require that the concepts be integrated within ego state theory and script theory. To arrive at an understanding of how the phenomena of shame and self-righteousness function within ego states, it is essential that the concepts being used be clearly defined. Berne (1972) recommended that theoretical discussions remain within a given set of concepts and definitions so that the definitions used "belong to the same framework or come from the same viewpoint" (p. 412). The following definitions of ego states are provided as a conceptual framework for such a theoretical exploration. Many of them draw from and rely on material I have previously published (see Erskine, 1980, 1988, 1991b, 1993; Erskine & Moursund, 1988).

Ego States

In 1961 Berne defined the collective Child ego states as an archaic ego consisting of fixations of earlier developmental stages: as "relics of the individual's own childhood" (p. 77). The Child ego state is the entire personality of the person as he or she was in that previous developmental period (Berne, 1958/1977, 1961, 1964). When functioning in a Child ego state the person perceives internal needs and sensations and the external world as he or she did at a previous developmental age. "This includes the needs, desires, urges, and sensations; the defense mechanisms; and the thought processes, perceptions, feelings, and behaviors of the developmental phase where fixation occurred" (Erskine, 1988, p. 17). The Child ego state fixations occurred when critical childhood needs for contact were not met, and the child's use of defenses against the discomfort of the unmet needs became habitual (Erskine, 1980).

The Parent ego states are the manifestations of introjections of the personalities of actual people as perceived by the child at the time of introjection (Erskine, 1988; Loria, 1988). Introjection is a defense mechanism (including disavowal, denial, and repression) frequently used when there is a lack of full psychological contact between a child and the adults responsible for his or her psychological needs. Introjection is an unaware identification with the beliefs, feelings, motivations, behaviors, and defenses of the other. The significant other is made part of the self (ego), and the conflict resulting from the lack of need fulfillment is internalized so that the conflict can seemingly be managed more easily (Perls, 1977; Rosenfeld, 1978).

Parent ego state contents may be introjected at any point throughout life and, if not reexamined in the process of later development, remain unassimilated or not integrated into the Adult ego state. The Parent ego states constitute alien chunks of personality, embedded within the ego and experienced phenomenologically as if they were one's own, but, in reality, they form a borrowed personality, potentially in the position of producing intrapsychic influences on the Child ego states.

The Adult ego state consists of current, age-consistent emotional, cognitive, and moral development; the ability to be creative; and the capacity for full, contactful engagement in meaningful relationships. The Adult ego state accounts for and integrates what is occurring moment-by-moment internally and externally, past experiences and their resulting effects, and the psychological influences and identifications with other significant people in one's life.

Archaic shame is an internal expression of an intrapsychic conflict between a reactive Child ego state and an influencing Parent ego state. When a Child ego state is active (either subjectively reportable or behaviorally observable), by theoretical inference a Parent ego state is cathected and intrapsychically influencing (Berne, 1961, 1964). "The individual manifests an attitude of child-like compliance" (Berne, 1961, p. 76) and/or may make use of childhood defenses such as avoidance, freezing, or fighting (Fraiberg, 1982/1983); ego splitting (Fairbairn, 1954); transformation of affect and reversal of aggression (Fraiberg, 1982/1983); and fantasy (Erskine, 1988, p. 18; Erskine & Moursund, 1988, p. 23).

Berne (1961) described the intrapsychic dynamics of ego states as representing "the relics of the infant who once actually existed, in a struggle with the relics of the parents who once actually existed" for it "reduplicates the actual childhood fights for survival between real people, or at least that is the way the patient experiences it" (p. 66).

The intrapsychic conflict is in part maintained by the child's need for relationship (Fairbairn, 1954), attachment (Bowlby, 1969), or contact (Erskine, 1989) and the fixated Child ego state's defense against full awareness of contact, attachment, and relationship needs. These needs are evident in the *psychological loyalty* to the intrapsychically influencing Parent ego state (Erskine, 1988, 1991b). The loyalty is in the defensive avoidance of the realization "My psychological needs were unmet" or in the unconscious fantasy "If I'm good enough, my needs will be met."

In the service of establishing a transactional analytic theory that describes the phenomena of shame and self-righteousness, the terms humiliation and humiliating transactions are used here to refer to interactions that occur between people when one person degrades, criticizes, defines, or ignores the other. The terms shame and self-righteousness are used to refer to the intrapsychic dynamics occurring within an individual that may be described as consisting of Parent ego state influence, compliance, and/or archaic systems of defense. When the sense of shame has become fixated, it represents an intrapsychic conflict *P·* between an influencing exteropsychic state of the ego and a compliant, defended *C* archaeopsychic state of the ego: that child who longed for relationship. "Fixation refers to a relatively enduring pattern of organization of affect, behavior, or cognition from an earlier stage of development which persists into and may dominate later life" (Erskine, 1991b, p. 69). It is the fixated defenses that keep the ego in separate states and interfere with integration of archaic experiences into an Adult ego (Erskine & Moursund, 1988).

A Defensive Fantasy

As a normal developmental process, young children often use fantasy as a way to provide controls, structure, nurturing, or whatever was experienced as missing or inadequate. The function of the fantasy may be to structure behavior as a protection from consequences or to provide love and nurturance when the real caretakers are cold, absent, or abusive. The fantasy serves as a buffer between the actual parental figures and the desires, needs, or feelings of the young child. In families or situations where it is necessary to repress an awareness of needs, feelings, and memories in order to survive or be accepted, the self-created fantasy may become fixated and not integrated with later developmental learning. Over time, the fantasy functions as a "reversal" of aggression (Fraiberg, 1982/1983, p. 73): The criticism, devaluation, and humiliation that the child may have been subject to are amplified and turned against the self as in self-criticism or self-abjection. Such shame-based fantasies serve to maintain an illusion of attachment to a caring relationship when the actual relationship may have been ruptured with humiliation.

Many clients report a persistent sense of shame accompanied by degrading self-criticism. They repeatedly imagine humiliating failures in performance or relationship. In fantasy they amplify the compliance with introjected criticism and humiliation while defending against memories of the original sadness at not being accepted as one is and the fear of abandonment because of who one is. When affect-laden memories of early traumatic humiliations are defensively repressed, they may reemerge in consciousness as fantasies of future failure or degradation. The self-criticism and fantasy of humiliating failure serve two additional functions: to maintain the disavowal of anger and to protect against the shock of possible forthcoming criticism and degradation.

Self-Righteousness: A Double Defense

Self-righteousness serves an even more elaborate function than the defensive aspects of shame. Self-righteousness is a self-generated fantasy (occasionally manifested in overt transactions) that defends against the pain of the loss of relationship while providing a pseudotriumph over the humiliation and an inflation in self-esteem. Whereas shame and self-criticizing fantasies leave the person feeling devalued and longing for a repair in the relationship, self-righteous fantasies are a desperate attempt to escape humiliation and to be free of shame by justifying oneself. Self-righteousness is: (1) a defense against the sadness and fear of humiliation, (2) an expression of the need to make an impact and to be taken seriously and treated respectfully, and (3) a defense against an awareness of the need for the other to repair the ruptured relationship (Bollas, 1987). The person fantasizes value for himself or herself, often by finding fault with others and then losing awareness of the need for the other. The self is experienced as superior.

As Alfred Adler described, a fantasy of superiority defends against memories of humiliation (Ansbacher & Ansbacher, 1956) and deflects the sense of shame outward. A clinical case example illustrates this concept. Robert, a 39-year-old married father of two, had been in group therapy for two-and-a-half years. Robert described that, while driving to work, he frequently fantasized arguing with his coworkers or department supervisor. He often elaborated these fantasies with an imagined long, well-articulated oratory before the board of directors. In these fantasized arguments he pointed out the errors of others, how their criticisms of Robert were wrong, and most importantly, how they made mistakes that he, Robert, would never make. In Robert's fantasy, the board of directors would be emotionally swayed by Robert's eloquent and convincing arguments. He would be exonerated of all criticism whereas the others would be blamed both for criticizing him and for their own failings. These obsessive fantasies were often initiated by some criticism at work that was not accompanied by an opportunity for Robert to explain his motivation. The lack of continued dialogue with people seemed to propel him into obsessive fantasy wherein he could debate with the other in front of an audience that, in the end, agreed that Robert was correct, even righteous.

These obsessive fantasies gradually diminished and finally ceased when we explored the humiliations he experienced repeatedly in early elementary school at a time when he had a speech impediment. Both teachers and other children made fun of his impediment. Although in psychotherapy he could not remember any of the specific taunts or mockery, he knew that he had been ridiculed. He had a constant sense that the reaction of others to him implied that "Something is wrong with you."

Over the years he painstakingly worked on improving his speech, overcame the impediment, and eventually developed impeccable diction. However, in compliance with the humiliation he had experienced as a child, he adopted the script belief "Something is wrong with me" as an explanation for his loss of close friendships with other children and approval from his teachers. He further defended against awareness of the script belief by perfecting his speech. Nevertheless, regardless of how perfect his speech became in adult life, whenever someone criticized him he would listen intently to their comments. The current criticisms would activate the emotional memories of earlier humiliations wherein the introjected criticisms would intrapsychically influence a Child ego state and potentiate the current criticisms. To comfort himself, on the way to work the next day, he would obsessively defend himself from his colleagues' or supervisor's remarks, longing for someone (the board of directors) to say he was right.

In Robert's case, the defensive process of disavowal of anger, compliance, transposition of affect, and fantasy became fixated in the same way that any defensive process does if it is not responded to early in its inception with an empathic and affectively attuned relationship (Erskine, 1991a, 1993). It was through respect for Robert's style of relating to people and a gentle and genuine inquiry into Robert's experience that he began to reveal the presence of his obsessive fantasies. The self-righteous fantasies defended against the natural desire for contact in relationship and his need for others to repair the ruptured relationship. Through attunement and empathic transactions he was able to experience the original shame—the sadness, fear, anger, and compliance in response to the humiliations. When expressing the sadness and fear at the loss of contact in his relationships with teachers and children, he rediscovered his longing to be connected with others. The defensive fantasies stopped. Tender involvement on the part of the therapist and other group members made it possible for Robert to experience his need for close emotional contact as natural and desirable.

The Script System

Berne's concepts of script have been explained and expanded on by many authors since they were first introduced (English, 1972; Erskine, 1980; Erskine & Zalcman, 1979; Goulding & Goulding, 1979; Holloway, 1977; Kahler with Capers, 1974; Steiner, 1971; Woollams, 1973). Each author presented his or her unique ideas and provided interesting theoretical perspectives, useful directions, and new dimensions to clinical practice. Yet only a few of these theoretical contributions were consistent with Berne's perspective on script as transference phenomena or his developmental and intrapsychic theory of ego states (Erskine, 1991b). Various models of ego states (Trautmann & Erskine, 1981) were used as the basis for script matrices without referring to Berne's original conceptualizations of ego states and without defining the rationale for reformulating ego state and script theory. Berne (1972) also contributed to this theoretical inconsistency by mixing concepts and models in his later writing. He lessened the impact of what his developmental and relational theories had to offer and thereby diminished his own creative extension of psychoanalytic and psychotherapy theory.

In the psychotherapy of shame and self-righteousness, as with many other psychological disturbances rooted in disturbances of relationship, the therapy is enhanced if the psychotherapist has a consistent and cohesive relationship-oriented theoretical basis for determining treatment planning and subsequent clinical interventions. Although several definitions of script exist in the transactional analysis literature (Cornell, 1988; Massey, 1989), the following definition of script (Erskine, 1980) is provided as a basis for correlating Berne's original definitions of ego states with an operational definition of life script and as ground for a consistent discussion of psychodynamics and psychotherapeutic methods: *Script is a life plan based on introjections and/or defensive reactions made under pressure, at any developmental age, which inhibit spontaneity and limit flexibility in problem solving and in relating to people.*

These introjections and/or defensive reactions occur under the pressure of failures in a contactful and supportive relationship. The needs for contact and related feelings of loss of relationship are denied and suppressed in the adoption of defensive reactions and introjections. This defensive process forms the "intrapsychic core of the script" (Erskine, 1980, p. 104).

Since its initial presentation in 1975 by Erskine and Zalcman and its publication in 1979 as "The Racket System: A Model for Racket Analysis" (Erskine & Zalcman), it has become clear that the American term "racket" does not directly translate into other languages. In the service of providing an international uniformity in transactional analysis theory and terminology, I recommend using the term *script system* rather than racket system and *intrapsychic analysis* rather than racket analysis. The concepts remain the same; only the terms are different.

The script system (originally published as the racket system) provides a model for understanding the systemic dynamics among the intrapsychic, behavioral, and physiological dimensions of life script. The script system diagrams how the intrapsychic reactions (defensive conclusions and decisions) and introjections that form the core of a life script are organized as script beliefs; how these core beliefs are manifested in behavior, fantasy, and physiological tensions; and how an individual structures his or her perceptions and interpretations of experience to provide reinforcement of script beliefs. It graphically depicts a cross section of the script—how the life script is lived out in the here and now.

The script system correlates with ego state theory while providing an alternative perspective on the organization of introjections and/or defensive reactions—the exteropsychic and archaeopsychic fixations of the ego. These fixations, in the form of script beliefs, serve as cognitive defenses against awareness of the needs and feelings present at an earlier age when need-fulfilling interpersonal contact was missing and script beliefs were formed or introjected. When operational, the script system depicts contamination of the Adult ego by Parent and Child ego states.

The script system is defined as a "self-reinforcing, distorted system of feelings, thoughts and actions maintained by script-bound individuals" (Erskine & Zalcman, 1979, p. 53). In a child's attempt to make sense of the experience of a lack of contact in relationship he or she is faced with answering the question: "What does a person like me do in a world like this with people like you?" When the child is under pressure from a lack of contact in relationship that acknowledges, validates, or fulfills needs, each of the three parts of this question may be answered with a defensive reaction and/or the unconscious defensive identification with the other that constitutes introjection. When the introjections and the defensive conclusions and decisions are not responded to by a contactful, empathic other person, they often become, in an attempt to gain self-support, fixated beliefs about self, others, and the quality of life—the core of the life script. These script beliefs function as a cognitive defense against awareness of the feelings and needs for contact in relationship that were not adequately responded to at the time when the script beliefs were formed. The presence of script beliefs indicates a continuing defense against the awareness of needs for contact in relationship and the full memory of disruptions in relationship.

The script display consists of all the overt and internal behaviors that are manifestations of the script beliefs and denied feelings and needs. The script display also includes the reported internal experiences of physiological tension and the fantasies that support the script beliefs by providing reinforcing experiences. The reinforcing experiences are the selected recall of transactions, fantasy, and bodily sensations that reinforce the script belief. Those experiences that do not reinforce the script beliefs are often negated (Erskine & Moursund, 1988, pp. 33-36).

In Robert's case, during elementary school he adopted the core script belief "Something is wrong with me" in compliance with the humiliation by the children and teachers and as a pseudosatisfaction of his need to be accepted by them. From the perspective of ego state theory, the core of Robert's sense of shame consists of a child's defensive transposition of sadness and fear, a disavowal of anger at not being treated respectfully, a fixated diminished self-concept in compliance with the introjected criticism, and a child's need for contact-in-relationship. This natural need for relationship keeps the Child ego states dependent and loyally attached to a Parent ego state and ensures compliance with the introjected humiliation. When the pain of not being accepted as one is becomes too great, as in Robert's situation, a defensive self-righteous fantasy may be used to deny the need for relationship while simultaneously expressing the need to make an impact and be treated respectfully.

From the perspective of script theory, the sense of shame is comprised of the core script belief "Something's wrong with me" that serves as a cognitive defense against awareness of the needs for relationship and the feelings of sadness and fear present at the time of the humiliating experiences.

When the script belief "Something's wrong with me" is operational, the overt behaviors of the script display are often those that are described as inhibited or inadequate: shyness, lack of eye contact in conversation, lack of self-expression, diminished expression of natural wants or needs, or any inhibition of natural expression of one's self that may be subject to criticism.

Fantasies may include anticipating inadequacy, failures in performance, or criticism that concludes with a reinforcement of the script belief "Something is wrong with me." Other fantasies may involve a rehashing of events and reshaping memory in such a way as to reinforce the core script beliefs. In some cases, the script belief is manifested in physiological restrictions such as headaches, stomach tensions, or other physical discomforts that inhibit the individual from behaving in a way that might be subject to humiliating comments from others, while simultaneously providing internal evidence that "Something's wrong with me." Often old memories of humiliating experiences are repeatedly recalled to maintain a homeostasis with core script beliefs and denial of the original needs and feelings. Yet in inhibiting one's self or in self-criticizing fantasies, the need for contact in relationship remains as an unaware hope for the reestablishment of a contactful relationship and for full acceptance by the other. It is as if he were saying to those who did the ridiculing, "If I become what you define me to be, then will you love me?"

Robert, as an example of someone using the dynamics of a double defense of self-righteousness, entered therapy unaware of any hope or need for relationship. His script display appeared to be the opposite of his script belief: He perfected his speech and behavior in such a way that there was no external evidence that "Something's wrong with me." His fantasies were self-righteous, focusing on what was wrong with the other. He remained hypersensitive to criticism with an unaware longing for someone in authority to tell him he was OK.

"Something's Wrong with Me"

The compounded and continual reinforcement of the script belief "Something is wrong with me" presents the therapist with complex challenges specific and unique to the psychotherapy of shame and self-righteousness. In many clinical cases this particular script belief is inflexible in response to the frequently used transactional analysis methods of explanation, confrontation, and interpretation; programmed redecision; an emphasis on behavioral change; or dogmatic reparenting. Each of these sets of methods provides only partial or temporary change in the frequency or the intensity of the complex script belief that is at the core of shame and self-righteousness. In fact, the very use of these methods frequently communicates "Something is wrong with you," which then can reinforce the core script belief, increase denial of the need for contact in relationship, and thereby increase the sense of shame or self-righteousness.

Through the use of methods that emphasize respect (Erskine & Moursund, 1988); empathic transactions (Clark, 1991); emotional engagement (Cornell & Olio, 1992); and gentle inquiry, affective attunement, and involvement (Erskine, 1991a; Erskine, 1993; Erskine & Trautmann, 1993), the opportunity for reinforcement of the script belief during the therapy process is considerably lessened.

In order to facilitate treatment planning and refine clinical interventions, it is essential to distinguish the *intrapsychic functions* as well as the historical origins of the core script belief. The complex historical origin of "Something is wrong with me" within the Child ego states can be understood from three perspectives:
   – messages with compliant decisions,
   – conclusions in response to an impossibility, and
   – defensive reactions of hope and control.
Each of the ways in which the script belief was formed has unique intrapsychic functions that require specific emphasis in psychotherapy.

The concept of injunction and counterinjunctions, malevolent attributions, and lethal parental messages with corresponding compliant decisions is well-established in the theory of script formation (Berne, 1972; Goulding & Goulding, 1979; Steiner, 1971). In the face of a potential loss of relationship, a child may be forced to make a defensive, compliant decision to accept as his or her identity the definition of those on whom he or she is dependent. This may be an adaptation to and compliance with overt or implicit messages of "Something's wrong with you.'" In many cases the message is delivered in the form of a criticizing question, "What's wrong with you?" The psychological message is, "You wouldn't be doing what you are doing if you were normal (or OK)." Such criticism fails to value the child's natural and spontaneous behavior, understand the child's motivation, or investigate what may be missing in the relationship between the child and the person doing the criticizing. A child who forms such a script belief in compliance with criticism may become hypersensitive to criticism, fantasize anticipated criticisms, and collect reinforcing memories of past criticisms. The intrapsychic function is to maintain a sense of attachment in the relationship at the expense of a loss in natural vitality and the excitement of spontaneity.

When children are faced with an impossible task, they often conclude, "Something's wrong with me." With such a conclusion they can defend against the discomfort of the missing contact needs and maintain a pseudosemblance of relationship. Dysfunctional families often present impossible demands to children. It is impossible for a young child to stop an alcoholic parent from getting drunk, or for a baby to cure depression, or for an elementary school child to be a marriage therapist. It is impossible for a child to change gender to satisfy a parent's desire to have a dream fulfilled. Each of these examples represents a reversal of the caretaker's responsibility for the welfare of the child and a loss of contact in relationship. Further disruptions in relationship are experienced as "my fault," and they deflect from awareness of needs and feelings present when the welfare of the child is not being honored.

The script belief "Something is wrong with me" may be formed in a third way—as a defensive reaction of control and hope, the hope for a continuing and contactful relationship. When family relationships are dysfunctional, a child, needing contact in relationship, may imagine that the caretaker's problems are the child's fault: "I made dad get drunk," or "I made mother get depressed," or "I caused the sexual abuse to happen . . . so, therefore, something must be wrong with me!" By taking the blame, the child is not only the source of the problem, but can also imagine being in control of solving the problem: "I'll be very good," "I'll hurry up and grow up," "I can go to therapy to get fixed," or "If things get very bad I can kill myself because it is all my fault." The function of such reactions is to create a hopeful illusion of need-fulfilling caretakers that defends against the awareness of a lack of need fulfillment within the primary relationships. The caretakers are experienced as good and loving, and any ignoring, criticizing, beating, or even raping is because "Something's wrong with me." Here the core script belief may function as a defensive control of the feelings of vulnerability in relationship.

Within the Child ego states, each of these three origins of the core script belief has specific *intrapsychic functions of identity, stability, continuity, and predictability*. With a particular person there may be only one way the script belief was formed. Frequently, however, the core script beliefs have more than one origin and multiple intrapsychic functions. Any combination of these three defensive reactions made under pressure increases the complexity of the functions. The core script belief "Something's wrong with me" is often compounded by these multiple functions.

It is essential in an in-depth psychotherapy of script cure to assess the origins and intrapsychic functions of a script belief and to value the significance of how those multiple functions help the client to maintain psychological homeostasis. The psychotherapy of shame and self-righteousness is complex because of the compounded and continually reinforcing multiple intrapsychic functions. Merely to identify a script belief and attempt methods of change or redecision overlooks the psychological functions in forming and maintaining the script belief. Such efforts may increase the intensity of the intrapsychic function and may make the fixed core of the script less flexible. A respectful and patient inquiry into the client's phenomenological experience is required to learn the unique combination of intrapsychic functions. It is *the task of a relationship-oriented psychotherapist to establish an affective, developmental attunement and involvement that provides for the transferring of defensive intrapsychic functions to the relationship with the therapist.* Through the therapist's consistency, dependability, and responsibility in contact-in-relationship, the client can relax defensive processes and integrate fragmented states of the ego (Erskine, 1991a). The functions are once again provided through contact in an interpersonal relationship and are no longer a self-protective function.

Shame in the Parent Ego States

When the core script belief within a Child ego state is formed either as compliant decisions, conclusions in response to an impossibility, defensive reactions of hope and control, or any combination of these three, there is most likely an absence of a caring, understanding, and communicating relationship. When there is a lack of full psychological contact between a child and the adults responsible for his or her welfare, the defense of introjection is frequently used. Through the defensive, unaware identification that constitutes introjection, the beliefs, attitudes, feelings, motivations, behaviors, and defenses of the person on whom the child is dependent are made part of the child's ego in the form of a fragmented, exteropsychic state. The function of introjection is to reduce the external conflict between the child and the person on whom the child depends for need fulfillment. The introjected Parent ego state may be active in transactions with others, intrapsychically influencing, or phenomenologically experienced as self.

An active Parent ego state may transact with family members or colleagues as the introjected other once did, for example, communicating, "Something's wrong with you!" The function of such a transaction is to provide temporary relief in a Child ego state from the internal criticism of a Parent ego state and to continue denial of the original need for contact-in-relationship.

The intrapsychically influencing Parent ego state is a replay of the criticism introjected in the past. It perpetuates the cycle of compliance with the criticism and the defensiveness of sadness and fear within a Child ego state. This defensive cycle of shame functions to maintain an illusion of attachment and loyalty to the person with whom the child was originally longing for a contactful relationship.

Shame in the Parent ego state not only may be active and/or influencing, but it may also be experienced as self. The parent's sense of shame may have been introjected. With the cathexis of the introject the shame is misidentified as one's own (Erskine, 1977). The script belief "Something's wrong with me" may actually exist in a Parent ego state. The cycle of shame—compliance with the criticism, transposition of sadness and fear, the disavowal of anger, and longing for relationship—may be mother's or father's. Defensive self-righteousness may also be the result of the cathexis of an introjection.

For example, for years Susan suffered with a debilitating shame related to her own sense of inadequacy, having a mother who was alternately depressed and angry, and the fear that she would someday be "crazy" too. The initial phase of therapy acknowledged her own needs for attention, validated the emotional neglect of her childhood, and normalized the defensive process of "Something's wrong with me." Psychotherapy then focused on the introjected shame that was originally mother's. With a contact-oriented, in-depth psychotherapy with the Parent ego state that emphasized inquiry, attunement, and involvement, Susan was able to vividly remember wanting to bear the burden for her mother so her mother could be free of suffering. During a Child ego state to Parent ego state dialogue, she succinctly described the process: "I love you so much, Mom, I'll carry your shame for you!"

Clinical Interventions

The psychotherapy of shame and self-righteousness begins with the therapist newly discovering each client's unique psychodynamics. Each shame-based client will present a different cluster of behaviors, fantasies, intrapsychic functions, and self-protective defenses. The theoretical perspectives described in this article are generalizations from clinical practice and the integration of several theoretical concepts. The theory is not meant to represent a statement of what is, but rather to serve as a guide in the therapeutic process of inquiry, attunement, and involvement. Importantly, the phenomena of shame and self-righteousness explained from the perspective of transactional analysis theory may encourage transactional analysts to explore with each client his or her unique experience of shame and to adopt a relationship-oriented psychotherapy approach.

A patient, respectful inquiry into the client's phenomenological experience will provide both the client and the therapist with an ever-increasing understanding of *who the client is* and the experiences to which he or she has been subjected. The process of inquiring must be sensitive to the client's subjective experience and unaware intrapsychic dynamics to be effective in discovering and revealing needs, feelings, fantasies, and defenses. A major focus of a gentle inquiry is the client's self-discovery of longing for relationship, interruptions to contact (both internally and externally), and memories that in the past necessarily have been excluded from awareness. An important but lesser focus is the psychotherapist's increased understanding of the client's phenomenological experience and intrapsychic functioning. In many cases it has been important to clients to discover that the therapist is genuinely interested in listening to them and in knowing who they are. Such discoveries about the relationship with the psychotherapist present a juxtaposition (Erskine, 1991a, 1993) between the contact available in the here and now and the memory of what may have been absent in the past. The juxtaposition presents an opportunity to acknowledge what was needed and to validate that feelings and self-esteem may well be related to the quality of relationship with significant others.

Shame may be a significant dynamic in most relationship difficulties, including depression, anxiety, obesity, addictions, and characterological presentations. The therapist's attunement to the unexpressed sense of shame provides the opportunity for clients to reveal their inner processes of feelings, fantasies, desires, and defenses. Attunement involves a sense of being fully aware of the developmentally based needs, affect, and self-protective dynamics—a kinesthetic and emotional sensing of what it is like to live with their experiences. Attunement occurs when the therapist honors the client's developmental level of coping with shame and avoids defining or categorizing the client's fantasies, motivations, or behavior. Attunement also involves sensitively communicating to the client that the therapist is aware of the client's inner struggles—that the client is not all alone in the sadness at not having been accepted *as one is* and in the fear of loss of relationship because of *who one is*. The therapeutic processes of attunement and involvement acknowledge the difficulty in revealing one's inner confusion and struggles, value the desperate attempt at self-support and coping, and simultaneously provide a sense of the therapist's presence.

Some shame-based clients will not have had the experience of talking about needs or have a sense of language that is related to affect and inner processes. In some families, to have needs or express emotion may result in the child being ignored or ridiculed. When there has been a lack of attunement, acknowledgment, or validation of needs or feelings within the family or school system, the client may have no language of relationship with which to communicate about his or her affect and needs (Basch, 1988; Tustin, 1986). There is often an absence in such family or school systems of the interpersonal affective contact (a nonverbal transaction) in which the expression of affect by one person in relationship stimulates a corresponding affect of reciprocity in the other.

Affect is transactional-relational in its nature, requiring a corresponding affect in resonance. The expression of the affect sadness requires the reciprocal affect of compassion and possible acts of compassion; the expression of the affect anger requires the reciprocal affects of attentiveness, seriousness, and responsibility and perhaps acts of correction; the expression of the affect fear requires reciprocal affects and actions related to security; and the expression of the affect joy requires the reciprocal affects of vitality and expression of pleasure.

Attunement includes the therapist's sensing of the client's affect, and in reciprocity he or she is stimulated to express a corresponding affect and resonating behavior, a process similar to the one Stern (1985) described in healthy interaction between an infant and his or her mother. The reciprocal affect in the therapist may be expressed by acknowledging the client's affect and leads to validation that affect has a function in their relationship. It is essential that the therapist be both knowledgeable of and attuned to the client's developmental level in the expression of emotions. The client may need to have his or her affect and needs acknowledged but lack the social language to express the emotions in conversation. It may be necessary for the therapist to help the client name his or her feelings, needs, or experiences as an initial step in gaining a sense of making an impact in relationship.

Involvement begins with the therapist's commitment to the client's welfare and a respect for his or her phenomenological experiences. It evolves from the therapist's empathic inquiry into the client's experience and is developed through the therapist's attunement with the client's affect and validation of needs. Involvement is the result of the therapist being fully contactful with and for the client in a way that corresponds to the client's developmental level of functioning (Clark, 1991).

Shame and self-righteousness are defensive processes wherein an individual's worth is discounted, and the existence, significance, and/or solvability of a relationship disturbance is distorted or denied. A therapist's involvement using acknowledgment, validation, normalization, and presence diminishes the internal discounting (Schiff & Schiff, 1971) that is part of the defensive denial accompanying shame.

Through sensitivity to the manifestation of shame and in understanding the intrapsychic functions of shame and self-righteousness, a psychotherapist can guide a client to acknowledge and express feelings and needs for relationship. Acknowledgment is the therapeutic antidote to discounting the existence of a disturbance in relationship. Acknowledgment becomes internal and dissolves the denial of affect or needs when given by a receptive other who knows and communicates about needs and feelings.

Therapeutic validation occurs when the client's sense of shame, diminished self-worth, and defensive fantasies are experienced as the effect of significant relationship disturbances. Validation is the cognitive linking of cause and effect, the therapeutic response to discounting the significance of a disturbance in relationship. Validation provides a client with an enhanced value of phenomenological experience and therefore an increased sense of self-esteem.

Normalization involves depathologizing and countering the discounting of the solvability of a relationship disturbance. Many clients as children were told "Something's wrong with you" or, when faced with the impossibility of being responsible for their parents' welfare, they concluded "Something's wrong with me." The burden of responsibility for the rupture in the relationship was falsely placed on the child and not on a grown-up caretaker. The therapeutic antidote to discounting the solvability of a problem is the assigning of responsibility for the relationship. It is imperative that the therapist communicate that a client's experience of shame, self-criticism, or anticipated ridicule are normal defense reactions to being humiliated or ignored, and that these responses are not pathological.

The assignment of responsibility may begin with a therapist actively taking responsibility for any breach in the therapeutic relationship. Most therapeutic breaks occur when a therapist fails to attune to the client's affective or nonverbal communication (Kohut, 1984). When a client bears the responsibility for the relationship, the discounting of the solvability continues and the sense of shame is reinforced. It may be necessary for a therapist to take total responsibility for not understanding the client's phenomenological experience, not valuing his or her defensive process, or not being attuned to the client's affect and needs.

Presence is the therapeutic involvement that serves as an antidote to the discounting of an individual's self-worth. Therapeutic presence is provided through sustained empathic inquiry (Stolorow, Brandchaft, & Atwood, 1987) and consistent attunement to the developmental level of affect and needs. Presence involves the therapist's attentiveness and patience. It communicates that the psychotherapist is responsible, dependable, and reliable. Presence occurs when the behavior and communication of the therapist at all times respects and enhances the client's worth. Presence is enhanced by the therapist's willingness to be impacted by the client's affect and phenomenological experience—to take the client's experience seriously.

The psychotherapist's involvement through transactions that acknowledge, validate, and normalize the client's phenomenological experience is the antidote to the toxicity of discounting the existence, significance, or responsibility for solving the disruptions of contact in the relationship. The dependable, attuned presence of the therapist is the antidote to discounting the worth of the individual (Bergman, 1991; Jordan, 1989; Miller, 1986, 1987; Surrey, 1985).

The effective psychotherapy of shame and self-righteousness requires a therapist's commitment to contact-in-relationship, a commitment of patience, and an understanding that such therapy is complex and requires a considerable amount of time. Inquiry, attunement, and involvement involve a mental orientation, a way of being in relationship, as well as sets of therapeutic skills. When used in resonance with the developmental level of a client's functioning, they are methods of providing a caring, understanding relationship that allows a client to express a sense of self-value that may never have been expressed before. Inquiry, attunement, and involvement are descriptions of respectful interactions that foster contact-in-relationship. It is through a contact-oriented, relationship psychotherapy that protective dynamics of shame and self-righteousness are revealed and dissolved. A psychotherapeutic focus on contact-in-relationship enhances an individual's sense of OKness.

REFERENCES

Ansbacher, H. L., & Ansbacher, R. R. (1956). *The individual psychology of Alfred Adler.* New York: Basic Books.

Bach, S. (1985). *Narcissistic states and the therapeutic process.* New York: Jason Aronson.

Basch, M. (1988). *Understanding psychotherapy: The science behind the art.* New York: Basic Books.

Bergman, S. J. (1991). *Men's psychological development: A relational perspective.* Work in Progress, No. 48. Wellesley, MA: Stone Center Working Paper Series.

Berne, E. (1961). *Transactional analysis in psychotherapy: A systematic individual and social psychiatry.* New York: Grove Press.

Berne, E. (1964). *Games people play: The psychology of human relationships.* New York: Grove Press.

Berne, E. (1972). *What do you say after you say hello?: The psychology of human destiny.* New York: Grove Press.

Berne, E. (1977). Transactional analysis: A new and effective method of group therapy. In P. McCormick (Ed.), *Intuition and ego states* (pp. 145-158). San Francisco: TA Press. (Original work published in *The American Journal of Psychotherapy, 12,* 735-743, 1958)

Bollas, C. (1987). *The shadow of the object.* New York: Columbia University Press.

Bowlby, J. (1969). *Attachment: Vol. 1 of Attachment and loss.* New York: Basic Books.

Bursten, B. (1973). Some narcissistic personality types. *International Journal of Psycho-analysis, 54,* 287-300.

Clark, B. D. (1991). Empathic transactions in the deconfusion of child ego states. *Transactional Analysis Journal, 21,* 92-98.

Cornell, W. F. (1988). Life script theory: A critical review from a developmental perspective. *Transactional Analysis Journal, 18,* 270-282.

Cornell, W. F., & Olio, K. A. (1992). Consequences of childhood bodily abuse: A clinical model for affective interventions. *Transactional Analysis Journal, 22,* 131-143.

English, F. (1972). Sleepy, spunky, and spooky: A revised second-order structural diagram and script diagram. *Transactional Analysis Journal, 2*(2), 64-67.

English, F. (1975). Shame and social control. *Transactional Analysis Journal, 5,* 24-28.

Erikson, E. (1950). *Childhood and society.* New York: Norton.

Erikson, E. (1959). Identity and the life cycle. *Psychological Issues, 1,* 18-171.

Erikson, E. (1968). *Identity: Youth and crisis.* New York: Norton.

Ernst, F. H., Jr. (1971). The OK corral: The grid for get-on-with. *Transactional Analysis Journal, 1*(4), 33-42.

Erskine, R. G. (1971). *The effects of parent-child interaction on the development of a concept of self: An Eriksonian view.* Unpublished manuscript, Purdue University, Department of Clinical Psychology, Lafayette, Indiana.

Erskine, R. G. (1977). The fourth degree impasse. In C. Moiso (Ed.), *TA in Europe: Contributions to the European Association of Transactional Analysis Summer Conferences, 1977-1978* (pp. 33-35). Geneva, Switzerland: European Association for Transactional Analysis.

Erskine, R. G. (1980). Script cure: Behavioral, intrapsychic and physiological. *Transactional Analysis Journal, 10,* 102-106.

Erskine, R. G. (1988). Ego structure, intrapsychic function, and defense mechanisms: A commentary on Eric Berne's original theoretical concepts. *Transactional Analysis Journal, 18,* 15-19.

Erskine, R. G. (1989). A relationship therapy: Developmental perspectives. In B. R. Loria (Ed.), *Developmental theories and the clinical process: Conference proceedings of the Eastern Regional Transactional Analysis Association conference* (pp. 123-135). Madison, WI: Omnipress.

Erskine, R. G. (1991a). The psychotherapy of dissociation: Inquiry, attunement and involvement. In B. R. Loria (Ed.), *The Stamford papers: Selections from the 29th annual ITAA conference* (pp. 53-58). Madison, WI: Omnipress.

Erskine, R. G. (1991b). Transference and transactions: Critique from an intrapsychic and integrative perspective. *Transactional Analysis Journal, 21,* 63-76.

Erskine, R. G. (1993). Inquiry, attunement, and involvement in the psychotherapy of dissociation. *Transactional Analysis Journal, 23,* 184-190.

Erskine, R. G., & Moursund, J. P. (1988). *Integrative psychotherapy in action.* Newbury Park, CA: Sage Publications.

Erskine, R. G., & Trautmann, R. L. (1993). The process of integrative psychotherapy. In B. R. Loria (Ed.), *The boardwalk papers: Selections from the 1993 Eastern Regional Transactional Analysis Association conference* (pp. 1-26). Madison, WI: Omnipress.

Erskine, R. G., & Zalcman, M. J. (1975, August). *Rackets: Beliefs and feelings.* Presentation at the 13th International Transactional Analysis Conference, San Francisco, CA.

Erskine, R. G., & Zalcman, M. J. (1979). The racket system: A model for racket analysis. *Transactional Analysis Journal, 9,* 51-59.

Fairbairn, W. R. D. (1954). *Psychoanalytic studies of the personality.* New York: Basic Books.

Fraiberg, S. (1983, Fall). Pathological defenses in infancy. *Dialogue: A Journal of Psychoanalytic Perspectives,* 65-75. (Original work published in *Psychoanalytic Quarterly, 51,* 612-635, 1982)

Goldberg, C. (1990). The role of existential shame in the healing endeavor. *Psychotherapy, 27,* 591-599.

Goldberg, C. (1991). *Understanding shame.* Northvale, NJ: Jason Aronson.

Goulding, M. M., & Goulding, R. L. (1979). *Changing lives through redecision therapy.* New York: Brunner/Mazel.

Holloway, W. H. (1977). Transactional analysis: An integrative view. In G. Barnes (Ed.), *Transactional analysis after Eric Berne: Teachings and practices of three TA schools* (pp. 169-221). New York: Harper's College Press.

Horowitz, M. (1981). Self-righteous rage and attribution of blame. *Archives of General Psychiatry, 38,* 1233-1238.

Jordan, J. V. (1989). *Relational development: Therapeutic implications of empathy and shame.* Works in Progress (No. 39). Wellesley, MA: Stone Center Working Paper Series.

Kahler, T., with Capers, H. (1974). The miniscript. *Transactional Analysis Journal, 4*(1), 26-42.

Kaufman, G. (1989). *The psychology of shame.* New York: Springer.

Klein, M. (1992). The enemies of love. *Transactional Analysis Journal, 22,* 76-81.

Kohut, H. (1977). *The restoration of the self: A systematic approach to the psychoanalytic treatment of narcissistic personality disorder.* New York: International Universities Press.

Kohut, H. (1978). Thoughts on narcissism and narcissistic rage. In P. Ornstein, (Ed.), *The search for the self: Selected writings of Heinz Kohut, 1950-1978* (Vol. 2) (pp. 615-658). New York: International Universities Press.

Kohut, H. (1984). *How does analysis cure?* Chicago, IL: University of Chicago Press.

Lewis, H. B. (1971). *Shame and guilt in neurosis.* New York: International Universities Press.

Lewis, H. B. (1987). Shame and the narcissistic personality. In D. L. Nathanson (Ed.), *The many faces of shame* (pp. 93-132). New York: Guilford.

Loria, B. R. (1988). The parent ego state: Theoretical foundations and alterations. *Transactional Analysis Journal, 18,* 39-46.

Lynd, H. (1958). *On shame and the search for identity.* New York: Wiley.

Massey, R. F. (1989). Script theory synthesized systemically. *Transactional Analysis Journal, 19,* 14-25.

Miller, J. B. (1986). *What do we mean by relationship?* Works in Progress (No. 22). Wellesley, MA: Stone Center Working Paper Series.

Miller, J. B. (1987). *Toward a new psychology of women* (2nd ed.). Boston: Beacon.

Modell, A. H. (1986). A narcissistic defense against affects and the illusion of self-sufficiency. In A. P. Morrison (Ed.), *Essential papers on narcissism* (pp. 293-307). New York: New York University Press.

Morrison, A. P. (1986). Shame, ideal self, and narcissism. In A. P. Morrison (Ed.), *Essential papers on narcissism* (pp. 348-371). New York: New York University Press.

Morrison, A. P. (1987). The eye tuned inward: Shame and the self. In D. L. Nathanson (Ed.), *The many faces of shame* (pp. 271-291). New York: Guilford.

Nathanson, D. (1992). *Shame and pride: Affect, sex, and the birth of the self.* New York: Norton.

Perls, L. (1977, July). *Conceptions and misconceptions in Gestalt therapy.* Keynote address presented at the European Association for Transactional Analysis Conference, Seefeld, Austria.

Reich, A. (1986). Pathologic forms of self-esteem regulation. In A. P. Morrison (Ed.), *Essential papers on narcissism* (pp. 44-60). New York: New York University Press.

Rosenfeld, E. (1978). An oral history of Gestalt therapy, Part I: A conversation with Laura Perls. *The Gestalt Journal, 1*(1), 8-31.

Schiff, A. W., & Schiff, J. L. (1971). Passivity. *Transactional Analysis Journal, 1*(1), 71-78.

Steiner, C. (1971). *Games alcoholics play: The analysis of life scripts.* New York: Grove Press.

Stern, D. N. (1985). *The interpersonal world of the infant: A view from psychoanalysis and developmental psychology.* New York: Basic Books.

Stolorow, R. D., Brandchaft, B., & Atwood, G. (1987). *Psychoanalytic treatment: An intersubjective approach.* Hillsdale, NJ: The Analytic Press.

Sullivan, H. S. (1954). Problems of communication in the interview. In H. S. Perry & M. L. Gawel (Eds.), *The psychoanalytic interview* (pp. 206-226). New York: Norton.

Surrey, J. L. (1985). *The "self-in-relation": A theory of women's development.* Works in Progress (No. 13). Wellesley, MA: Stone Center Working Paper Series.

Tomkins, S. (1962). *Affect, imagery, consciousness: Vol. 1. The positive affects.* New York: Springer.

Tomkins, S. (1963). *Affect, imagery, consciousness: Vol. 2. The negative affects.* New York: Springer.

Tomkins, S. (1991). *Affect, imagery, consciousness: Vol. 3. The negative affects: Anger and fear.* New York: Springer.

Trautmann, R. L., & Erskine, R. G. (1981). Ego state analysis: A comparative view. *Transactional Analysis Journal, 11*, 178-185.

Tustin, F. (1986). *Autistic barriers in neurotic patients.* London: Karnac.

Wallace, B., & Nosko, A. (1993). Working with shame in the group treatment of male batterers. *International Journal of Group Psychotherapy, 43*, 45-61.

Wilson, S. D. (1990). *Release from shame: Recovery for adult children of dysfunctional families.* Downers Grove, IL: Interuniversity Press.

Wolf, E. S. (1988). *Treating the self: Elements of clinical self psychology.* New York: Guilford.

Woollams, S. J. (1973). Formation of the script. *Transactional Analysis Journal, 3*(1), 31-37.

Wurmser, L. (1981). *The mask of shame.* Baltimore: John Hopkins University Press.

Wurmser, L. (1987). Shame—The veiled companion of narcissism. In D. L. Nathanson (Ed.), *The many faces of shame* (pp. 64-92). New York: Guilford.

This article was originally published in the Transactional Analysis Journal, *Volume 24, Number 2, April 1994, pp. 86-102. The author gratefully acknowledges the members of the Professional Development Seminars of the Institute for Integrative Psychotherapy for sharing personal experiences and for their professional involvement in formulating the ideas in this article. Portions of this article were presented at the Symposium on the Treatment of Shame at the joint conference of the International Transactional Analysis Association and the USA TA Association in Minneapolis, Minnesota, in October of 1993.*

The Dynamics of Shame:
A Roundtable Discussion

Richard G. Erskine, Barbara Clark,
Kenneth R. Evans, Carl Goldberg, Hanna Hyams,
Samuel James, and Marye O'Reilly-Knapp

Editor's Note: At the joint meeting of the International Transactional Analysis Association's 31st Annual Conference and the USA Transactional Analysis Association in Minneapolis, Minnesota, October 12-17, 1993, a symposium was held on "The Dynamics of Shame" to explore a topic that has not received adequate attention in the transactional analysis literature. This continuing education symposium presented various theoretical perspectives on shame, explored how the concept can be explained within transactional analysis theory, and examined clinical methods relative to the treatment of shame. The two-day symposium included a series of four lectures and seven workshops that served as a basis for this roundtable discussion. In keeping with the theme of this issue of the Journal *and to provide an interface with the continuing education program of the conference, the following excerpts from the roundtable conversation were edited by Richard G. Erskine. The roundtable followed a speech by Barbara Clark entitled, "How Do I Shame Thee? Let Me Count the Ways" (see James, 1993), and a paper by Richard Erskine entitled "Shame: A Transactional Analysis Perspective" (see James, 1993).*

The faculty for the symposium and members of the roundtable discussion were Barbara Clark, Ph.D.; Kenneth Evans, B.Sc., D.S.A.; Carl Goldberg, Ph.D.; Hanna Hyams, M.A.; Samuel James, Ed.D.; and Marye O'Reilly-Knapp, D.N.Sc. Richard G. Erskine, Ph.D., served as symposium coordinator and roundtable moderator.

Richard: Let me start by talking about my own feelings. I usually don't write a speech, but I decided to write this one because of the personal nature of this topic and how deeply it effects everyone. I am more nervous than I normally am because I want you all to like and appreciate what I have to say. I'd like to open this discussion by asking each panel member to describe what he or she is feeling. Maybe if we start with the affective level, we can get into the content.

Hanna: For me this symposium is a celebration. I have a feeling of joy because for the last eight years I've been working alone, teaching, and doing workshops on shame. Today I have the feeling and the hope that the family joins me!

Sam: With regard to shame, I feel that my feelings go up and down. It is such a troubling issue to look at. One must be willing to tolerate the toxic effects, but along with them, I think, comes a great deal of freedom. If one can really look at and integrate the shame part of one's life, I think it has a very humbling, appreciative effect that makes people much more interested in generativity. Erikson (1950) said the last stage of life is despair versus integrity. I think that those who deal with shame move more toward the position of integrity—that is, making peace with themselves—whereas those who fail to make peace with the issue of shame become more despairing. They feel rather cheated—this living experience is rather an absurd joke. So, I feel deeply about this. I am always troubled by it. It's an issue I feel I never make real peace with in the sense that I can enter into it with some sense of security, because I never really know where it is going to take me. So, I find myself rather apprehensive about these issues. It, indeed, is a journey, but one I usually take cautiously.

Ken: I have a profound shame-based system and, at some points in my life, it's been like a crucifixion. At the moment I am swinging between excitement and terror.

Marye: I am thinking about my own personal struggles with shame as well as clients who have taught me about the concept of shame. Shame impacts on internal experiences and also relationships with others. I am both excited and scared and hope that all of us will come away with a far richer experience of this issue.

Carl: It looks like I am going to be the gadfly. I was feeling uncomfortable and irritable. Shame has been presented as an infidel—a terrible thing that some people do to other people. I think this goes back to the problem I had with my own training, in which guilt was the villain, the cause of human suffering. Shame now has that role—as if there are some awful people who shame other people. It is one-sided. It seems to me that the morality of shame is where we are all victims. There is an intersubjective realm. How can we view shame as interpersonal when we talk about it in a one-sided way? For example, this occurs when we assume the therapist is responsible for everything that happens in therapy, or the parent is the one who does these awful things to children. My interest in shame is from the perspective of a very different morality: We are all human sufferers and there are not really victims and perpetrators—we are all victims of each other. Until we realize that, we are returning to the morality of guilt, which has done awful things to the way that we live and the way that we understand other people.

Barbara: I am interested in what you're saying, Carl, and want to hear more about us all being victims. I have heard us talking today about shame being a relationship problem or intersubjectivity. What we don't want to lose sight of is that admiration is also part of this whole process. Children admire their parents and teachers, and they are thus vulnerable to how parents or teachers respond to them.

Ken: Shame is neutral as an affect. I don't think it is curable. I am always going to feel the emotion of shame. I don't like it, but for me it is a fact. The difference is that I no longer believe that I am a shameful person. So the emotion, the affect, is morally neutral. It is the thoughts we put on it that mess us up.

Marye: I do not identify shame as so awful that no one should have to experience it. However, what interests me is to think of shame as an affect in which the intensity can be destructive and damaging.

Hanna: The problem we are not dealing with is that we don't see shame globally. Each one of us expressed aspects of shame. You, Sam, touched the problem of the split that each of us is born with—the struggle between goodness and badness—and what each of us has to do to heal that and become whole.

Carl: Barbara, in your speech prior to this roundtable you gave a personal example of how you were shamed in first grade by the teacher when you didn't perform the way she expected you to. I think you movingly described the position of the victim, the child who is suffering. However, many of us have been parents and teachers. We know what it is like to be the person in charge. What did your teacher feel? Maybe she felt shamed by you. I would bet, Barbara, you were one of her pet students. And she really liked the fact that you looked up to her. It was an important part of her self-esteem as a teacher. And then you did something that shocked her. She thought she had done a very good job, particularly with you, but now you were misbehaving. How did she feel? Wasn't she also a victim of your shaming? What I am talking about is the subtext in the shame. Unless we look at the intersubjective shame that goes on, I think the picture is very one-sided.

Sam: I don't think there is any way that human beings are going to stop shaming one another or that we are going to stop shaming ourselves. To establish a shame-free environment is not the point. We aren't going to be any more successful at that than we are at eliminating happiness or anger or any other affect. The point is to understand those parts of the shaming experience that leave one isolated, defeated, and feeling fundamentally bad and flawed. I find with a lot of shame-prone patients that when I get attuned with them they change. So, it is a process of trying to find out who they are and what's going on. Attunement is terrifying because it is based so much on power and dominance. Toxic shame is a political act. Secondary shame is more about learning. I shame my kids. I feel bad about it. And when the dust settles, I usually 'fess up and talk with them about what went on. That's how I have made peace with shame—at least to this point. Because I don't have control over the shame aspect without giving up the passion of my feelings for my kids, and that seems too high a price. What I can be is responsible when I am shaming someone, admit it, and try to reestablish a connection, especially with children. And I think what I try to do in my practice is to look at it in some responsible learning format as opposed to something I am trying to exclude.

Richard: I also find that when I take the time to genuinely inquire and be attuned to where people are, they talk about shame. They no longer carry the toxicity of it. Yes, the memories are always there. I hope that all of our memories remain as a resource library in our lives, particularly for those of us who are psychotherapists. We need that resource library in order to be empathic. When I say to myself, "I am probably not connecting with this person right now," I put the responsibility back on myself. I think a lot of humiliation goes on when people don't take the responsibility for how they hurt other people.

Barbara: I was thinking about the concept of eliminating shame. I don't see it as possible, either. I see shame as an innate affect that is there to protect us. As I studied shame and worked in psychotherapy I learned to make a different meaning intrapsychically when I feel shame. I expect that I am going to feel shame if I am exposed in some way. If I had fallen off the podium this morning, I guarantee you I would have felt shame, but the meaning that I would have made of that experience is that it is normal to feel shame. It is not that I am defective. I may make a mistake and I feel shame about it, but I am not defective. The freeing part for me is to differentiate the meaning of the shame experience in my personal life, my professional life, and with my clients. As I was preparing this talk my husband asked me how it was going. He is very supportive—he knows that I get nervous before these talks. I told him that for the first time in my life I would be in front of people and not be afraid that there is something wrong with me. Some people will like it, some people will not like it, some will be neutral—but that is about the information, it is not about my worth. I think the meaning-making has made a difference for me.

Ken: The negative aspect of shame for me is an inner revulsion—a dying inside. I would say it is a defense against extinction—physical and psychological extinction.

Hanna: I agree with you, Ken. In my practice and my own life, I see shame as a survival mechanism. I think the pain is really what we are talking about. In a sense we all have shame, but the degree of shame is tied to the degree of pain. It is so easy to shame little children because they are helpless.

Marye: I am triggered by your earlier words, Ken—an inner death of the self. I think about shame as a discounting of the Self.

Ken: I was listening intently to how in his speech prior to this roundtable Richard described the therapeutic relationship, and I was thinking about Barbara's article on empathic transactions in the deconfusion of Child ego states (Clark, 1991). There seems to be an evolution in the role of the therapist. There has been a parallel development in Gestalt psychotherapy—a moving away from what was a highly confrontive and shaming form of therapy in the 1970s. The move now is to a form of therapy that focuses much more on a dialogic, existential encounter with the client—a greater focus on relationship. I see an exciting parallel development with empathic transactions, reciprocity, and dialogic encounter. Gestalt therapy currently is an I-Thou dialogic experience.

Richard: My opinion about the therapeutic need for affective attunement and gentle inquiry is the result of my therapeutic failures. When I take the time to ask, "How have I missed you? Where did I miss you?" clients talk about where they were missed in the therapeutic process. I have to take that seriously.

Carl: The problem is that there is a certain artificiality involved in getting material in therapy. Richard, in your speech you made the assumption, and I think everyone in the audience will agree with you, that the interpersonal realm is more basic, more fundamental than the Self. And I think that is also why you say that shame protects the Self from humiliation. I see it as reversed.

Richard: I don't think we can have a Self without an interpersonal relationship. We can't have the interpersonal without Self. A baby is born as an organism, and the Self emerges out of an interpersonal relationship that furthers a sense of Self.

Carl: But there is a private shame that has to do with the Self that only the Self knows. It is more painful and more profound than anything that is experienced interpersonally.

Sam: I agree with you, Carl. I think one of the reasons there are a lot of empathic failures with patients who experience private shame is that they feel hopeless. It is very hard and painful for the therapist to sit with their hopelessness and be empathic. This is one of the reasons that we have trouble staying focused with them. I think the trauma literature is helpful; for example, Herman (1992) talks about being a team if you are going to deal with hopelessness. Therapists need a place where they can talk about what they are doing—such as peer supervision—but at a more emotional level. With that comes the opportunity for the therapist to be a representative in the therapy and not just an individual in the therapy. Hopelessness is something we all feel. And despair also. It is part of being alive and being a human being—our own limits as clinicians, as people. We can't wander in where angels fear to tread unless we are supported ourselves, or we will miss the patient and put our survival ahead of theirs.

Ken: Yes, it is easier to get active, to problem solve in helping the client to feel OK, than it is to actually live. It's a journey with the client who is in despair, and that's the time when they need the therapist most. It's the most difficult time for the therapist, but absolutely fruitful.

Hanna: I agree with you, Ken. And at some point we actually enter into the same role with the client as the parent played—the parent who was despairing and could not deal with the situation. But we have some other means, maybe, to take a little distance, to individuate ourselves from the problem, or otherwise we are no good to the client, either.

Comments from the Audience

Wayne Carpenter: I appreciate all of your input. It seems to me we are talking about two things, the first being inherent, perhaps biological, or relational because of our dependency needs as human beings. Shame is a fact of life. Second, I am hearing that we are proposing psychological interventions that are better tailored to what I have heard described as toxic shame—the shame that debilitates rather than helps us to be organized in a human community—the shame that ties us up and leaves us incapable, the shame that used to keep me from standing up at conferences and doing this. I'm interested in your responses.

Carl: I think a distinction has to be made. Several of us are talking about existential shame—a fact of life—and others are talking about a biological reality. And the treatment is very different. But talking about the inevitability of shame and the existential condition and bearing that with your patient is a very different kind of treatment.

Marye: As a nurse I am concerned about how often we separate the biological from the psychological. If we don't consider the body as well as the mind, then we are fragmenting the individual. The treatment for shame has intrapsychic, physiological, and interpersonal components.

Ken: In Gestalt therapy, for many years we have been bedeviled by what is figure and ignored that which is the ground. Interventions and technique are very much a part of the figure. I think what is really healing is the ground—that is, the relationship over time.

Jeanne Wiger: In thinking about what you were saying about figure and ground, and what was said earlier about the need to be there when clients are going through the hopelessness, part of the problem I run into, and the reason I find myself tempted to move away, is the feeling of not doing anything during that time. There is importance in just being there. I'd like to hear some comments on that.

Richard: That is what I meant when I talked in my speech earlier about the affects of reciprocity. I think what is necessary when someone is sad is that reciprocity of compassion, then perhaps doing something compassionately. Often it doesn't require action, but it does require that affect within us. When someone is angry at us, what is needed is an affective response of responsibility, of attentiveness, of taking them seriously—and then, maybe, some active correction. But we have to sit with our own affect of reciprocity in their presence. And that is what is contactful.

Jeanne Wiger: For me, then, it's giving myself permission to know the value and importance of that and not to discount it.

Barbara: When you are in relationship and being there with the client you are doing something. We need to be emotionally present—it's what children need when they are upset—they need your presence. They don't need for you to do something. They need for you to be there with them and experience and understand what they are experiencing. I think it is the same in psychotherapy. We are doing what we need to be doing when we are there with the client emotionally.

Hanna: I think we are talking about different levels. I agree that some people need just that. But there are some people who have difficulty expressing anything. They have a harder time if you are just there—they need more than just being. It is important to realize that without our being there first we can't do anything, but sometimes they need to throw some mud on us—and how we meet that challenge involves more than just being there.

Barbara: Yes, we have to respond to where the client is developmentally.

Ken: One of the wonderful things about being a psychotherapist is being with someone when they are going through hell and seeing them survive and grow beyond it. In the midst of all this shame and despair, I have a tremendous faith in human nature.

Patricia Rincon Gallardo: I work in organizations. I am not a clinician. But what Richard said is very important. One can be attuned and compassionate in many ways. In organizations, I work from that attunement. It really opens people up to saying things to me, even more than to clinicians—things that they are scared away from saying because they feel that they are not understood. Sometimes when people are not compassionate, they confront others too quickly on their rackets and games. What I am learning is that the shame some people feel is manifested in self-righteousness. The patient is blamed for whatever is not working.

Ed Zerin: I like what you said, Hanna. We not only have to be *there*, we *do* have to *be* there. In addition to being there, if I share with people certain stories, certain mythologies, and I share with them some of my own shame, I can be effective with them. That gives them permission to open up. I have had many patients look at me starry-eyed and say, "You did that—my goodness!" This summer when we were lecturing I shared something very personal in the group and people said, "I would never talk about it before, but I want to talk to you about it."

Carl: I would go a step further and agree with what you are all saying. People who are shamed come from cloistered lives, very narrow lives. What is necessary is to teach them skills, because without this they feel incompetent to try things. They only do things they are exceptional at doing. They won't attempt things that they don't do very well. One of the roles that the therapist needs to play with shame-prone people is to teach them skills, give them homework, and not simply just be there with them.

George Fling: A lot of the shaming that goes on is not just what happens between parents and children or between teachers and students or between therapists and clients, but we also have shaming that occurs on a societal level—in terms of how women are treated, how men are treated, poverty, and things like that. I am not at all sure how to address that as a therapist, but I want to acknowledge that this is a lot broader than just an interpersonal issue.

Richard: Perhaps that is the best way, George, to acknowledge that there is such a thing as societal shaming. In closing, I'd like to thank the roundtable members and the audience for this stimulating discussion.

REFERENCES
Clark, B. D. (1991). Empathic transactions in the deconfusion of child ego states. *Transactional Analysis Journal, 21*, 92-98.
Erikson, E. (1950). *Childhood and society.* New York: Norton.
Herman, J. (1992). *Trauma and recovery.* New York: Basic Books.
James, N. L. (Ed.). (1993). *The Minneapolis papers: Selections from the 31st annual ITAA conference.* Madison, WI: Omnipress.

This article was originally published in the Transactional Analysis Journal, *Volume 24, Number 2, April 1994, pp. 80-85.*

A Relationship Therapy: Developmental Perspectives

Richard G. Erskine

Relationships between people are built on contact. Contact constitutes the primary motivating experience of human behavior. Contact is simultaneously internal and external: It involves an awareness of needs, hungers, and urges that occur within the organism and a reaching to the environment to satisfy those inner sensations. As a result people are further motivated by the need to establish and maintain relationships.

The concept of contact and its role in establishing and maintaining human relationships was first articulated in the psychotherapy literature by Laura and Frederick Perls (Perls, 1944; Perls, Hefferline, & Goodman, 1951), who challenged the psychoanalytic focus on the primacy of Oedipal conflicts and urged psychotherapists to take into account early infant-parent interactions and interruptions to contact (fixed defenses or fixed gestalten) as a major source of psychological disturbance in adulthood.

Fairbairn's (1952) premise that people are motivated by the need to establish and maintain relationships and that this is accomplished through human contact was in direct opposition to Freud's (1905/1953) drive theory, in which the sexual and death instincts were thought to motivate all behavior. Although Melanie Klein (1964) wrote about the importance of the first months of life, her theoretical positions continued to be based on drive theory and her own assumptions regarding the infant's inner processes. She did not take into account the significance of direct contact between infant and caretaker in the formation of ego or a sense of self.

Erik Erikson (1950) laid a theoretical foundation for an understanding of human behavior that led away from drive theory toward a theory of interpersonal relations. He described the profound helplessness of the human infant as the force evoking reciprocal nurturing responses from parents. His stages of human development over the entire life cycle describe the formation of identity (ego) as an outgrowth of interpersonal relations (trust vs. mistrust, autonomy vs. shame and doubt, etc.). However, he did not limit the formation of ego, identity, and ensuing relationships to childhood (for example, intimacy vs. isolation, generativity vs. stagnation). He provided a theoretical basis that lights the way for a relationship therapy that focuses not only on early childhood and the fixation of those primary relationships, but on the ways in which relationships are of utmost significance in continuing to redefine one's sense of self (identity) throughout the entire life span.

Harry Stack Sullivan's (1953) approach to interpersonal therapy comes closest to relating to the person without theoretical formulations tied to particular developmental stages. Most other theorists focus exclusively on the value of early childhood relationships or explain human dynamics from other conceptual positions.

Margaret Mahler's (1968; Mahler, Pine, & Bergman, 1975) descriptions of the stages of early child development placed importance on the relationship between mother and infant and stressed the periods of symbiosis and rapprochement as crucial in ego formation. Her research, however, did not include observations of the first few months of life; she dismissed the subtlety of contact in this period by describing it as the autistic stage—an unfortunate description that has led some clinicians to place less emphasis on the interactions of this period of time in the formation of a person's sense of self. Her collaborator, Fred Pine (1985), in his description of the importance of the "quiet moments" in psychotherapy, attempted to rectify this potential therapeutic oversight.

Stern's (1985) recent compilation of research on early infant behavior underscores the observations that humans are contact-seeking from the first moments of life and that it is out of the reciprocity of contact between infant and caretaker that the ego or sense of self begins to emerge. These infant-caretaker contacts are experienced at first viscerally, later affectively, and much later, cognitively, and they form the basic internal sense of relationship with people.

Bowlby (1969, 1973, 1980), in drawing on both animal and human infant studies, emphasized the significance of early as well as prolonged physical bonding in the creation of a visceral core from which all experiences of self and other emerge. Early, as well as continuous, physical contact between infant and caretaker produces a bonding that continues throughout the life cycle as visceral memory traces. When such contact does not occur in accordance with the child's needs, or if the handling of the child is harsh, there is a physiological defense against the loss of contact. These physiological defenses, if fixated, form the core of the life script—what has been described as the physiological level of script (Erskine, 1980).

The person's sense of self and others, then, is not composed of visceral experiences of contact that are need fulfilling, but rather, is composed of physiological experiences that are defensive. These core experiences may have an effect in shaping future experiences.

Selma Fraiberg (1983) described the presence in early childhood of the defenses of freezing, turning away, fighting, and transformation of affect. These are defenses that are present prior to cognition and are experienced physically and affectively.

Drawing on Fairbairn's (1952) concept that the establishment of relationships is the ultimate goal of human behavior, both Guntrip (1971) and Winnicott (1965) implied a course of psychotherapy that is relational rather than interpretive (classical psychoanalysis), explanatory (some applications of transactional analysis), or change-oriented (behavior therapy). The basic tenet of a relationship therapy is that the core sense of self is inherently tied to the child's relationship to parents and, in the earliest years particularly, to the relationship with mother or the substitute primary caretaker. These relationships form the foundation for relating to people and the world. Through the use of contact in the relationship between client and therapist, where old defensive patterns are no longer necessary, intrapsychic reorganization occurs.

Eric Berne (1961, 1972), in laying out his theory of script, described the etiology of psychological dysfunction as possibly beginning with "mother's milk," elaborated on with series of interactions on the changing table, and which are again repeated in similar ways throughout the preschool years as parents attempt to socialize the child.

In describing his structural concept of ego states, Berne (1961) defined the *natural* Child as free of internalized influence and the *adaptive* Child as under the internal influence of an introjected parent. (For elaboration on the distinction between *adaptive* and *natural* Child from Adapted Child and Natural Child in transactional analysis terminology, see Erskine, 1988; Loria, 1988; and Trautmann & Erskine, 1981.) Berne's concepts of *natural* and *adaptive* parallel Winnicott's (1965) theory of true self and false self.

Winnicott (1965, p. 99) based his explanation of psychopathology on the idea of a false self, which is the cumulative result of the caretakers' failure to serve as a protective shield against both external and internal overwhelming stimuli that impinge on the child. (Freud [1920/1955], in *Beyond the Pleasure Principle*, described the importance of a protective shield from a drive-theory perspective, but did not relate it, as Winnicott did, to the mother or caretaker who safely guards the child from excessive stimuli.)

The primary caretaker's serving as a protective shield creates what Winnicott (1965, p. 148) called a good-enough holding environment and allows for the infant's inner reality to serve as a core in the development of a sense of self. The failure of the parents to regulate stimuli, to serve as a protective shield, to create a good enough holding environment (all parallel terms) are referred to by Winnicott (1965) as impingements.

Impingements are destructive of true ego integration and lead to primitive defensive organization and functioning: in essence, a loss of contact with internal processes and a loss of contact with others in the environment.

The adaptations, the defenses, what Winnicott called the "False Self," hide the person's inner reality. In a relationship therapy it is through the therapist's inquiring into the person's experience that the person comes to know his or her own "hidden" or "lost" inner experience.

The focus in such a therapy is on the internalized early relationships, as seen in introjections, survival reactions, script beliefs, and defense mechanisms that are at work in the creation and maintenance of relationships today.

In a relationship therapy the concept of contact is the theoretical basis from which clinical interventions are derived. Transference, regression, activation of introjection, and the presence of defense mechanisms are all understood as indications of previous contact deficits. A major goal of therapy, then, is to use the therapist-client relationship—the ability to create full contact in the present—as a stepping-stone to healthier relationships with other people and a satisfying sense of self.

Through respect, kindness, and contactful listening we establish a personal presence and allow for an interpersonal relationship that provides affirmation of the client's integrity

(Erskine & Moursund, 1988). This respectfulness may be best described as a consistent invitation to interpersonal contact between client and therapist, with simultaneous support for the client to contact his or her internal experiences and receive an external recognition of those experiences. Contact is enhanced through a genuine interest in the client's welfare and a respect for his or her unfolding experiences.

REFERENCES

Berne, E. (1961). *Transactional analysis in psychotherapy: A systematic individual and social psychiatry.* New York: Grove Press.

Berne, E. (1972). *What do you say after you say hello?: The psychology of human destiny.* New York: Grove Press.

Bowlby, J. (1969). *Attachment. Vol. 1 of Attachment and loss.* New York. Basic Books.

Bowlby, J. (1973). *Separation: Anxiety and anger. Vol. 2 of Attachment and loss.* New York. Basic Books.

Bowlby, J. (1980). *Loss: Sadness and depression. Vol. 3 of Attachment and loss.* New York: Basic Books.

Erikson, E. (1950). *Childhood and society.* New York: Norton.

Erskine, R. (1980). Script cure: Behavioral, intrapsychic and physiological. *Transactional Analysis Journal, 10*, 102-106.

Erskine, R. (1988) Ego structure, intrapsychic function, and defense mechanisms: A commentary on Eric Berne's original theoretical concepts. *Transactional Analysis Journal, 18*, 15-19.

Erskine, R. G., & Moursund, J. P. (1988). *Integrative psychotherapy in action.* Newbury Park, CA: Sage Publications.

Fairbairn, W. R. D. (1952). *An object-relations theory of the personality.* New York: Basic Books.

Fraiberg, S. (1983, Fall). Pathological defenses in infancy. *Dialogue: A Journal of Psychoanalytic Perspectives, 65*-75.

Freud, S. (1953). Three essays on the theory of sexuality. In J. Strachey (Ed. and Trans.), *The standard edition of the complete psychological works of Sigmund Freud* (Vol. 7, pp. 125-245). London: Hogarth Press. (Original work published 1905)

Freud, S. (1955). Beyond the pleasure principle. In J. Strachey (Ed. and Trans.), *The standard edition of the complete psychological works of Sigmund Freud* (Vol. 18, pp. 3-64). London: Hogarth Press. (Original work published 1920)

Guntrip, H. (1971). *Psychoanalytic theory, therapy and the self.* New York: Basic Books.

Klein, M. (1964). *Contributions to psychoanalysis 1921-1945.* New York: McGraw Hill.

Loria, B. R. (1988). The parent ego state: Theoretical formulations and alterations. *Transactional Analysis Journal, 18*, 39-46.

Mahler, M. (1968). *On human symbiosis and the vicissitudes of individuation.* New York: International Universities Press.

Mahler, M., Pine, F., & Bergman, A. (1975). *The psychological birth of the human infant: Symbiosis and individuation.* New York: Basic Books.

Perls, F. S. (1944). *Ego, hunger and aggression: A revision of Freud's theory and method.* Durban, South Africa: Knox Publishing.

Perls, F. S., Hefferline, R. F., & Goodman, P. (1951). *Gestalt therapy: Excitement and growth in the human personality.* New York: Julian Press.

Pine, F. (1985). *Developmental theory and clinical process.* New Haven: Yale University Press.

Stern, D. (1985). *The interpersonal world of the infant: A view from psychoanalysis and developmental psychology.* New York: Basic Books.

Sullivan, H. . (1953). *The interpersonal theory of psychiatry* (H. S. Perry & M. L. Gawel, Eds.). New York: Norton.

Trautmann, R., & Erskine, R. (1981). Ego state analysis: A comparative view. *Transactional Analysis Journal, 11*, 178-185.

Winnicott, D. W. (1965). *The maturational processes and the facilitating environment: Studies in the theory of emotional development.* New York: International Universities Press.

This article was originally published in B. B. Loria (Ed.), Developmental Theories and the Clinical Process: Conference Proceedings of the Eastern Regional Transactional Analysis Conference *(pp. 123-135), Madison, WI: Omnipress, 1989.*

The Process of Integrative Psychotherapy

Richard G. Erskine and Rebecca L. Trautmann

Just as people and relationships are dynamic processes, so is the development of theory, originating as it does from the dynamic process of the individual theorist(s) and from the dynamic process of each therapeutic relationship that guides and informs that theory. Thus we would like to take the opportunity in this article to talk about how integrative psychotherapy has developed and how we think about it and practice it today in 1993.

The term "integrative" in integrative psychotherapy has a number of meanings. It refers to the process of integrating the personality: helping the client to assimilate and harmonize the contents of his or her ego states, relax the defense mechanisms, relinquish the life script, and reengage the world with full contact. It is the process of making whole: taking disowned, unaware, unresolved aspects of the ego and making them part of a cohesive self. Through integration it becomes possible for people to have the courage to face each moment openly and freshly, without the protection of a preformed opinion, position, attitude, or expectation.

"Integrative" also refers to the integration of theory, the bringing together of affective, cognitive, behavioral, physiological, and systems approaches to psychotherapy. The concepts are utilized within a perspective of human development in which each phase of life presents heightened developmental tasks, need sensitivities, crises, and opportunities for new learnings. Integrative psychotherapy takes into account many views of human functioning: psychodynamic, client-centered, behaviorist, family therapy, Gestalt therapy, Reichian, object relations theories, psychoanalytic self psychology, and transactional analysis. Each provides a valid explanation of behavior, and each is enhanced when selectively integrated with the others. The psychotherapeutic interventions are based on research-validated knowledge of normal developmental process and the theories describing the self-protective defensive processes used when there are interruptions in normal development.

The ABC's and P

The preliminary ideas of integrative psychotherapy were first presented by Richard Erskine in 1972 in lectures at the University of Illinois. An outline of these ideas was published in the article, "The ABC's of Effective Psychotherapy" (Erskine, 1975) and are then elaborated on in the article, "Script Cure" (Erskine, 1980). Some of the clinical methods that will be briefly described here are presented transaction-by-transaction in *Integrative Psychotherapy in Action* (Erskine & Moursund, 1988).

The focus of integration is on three primary dimensions of human functioning and therefore of psychotherapeutic focus: cognitive, affective, and behavioral. The cognitive theories stress the mental processes of a person and focus on the question, "Why?" The cognitive approach explains and provides a model of understanding. Why do we have the problems that we have? Why does our mind work the way it does? It assumes that psychotherapy is an intellectual process, and when the client comes to understand why he or she behaves and thinks in a particular manner, he or she will solve the conflicts involved.

Significantly different from the cognitive is the behavioral approach, which deals with the question of "What?" Behavioral therapy describes what exists and attempts to shape appropriate behavior. What is the specific problem? What contingencies shaped and now maintain the behavior? What changes are necessary in the reward system to produce new behavior? And since behavioral therapy emerged out of experimental psychology, there is a great deal of attention given to what measures are to be applied to evaluate the changes made. The application of behavioral therapy involves a shift away from the question of "Why?" and instead is focused on "What?" The goal of behavioral therapy is to identify and reinforce desired behaviors.

Both cognitive and behavioral therapy are significantly different from an affective psychotherapy. An affective approach deals with the question "How?" How does a person feel? Here the focus is on the internal experiential process: how each person emotionally experiences what has happened. The major focus is not on the "Why" of cognitive therapy or the "What" of behavioral therapy, but on "How" we emotionally experience ourselves in the here and now. A basic premise in affective therapy is that people are out of touch with their feelings. It is assumed that removing blocks to emotions and fully expressing repressed affect will produce an emotional closure and provide for a fuller range of affective experiences.

In addition to the dimensions of affect, behavior, and cognition, we have included the physiological dimension. As many of the mind/body theories and modalities have developed, including the research on psychoneuroimmunology, it became imperative to include a focus on the body as an integral aspect of psychotherapy. Disturbances in affect or cognition can adversely affect the body just as physiological dysfunction can impact changes in behavior, affect, and cognition.

The affective, behavioral, cognitive, and physiological foundations of the human organism are viewed from a systems perspective—a cybernetic model wherein any dimension has an interrelated effect on the other dimensions. Just as the individual is affected by others in a family or work system, they in turn contribute to the uniqueness of the system. In a similar systemic way the intrapsychic and observable dimensions of an individual are inherently influenced in the psychological function of the individual. The systems perspective leads to the question, "What is the function of a particular behavior, affect, belief, or body gesture on the human organism as a whole?" A major focus of an integrative psychotherapy is on assessing whether each of these domains—affective, behavioral, cognitive, and physiological—are open or closed to contact and in the application of methods that enhance full contact (see Figure 1).

Contact

A major premise of integrative psychotherapy is that contact constitutes the primary motivating experience of human behavior. Contact is simultaneously internal and external:

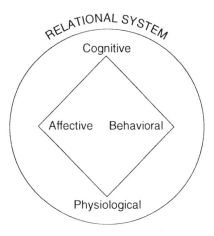

Figure 1
The Self-in-Relationship System

It involves the full awareness of sensations, feelings, needs, sensorimotor activity, thought, and memories that occur within the individual and a shift to full awareness of external events as registered by each of the sensory organs. With full internal and external contact, experiences are continually integrated. To the degree that the individual is involved in full contact, needs will arise, be experienced, and be acted on in relation to the environment in a way that is organically healthy. When a need arises, is met, and is let go, the person moves on to the next experience. When contact is disrupted, however, needs are not met. If the experience of need arousal is not closed naturally, it must find an artificial closure. These artificial closures are the substance of reactions and decisions that may become fixated. They are evident in the disavowal of affect, habitual behavior patterns, neurological inhibitions within the body, and the beliefs that limit spontaneity and flexibility in problem solving and relating to people.

Each defensive interruption to contact impedes full awareness. It is the fixation of interruptions in contact, internally and externally, that is the concern of integrative psychotherapy.

Relationships

Contact also refers to the quality of the transactions between two people: the full awareness of both one's self and the other, a sensitive meeting of the other, and an authentic acknowledgment of one's self. Relationships between people are built on contact, the primary motivation for establishing and maintaining relationships.

Integrative psychotherapy makes use of many perspectives on human functioning. For a theory to be integrative it must also separate out those concepts and ideas that are not theoretically consistent in order to form a cohesive core of constructs that inform and guide the psychotherapeutic process. The single most consistent concept in the psychology and psychotherapy literature is that of relationship (Erskine, 1989). From the inception of a theory of contact by Laura and Frederick Perls (Perls, 1944; Perls, Hefferline, & Goodman, 1951) to Fairbairn's (1952) premise that people are relationship-seeking from the beginning and throughout life, to Sullivan's (1953) emphasis on interpersonal contact, to Guntrip's (1971) and Winnicott's (1965) relationship theories and corresponding clinical applications, to Berne's (1961, 1972) theories of ego states and script, to Rogers's (1951) focus on client-centered therapy, to Kohut (1971, 1977) and his followers' (Stolorow, Brandchaft, & Atwood, 1987) application of "sustained empathic inquiry" (p. 10), to the relationship theories developed by the Stone Center (Bergman, 1991; Miller, 1986; Surrey, 1985), there has been a succession of teachers, writers, and therapists who have emphasized that relationship—both in the early stages of life as well as throughout adulthood—are the source of that which gives meaning and validation to the self.

The literature on human development also leads to the premise that the sense of self and self-esteem emerge out of contact in relationship. Erikson's (1950) stages of human development over the entire life cycle describe the formation of identity (ego) as an outgrowth of interpersonal relations (trust vs. mistrust, autonomy vs. shame and doubt, etc.). Mahler's (1968; Mahler, Pine, & Bergman, 1975) descriptions of the stages of early child development place importance on the relationship between mother and infant. Bowlby (1969, 1973, 1980) has emphasized the significance of early as well as prolonged physical bonding in the creation of a visceral core from which all experiences of self and other emerge. When such contact does not occur in accordance with the child's needs there is a physiological defense against the loss of contact, poignantly described by Fraiberg in "Pathological Defenses in Infancy" (1983).

From a theoretical foundation of contact in relationship coupled with Berne's concept of ego states (particularly Child ego states) comes a natural focus on child development. The works of Daniel Stern (1985) and John Bowlby (1969, 1973, 1980) are presently most influential, largely because of their emphasis on early attachment and the natural, lifelong need for relationship. Based on his research on infants, Stern delineated a system for understanding the development of the sense of self, with this sense of self emerging out of four domains of relatedness: emergent relatedness, core relatedness, intersubjective relatedness, and verbal relatedness. As we take this view of the developing person into our psychotherapy practice, we have a deep appreciation for the vitality and active constructing that is so much a part of who our client is. By looking at the client simultaneously from the perspective of what a child needs and how he or she processes experiences as well in terms of these being ongoing life processes, we use our self in a directed way to assist the process of developing and integrating. What is frequently very significant in the psychotherapy is the process of attunement, not just to discrete thoughts, feelings, behaviors, or physical sensations, but also to what Stern (1985) termed "vitality affects" (p. 54), such that we try to create an experience of unbroken feeling-connectedness. The sense of self and the sense of relatedness that develop seem crucial to the process of healing, particularly when there have been specific traumas in the client's life, and to the process of integration and wholeness when aspects of the self have been disavowed or denied because of the failures of contact in relationship.

Psychological Constructs

Integrative psychotherapy correlates constructs from many different theoretical schools resulting in a unique organization of theoretical ideas and corresponding methods of clinical intervention. The concepts of contact-in-relationship, ego states, and life script are central to our integrative theory.

Ego States and Transference

Eric Berne's (1961) original concept of ego states provides an overall construct that unifies many theoretical ideas (Erskine, 1987, 1988). Berne (1961) defined the Child ego states as an archaic ego consisting of fixations of earlier developmental stages, as "relics of the individual's own childhood" (p. 77). The Child ego states are the entire personality of the person as he or she was in a previous developmental period (Berne, 1961, 1964). When functioning in a Child ego state the person perceives the internal needs and sensations and the external world as he or she did in a previous developmental age. This includes the needs, desires, urges, and sensations; the defense mechanisms; and the thought processes, perceptions, feelings, and behaviors of the developmental phase when fixation occurred. The Child ego state fixations occurred when critical childhood needs for contact were not met, and the child's use of defenses against the discomfort of the unmet needs became habitual.

The Parent ego states are the manifestations of introjections of the personalities of actual people as perceived by the child at the time of introjection (Loria, 1988). Introjection is a defense mechanism (including disavowal, denial, and repression) frequently used when there is a lack of full psychological contact between a child and the adults responsible for his or her psychological needs. By internalizing the parent with whom there is conflict, the conflict is made part of the self and experienced internally, rather than with that much-needed parent. *The function of introjection is in providing the illusion of maintaining relationship, but at the expense of a loss of self.*

Parent ego state contents may be introjected at any point throughout life and, if not reexamined in the process of later development, remain unassimilated or not integrated into the Adult ego state. The Parent ego states constitute an alien chunk of personality, embedded within the ego and experienced phenomenologically as if they were one's own, but, in reality, they form a borrowed personality, potentially in the position of producing intrapsychic influences on the Child ego states.

The Adult ego state consists of current, age-consistent emotional, cognitive, and moral development; the ability to be creative; and the capacity for full, contactful engagement in meaningful relationships. The Adult ego state accounts for and integrates what is occurring moment-by-moment internally and externally, past experiences and their resulting effects, and the psychological influences and identifications with significant people in one's life.

The object relations theories of attachment, regression, and internalized object (Bollas, 1979, 1987; Fairbairn, 1952; Guntrip, 1971; Winnicott, 1965) become more significant when integrated with the concepts of the Child ego states as fixations of an earlier developmental period and the Parent ego states as manifestations of introjections of the personality of actual people as perceived by the child at the time of introjection (Erskine, 1987, 1988, 1991).

The psychoanalytic self psychology concept of selfobject function (Kohut, 1971, 1977) and the Gestalt therapy concept of defensive interruptions to contact (Perls, Hefferline, & Goodman, 1951) can be combined within a theory of ego states to explain the continued presence of separate states of the ego that do not become integrated into an Adult ego state (Erskine, 1991).

Ego state theory also serves to define and unify the traditional psychoanalytic concepts of transference (Brenner, 1979; Friedman, 1969; Langs, 1976) and nontransferential transactions (Berne, 1961; Greenson, 1967; Lipton, 1977). Transference within an integrative psychotherapy perspective of ego states can be viewed as:
   1. the means whereby the client can describe his or her past, the developmental needs that have been thwarted, and the defenses that were erected to compensate;
   2. the resistance to full remembering and, paradoxically, an unaware enactment of childhood experiences (the repeated relationship);
   3. the expression of an intrapsychic conflict and the desire to achieve the satisfaction of relationship needs and intimacy in relationships (the therapeutically needed relationship); or
   4. the expression of the universal psychological striving to organize experience and create meaning.

This integrative view of transference provides the basis for a continual honoring of the inherent communication in transference as well as a recognition and respect that many transactions may be nontransferential (Erskine, 1991).

Script
The concept of script serves as the third unifying construct and describes how as infants and small children we begin to develop the reactions and expectations that define for us the kind of world we live in and the kind of people we are. Encoded physically in body tissues and biochemical events, emotionally, and cognitively in the form of beliefs, attitudes, and values, these responses form a blueprint that guides the way we live our lives (Erskine, 1980). Eric Berne termed this blueprint a "script" (1961, 1972), and Fritz Perls, innovator of Gestalt therapy, described a self-fulfilling, repetitive pattern (1944) and called it "life script" (Perls & Baumgardner, 1975). Alfred Adler referred to this as "life style" (Ansbacher & Ansbacher, 1956), Sigmund Freud used the term "repetition compulsion" to describe similar phenomena (1923/1961), and recent psychoanalytic writers have referred to a developmentally preformed pattern as "unconscious fantasy" (Arlow, 1969b, p. 8) and "schemata" (Arlow, 1969a, p. 29; Slap, 1987). In psychoanalytic self psychology the phrase "self system" is used to refer to recurring patterns of low self-esteem and self-defeating interactions (Basch, 1988, p. 100) that are the result of "unconscious organizing principles" termed "prereflexive unconscious" (Stolorow & Atwood, 1989, p. 373). Stern (1985), in analyzing research on infant and toddler development, conceptualizes these learned patterns as "representations of interactions that have been generalized (RIGs)" (p. 97).

Recent psychotherapy literature has described such blueprints as "self-confirmation theory" (Andrews, 1988, 1989) and as a self-reinforcing system of "a self-protection plan" referred to as the "script system" (Erskine & Moursund, 1988). The script system is divided into three primary components: script beliefs, script manifestations, and reinforcing experiences.

Script beliefs. In essence, the script answers the question, "What does a person like me do in a world like this with people like you?" Both the conscious and unconscious answers to this question form the script beliefs—the compilation of the survival reactions, RIGs (representations of interactions that have been generalized), decisions, conclusions, defenses, and reinforcements that occurred in the process of growing up. Script beliefs may be described in three categories: beliefs about self, beliefs about others, and beliefs about the quality of life. Once adopted, script beliefs influence what stimuli (internal and external) are attended to, how they are interpreted, and whether or not they are acted on. They become the self-fulfilling prophecy through which the person's expectations are inevitably proven to be true (Erskine & Zalcman, 1979).

The script beliefs are maintained in order (a) to avoid reexperiencing unmet needs and the corresponding feelings suppressed at the time of script formation and (b) to provide a predictive model of life and interpersonal relationships (Erskine & Moursund, 1988). Prediction is important, particularly when there is a crisis or trauma. Although the script is often personally destructive, it does provide psychological balance or homeostasis: It gives the illusion of predictability (Bary & Hufford, 1990; Perls, 1944). Any disruption in the predictive model produces anxiety: To avoid such discomfort, we organize our perceptions and experiences so as to maintain our script beliefs (Erskine, 1981).

Script manifestation. When under stress or when current needs are not met in adult life, a person is likely to engage in behaviors that verify script beliefs. These behaviors are referred to as the script manifestations and may include any observable behaviors (choice of words, sentence patterns, tone of voice, displays of emotion, gestures and body movements) that are the direct displays of the script beliefs and the repressed needs and feelings (the intrapsychic process). A person may act in a way defined by script beliefs, such as saying "I don't know" when believing "I'm dumb." Or he or she may act in a way that socially defends against the script beliefs, as, for example, excelling in school and acquiring numerous degrees as a way of keeping the "I'm dumb" belief from being discovered by others.

As part of the script display, individuals often have physiological reactions in addition to or in place of the overt behaviors. These internal experiences are not readily observable; nevertheless, the person can give a self-report: fluttering in the stomach, muscle tension, headaches, colitis, or any of a myriad of somatic responses to the script beliefs. Persons who have many somatic complaints or illnesses frequently believe that "something is wrong with me" and use physical symptoms to reinforce the belief—a cognitive defense that serves to keep the script system intact.

Script display also includes fantasies in which the individual imagines behaviors, either his or her own or someone else's, that lend support to script beliefs. These fantasied behaviors function as effectively as overt behaviors in reinforcing script beliefs/ feelings—in some instances, even more effectively. They act on the system exactly as though they were events that had actually occurred.

Reinforcing experiences. Any script display can result in a reinforcing experience—a subsequent happening that "proves" that the script belief is valid and thus justifies the behavior of the script display. Reinforcing experiences are a collection of emotion-laden memories, real or imagined, of other people's or one's own behavior; a recall of internal bodily experiences; or the retained remnants of fantasies, dreams, or hallucinations. Reinforcing experiences serve as a feedback mechanism to reinforce script beliefs. Only those memories that support the script belief are readily accepted and retained. Memories that negate script beliefs tend to be rejected or forgotten because they would challenge the belief and the whole defensive process.

Each person's script beliefs provide a distorted framework for viewing self, others, and the quality of life. In order to engage in script display, individuals must discount other options; they frequently will maintain that their behavior is the "natural" or "only" way they can respond. When used socially, script displays are likely to produce interpersonal experiences that, in turn, are governed by and contribute to the reinforcement of script beliefs.

Thus each person's script system is distorted and self-reinforcing through the operation of its three interrelated and interdependent subsystems: script beliefs/feelings, script displays, and reinforcing experiences. The script system serves as a defense against awareness of past experiences, needs, and related emotions while simultaneously being a repetition of the past.

Principles and Domains

Two principles guide all integrative psychotherapy. The first is our commitment to positive life change. Integrative psychotherapy is intended to do more than teach a client some new behaviors or a handful of coping skills designed to get him or her through today's crisis. It must somehow affect the client's life script. Without script change, therapy affords only temporary relief. We wish to help each client integrate his or her fixed perspectives into a flexible and open acceptance of learning and growing from each experience.

The second guiding principle is that of respecting the integrity of the client. Through respect, kindness, compassion, and maintaining contact we establish a personal presence and allow for an interpersonal relationship that provides affirmation of the client's integrity. This respectfulness may be best described as a consistent invitation to interpersonal contact between client and therapist, with simultaneous support for the client to contact his or her internal experience and receive recognition for that experience.

The four dimensions of human functioning that were outlined above—affective, behavioral, cognitive, and physiological—also indicate the domains in which therapeutic work occurs. Cognitive work takes place primarily through the therapeutic alliance between the client's Adult ego state and the therapist. It includes such things as contracting for change, planning strategies for change, and searching for insight into old patterns.

Behavioral work involves engaging the client in new behaviors that run counter to the old script system and that will evoke responses from others inconsistent with the collection of script-reinforcing memories. We sometimes assign "homework" so that the therapeutic experience can be extended beyond formal therapy sessions and during sessions invite clients to behave differently with us, with group members, and in fantasy with those people who helped him or her build and maintain the life script through the years.

Affective work, while it may involve current feelings, is more likely to involve archaic and/or introjected experiences. This is often experienced as going back to an age when the original introjects were taken on or life script decisions were made, or when those introjections or decisions were strongly reinforced. In this regressed state clients feel and think like a younger version of themselves, exhibiting many of the attitudes and decisions that went into the creation of their scripts. In this supported regression there is an opportunity to express the feelings, needs, and desires that have been repressed and to experiment with contact that might not before have been possible. The inhibiting decisions of years before are vividly recalled and can be reevaluated and redecided.

The fourth major avenue into script is the physical: working directly with body structures. As Wilhelm Reich (1945) pointed out, people live out their character structures in their physical bodies. Life script decisions inevitably involve some distortion of contact, and such distortions often carry with them a degree of muscular tension. Over time the tension becomes habitual and is eventually reflected in actual body structure. Working directly with this structure through muscle massage, altering breathing patterns, and/or encouraging or inhibiting movements, we can often help the client to access old memories and patterns and experience the possibility of new options.

We seldom limit a piece of work to a single domain; most work eventually involves several or all of them. This is another aspect of the integrative nature of our work. When a person is not defended against his or her own inner experience, he or she is able to integrate psychological functioning in all domains, taking in, processing, and sending out messages through each avenue and translating information easily from one to another internally.

Another way of looking at integrative psychotherapy is in terms of the primary ego state focus of the work. A given segment may deal primarily with Child, with Parent, with Child-Parent dialogue, or with Adult ego states. Work with the Child ego state usually opens with some sort of invitation to the client either to remember or to relive an old experience from childhood. In the Child ego state the client has direct access to old experiences and is able to relive those memories, which may be actual or representative. Through the process of remembering, reexperiencing the needs and feelings from that time, sometimes by expressing what was unexpressed, and having those needs and feelings responded to, the early fixated experience can become integrated. The invitation may be something like, "Go back to a time when you felt this way before," or it may involve invoking visual, auditory, and kinesthetic cues that assist the client in moving into old memories unavailable to Adult ego state awareness. Sometimes physical movement or massage work will stimulate the cathexis of earlier experiences. The therapist often paces and leads the client into childhood experiences through a series of verbal interchanges during which the Child ego state is increasingly elicited. Occasionally a structured relaxation exercise might be used.

Once the client is into the necessary experience, the therapist is then able to help the Child (with the Adult observing) to uncover the way in which the life script was formed and lived out through the years. The client remembers or relives the early trauma and the early unmet needs and reexperiences the process of reaction or decision through which he or she created a defensive, artificial closure to deal with those needs. This re-creation of an old scene is both the same as the original experience (the feelings, wants, and needs are felt again, along with the constraints that led to that early resolution) and different from the original, in that the presence of the observing Adult ego state and the supportive therapist create new resources and options that were not available before. It is these new resources that make possible a different decision this time (Goulding & Goulding, 1979). Because the self-in-the-world is literally experienced in a different way in the therapeutic regression, making a change in the archaic survival reaction or decision can break the old life script pattern. The client sees, hears, and feels self and the world in a new way and therefore can respond to self and others in new ways. Sometimes when there are no specific memories or no specific traumas, the Child is integrated through ongoing, consistent contact with the attuned therapist who responds to the client's needs in an acknowledging, validating, and normalizing manner. Such contact-in-relationship provides a therapeutic space for the client to drop the contact-interrupting defenses and relinquish script beliefs. This is the essence of the integration of the Child ego state into the Adult ego state.

When the script pattern is primarily linked to an internally influencing Parent ego state (introject), the client might be invited to cathect that Parent: to "be" Mom or Dad and to enter into a conversation with the therapist as Mom or Dad might have done (McNeel, 1976). The therapist first gets acquainted with the introjected Parent much as if a new and unknown person had actually come into the room. As the Parent ego state begins to experience and respond to the therapist's joining, the quality of the interaction gradually shifts into a more therapeutic mode, and the Parent is encouraged to deal with his or her own issues. This is working through the life script issues of the parenting person that the client has taken on as his or her own. Many of the methods used to treat the Child ego state may be used here if the Parent needs to deal with repressed experiences.

Or the therapist may intervene on behalf of the child involved—the client—to advocate for and provide protection if the introjected Parent is unyielding or continues to be destructive in some way. As the Parent begins to respond to challenges to his or her life script pattern, the introject loses its compulsive, binding quality. The thinking patterns, attitudes, emotional responses, defenses, and behavioral patterns that were introjected from significant others no longer remain as an unassimilated or exteropsychic state of the ego but are decommissioned as a separate ego state and integrated into an aware neopsychic or Adult ego (Erskine & Moursund, 1988).

Most enduring and problem-creating life script patterns are maintained by both Parent and Child ego states—that is, they contain elements of both Child decisions and Parent introjects. To facilitate full integration, a given piece of therapeutic work may involve both Parent and Child ego states, either in sequence (as the therapist deals first with the Parent, brings that segment to closure, and then helps the Child to explore and respond to the new information) or in the form of a dialogue between Parent and Child ego states.

Our work also incorporates direct interaction with the client's Adult ego state. This is particularly important for making contact, clarifying goals, and to serve as an observer and ally when working with the Child or Parent ego states. For some clients psychotherapy requires neither focus on fixated defense mechanisms or regression to childhood traumas that have been unresolved nor a decommission of introjections, but rather on the concerns of the adult life cycle. We evaluate what the client presents in light of developmental transitions, crises, age-related tasks, and existential experiences. When life cycle transitions and existential crises are respected as significant and the client has an opportunity to explore his or her emotions, thoughts, ideals, and borrowed opinions and to talk out possibilities, there emerges a sense of meaningfulness or purpose in life and its events.

Methods

Inquiry

Inquiry is a continual focus in contact-oriented, relationship-based psychotherapy. It begins with the assumption that the therapist knows nothing about the client's experience and therefore must continually strive to understand the subjective meaning of the client's behavior and intrapsychic process. Through respectful investigation of the client's phenomenological experience the client becomes increasingly aware of both current and archaic needs, feelings, and behavior. It is with full awareness and the absence of internal defenses that needs and feelings that were fixated due to past experiences can be integrated into a fully functioning Adult ego.

It should be stressed that the *process* of inquiring is as important, if not more so, than the content. The therapist's inquiry must be empathic with the client's subjective experience to be effective in discovering and revealing the internal phenomena (physical sensations, feelings, thoughts, meanings, beliefs, decisions, hopes, and memories) and uncovering the internal and external interruptions to contact.

Inquiry begins with a genuine interest in the client's subjective experiences and construction of meanings. It proceeds with questions from the therapist as to what the clients are feeling, how they experience both themselves and others (including the psychotherapist), and what conclusions they make. It may continue with historical questions as to when an experience occurred and who was significant in the person's life. Inquiry is used in the preparatory phase of therapy to increase the client's awareness of when and how they interrupt contact.

It is essential that the therapist understand each client's unique need for a stabilizing, validating, and reparative other person to take on some of the relationship functions that the client is attempting to manage alone. A contact-oriented relationship therapy requires that the therapist be attuned to these relationship needs and be involved, through empathic validation of feelings and needs and by providing safety and support.

Attunement

Attunement is a two-part process: the sense of being fully aware of the other person's sensations, needs, or feelings and the communication of that awareness to the other person. Yet more than just understanding, attunement is a kinesthetic and emotional sensing of the other; knowing their experience by metaphorically being in their skin. Effective attunement also requires that the therapist simultaneously remain aware of the boundary between client and therapist.

The communication of attunement validates the client's needs and feelings and lays the foundation for repairing the failures of previous relationships. Attunement is demonstrated by what we say, such as "that hurt," "you seemed frightened," or "you needed someone to be there with you." It is more frequently communicated by the therapist's facial or body movements that signal to the client that their affect exists, it is perceived by the therapist, it is significant, and it makes an impact on the therapist.

Attunement is often experienced by the client as the therapist gently moving through the defenses that have protected him or her from the awareness of relationship failures and the related needs and feelings, making contact with the long-forgotten parts of the Child ego state. Over time, this results in a lessening of external interruptions to contact and a corresponding dissolving of internal defenses. Needs and feelings can then be increasingly expressed with the comfort and assurance that they will be met with an empathic response. Frequently the attunement provides a sense of safety and stability that enables the client to begin to remember and to endure regressing into childhood experience, becoming fully aware of the pain of traumas, the failure of relationship(s), and the lost self.

It is not unusual, however, for the communication of attunement by the therapist to be met with a reaction of intense anger, withdrawal, or even further dissociation. The *juxtaposition* of the attunement by the therapist and the memory of the lack of attunement in previous significant relationships produces intense emotional memories of needs not being met. Rather than experience those feelings the client may react defensively with fear or anger at the contact offered by the therapist. The contrast between the contact available with the therapist and the lack of contact in their early life is often more than clients can bear, so they defend against the present contact to avoid the emotional memories.

It is important for the therapist to work sensitively with juxtaposition. The affect and behavior expressed by the client are an attempt to disavow the emotional memories. Therapists who do not account for the defensive reactions may misidentify the juxtaposition reaction as negative transference and/or experience intense counter-transference feelings in response to the client's avoidance of interpersonal contact. This concept helps therapists to understand the intense difficulty the client has in contrasting the current contact offered by the therapist with the awareness that needs for contactful relationship were unfulfilled in the past.

Juxtaposition reactions may signal that the therapist is proceeding more rapidly than the client can assimilate. Frequently it is wise to return to the therapeutic contract and clarify the purpose of the therapy. Explaining the concept of juxtaposition has been beneficial in some situations. Most often a careful inquiry into the phenomenological experience of the current interruption to contact will reveal the emotional memories of disappointment and painful relationships.

With the dissolution of the interruptions to contact, the relationship offered by the therapist provides the client with a sense of validation, care, support, and under-standing—"someone is there for me." This involvement by the therapist is an essential feature in the total dissolving of the defenses and a resolution and integration of traumas and unrequited relationships.

Involvement
Involvement is best understood through the client's perception—a sense that the therapist is contactful. It evolves from the therapist's empathic inquiry into the client's experience and is developed through the therapist's attunement with the client's affect and validation of his or her needs. Involvement is the result of the therapist being fully present, with and for the person, in a way that is appropriate to the client's developmental level of functioning. It includes a genuine interest in the client's intrapsychic and interpersonal world and a communication of that interest through attentiveness, inquiry, and patience.

Involvement begins with the therapist's commitment to the client's welfare and a respect for his or her phenomenological experiences. Full contact becomes possible when the client experiences that the therapist (1) respects each defense, (2) stays attuned to his or her affect and needs, (3) is sensitive to the psychological functioning at the relevant developmental ages, and (4) is interested in understanding his or her way of constructing meaning.

Therapeutic involvement that emphasizes acknowledgment, validation, normalization, and presence diminishes the internal discounting that is part of the defensive process. These engagements allow previously disavowed feelings and denied experiences to come to full awareness. The therapist's *acknowledgment* of the client's feelings begins with an attunement to his or her affect, even if it is unexpressed. Through sensitivity to the physiological expression of emotions the therapist can guide the client to express his or her feelings or to acknowledge that feelings or physical sensations may be the memory—the only memory available. In some situations the child may have been too young for the availability of linguistic and retrievable memory. In many cases of relationship failure the person's feelings were not acknowledged, and it may be necessary in psychotherapy to help the person gain a vocabulary and to voice those feelings. Acknowledgment of physical sensations and affect helps the client to claim his or her own phenomenological experience. Acknowledgment includes a receptive other who knows and communicates about the existence of nonverbal movements, tensing of muscles, affect, or even fantasy.

There are times in clients' lives when their feelings were acknowledged but were not validated. *Validation* communicates to the client that his or her affect or physical sensations are related to something significant in his or her experiences. Validation is making the link between cause and effect. Validation diminishes the possibility of the client internally discounting the significance of affect, physical sensation, memory, or dreams. It provides the client with an enhanced value of his or her phenomenological experience and therefore an increased sense of self-esteem.

Normalization means to depathologize clients' or others' categorization or definition of their internal experience or their behavioral attempts at coping. It may be essential for the therapist to counter societal or parental messages such as, "You're crazy for feeling scared," with "Anyone would be scared in that situation." Many flashbacks, bizarre fantasies, nightmares, confusion, panic, and defensiveness are normal coping phenomena in abnormal situations. It is imperative that the therapist communicate that the client's experience is a normal defensive reaction, not pathological.

Presence is provided through the psychotherapist's sustained empathic responses to both the verbal and nonverbal expressions of the client. It occurs when the behavior and communication of the psychotherapist, at all times, respects and enhances the integrity of the client. Presence includes the therapist's receptivity to the client's affect—to be impacted by his or her emotions, to be moved and yet to stay present with the impact of his or her emotions, not to become anxious, depressed, or angry. Presence is an expression of the psychotherapist's full internal and external contact. It communicates the psychotherapist's responsibility, dependability, and reliability.

Therapeutic involvement is maintained by the therapist's constant vigilance to providing an environment and relationship of safety and security. It is necessary that the therapist be constantly attuned to the client's ability to tolerate the emerging awareness of past experiences so that they are not overwhelmed once again in the therapy as they may have been in a previous experience. When the inquiring of the client's phenomenological experiences and the therapeutic regressions occur in surroundings that are calming and containing, the fixated defenses are further relaxed and the needs and feelings of the past experience(s) can be integrated.

The psychotherapist's involvement through transactions that acknowledge, validate, and normalize the client's phenomenological experiences and sustain an empathic presence fosters a *therapeutic potency* that allows the client to safely depend on the relationship with the psychotherapist. Potency is the result of engagement that communicates to the client that the therapist is fully invested in his or her welfare. Acknowledgment, validation, and normalization provide clients with permission to know their own feelings, value the significance of their affects, and relate them to actual or anticipated events. Therefore, such *therapeutic permission* to diminish defenses, to know his or her physical sensations, feelings, and memories and to reveal them must come only after clients experience protection within the therapeutic environment. Such *therapeutic protection* can be adequately provided only after there is a thorough assessment of the intrapsychic punishment and the client has a sense of safety that the therapist is consistently invested in his or her welfare. *Intrapsychic punishment* involves the child's perceived loss of bonding or attachment, shame, or threat of retribution. Protective interventions may include supporting a regressive dependency, providing a reliable and safe environment wherein the client can rediscover what has been lost to awareness, and pacing the therapy so the experiences may be fully integrated.

There are times when a client will attempt to elicit attunement and understanding by *acting out* a problem that he or she cannot talk out or express in any other way. Such acting out expressions are simultaneously both a defensive deflection of the emotional memories and also an attempt to communicate their internal conflicts. Confrontations or explanations can intensify the defenses, making the awareness of needs and feelings less accessible to awareness. Involvement includes a gentle, respectful inquiring into the internal experience of the acting out. The therapist's genuine interest in and honoring of the communication, which often may be without language, is an essential aspect of therapeutic involvement.

Involvement may include the therapist being active in facilitating the client's undoing repressive retroflections and activating responses that were inhibited, such as screaming for help or fighting back. The therapist's considered revealing of his or her internal reactions or showing compassion are further expressions of involvement. It may also include responding to earlier developmental needs in a way that symbolically represents need fulfillment, but the goal of a contact-oriented therapy is not in the satisfaction of archaic needs. This is an unnecessary and impossible task. Rather, the goal is the dissolving of fixated, contact-interrupting defenses that interfere with the satisfaction of current needs and full contact with self and others in life today. This is often accomplished by working within the transference to allow the intrapsychic conflict to be expressed within the therapeutic relationship and to be responded to with appropriate empathic transactions.

A contact-oriented psychotherapy through inquiry, attunement, and involvement responds to the client's current needs for an emotionally nurturing relationship that is reparative and sustaining. The aim of this kind of therapy is the integration of the affect-laden experiences and an intrapsychic reorganization of the client's beliefs about self, others, and the quality of life.

Conclusion

Contact facilitates the dissolving of defenses and the integration of the disowned parts of the personality. Through contact the disowned, unaware, unresolved experiences are made part of a cohesive self. In integrative psychotherapy the concept of contact is the theoretical basis from which clinical interventions are derived. Transference, ego state regression, activation of the intrapsychic influence of introjection, and the presence of defense mechanisms are all understood as indications of previous contact deficits. The four dimensions of human functioning—affective, behavioral, cognitive, and physiological—are an important guide in determining where someone is open or closed to contact and therefore of our therapeutic direction. A major goal of integrative psychotherapy is to use the therapist-client relationship—the ability to create full contact in the present—as a stepping-stone to healthier relationships with other people and a satisfying sense of self. With integration it becomes possible for the person to face each moment with spontaneity and flexibility in solving life's problems and in relating to people.

REFERENCES

Andrews, J. (1988). Self-confirmation theory: A paradigm for psychotherapy integration. Part I. Content analysis of therapeutic styles. *Journal of Integrative and Eclectic Psychotherapy, 7*(4), 359-384.

Andrews, J. (1989). Self-confirmation theory: A paradigm for psychotherapy integration. Part II. Integrative scripting of therapy transcripts. *Journal of Integrative and Eclectic Psychotherapy, 8*(1), 23-40.

Ansbacher, H. L., & Ansbacher, R. R. (1956). *The individual psychology of Alfred Adler.* New York: Atheneum.

Arlow, J. (1969a). Fantasy, memory, and reality testing. *Psychoanalytic Quarterly, 38,* 28-51.

Arlow, J. (1969b). Unconscious fantasy and disturbances of conscious experience. *Psychoanalytic Quarterly, 38,* 1-27.

Bary, B., & Hufford, F. (1990). The six advantages to games and their use in treatment planning. *Transactional Analysis Journal, 20,* 214-220.

Basch, M. (1988). *Understanding psychotherapy: The science behind the art.* New York: Basic Books.

Bergman, S. J. (1991). *Men's psychological development: A relationship perspective.* Works in progress (No. 48). Wellesley, MA: The Stone Center, Wellesley College.

Berne, E. (1961). *Transactional analysis in psychotherapy: A systematic individual and social psychiatry.* New York: Grove Press.

Berne, E. (1964). *Games people play: The psychology of human relationships.* New York: Grove Press.

Berne, E. (1972). *What do you say after you say hello?: The psychology of human destiny.* New York: Grove Press.

Bollas, C. (1979). The transferential object. *International Journal of Psychoanalysis, 60,* 97-107.

Bollas, C. (1987). *The shadow of the object: Psychoanalysis of the unthought known.* New York: Columbia Universities Press.

Bowlby, J. (1969). *Attachment. Vol. 1 of Attachment and loss.* New York. Basic Books.

Bowlby, J. (1973). *Separation: Anxiety and anger. Vol. 2 of Attachment and loss.* New York. Basic Books.

Bowlby, J. (1980). *Loss: Sadness and depression. Vol. 3 of Attachment and loss.* New York: Basic Books.

Brenner, C. (1979). Working alliance, therapeutic alliance, and transference. *Journal of the American Psychoanalytic Association, 27,* 137-158.

Erikson, E. (1950). *Childhood and society.* New York: Norton.

Erskine, R. (1975). The ABC's of effective psychotherapy. *Transactional Analysis Journal, 5*(2), 163-165.

Erskine, R. (1980). Script cure: Behavioral, intrapsychic and physiological. *Transactional Analysis Journal, 10,* 102-106.

Erskine, R. (1981, April). Six reasons people stay in script. Lecture. Professional Training Program, Institute for Integrative Psychotherapy, New York.

Erskine, R. G. (1987). A structural analysis of ego: Eric Berne's contribution to the theory of psychotherapy. In *Keynote Speeches: Delivered at the EATA Conference, July, 1986, Noordwikerhout, The Netherlands.* Geneva, Switzerland: European Association for Transactional Analysis.

Erskine, R. (1988). Ego structure, intrapsychic function, and defense mechanisms: A commentary on Eric Berne's original theoretical concepts. *Transactional Analysis Journal, 18,* 15-19.

Erskine, R. G. (1989). A relationship therapy: Developmental perspectives. In B. Loria (Ed.), *Developmental theories and the clinical process: Conference proceedings of the Eastern Regional Transactional Analysis conference* (pp. 123-135). Madison, WI: Omnipress.

Erskine, R. (1991). Transference and transactions: Critique from an intrapsychic and integrative perspective. *Transactional Analysis Journal, 21,* 63-76.

Erskine, R., & Moursund, J. (1988). *Integrative psychotherapy in action.* Newbury Park, CA: Sage Publications.

Erskine, R. G., & Zalcman, M. J. (1979). The racket system: A model for racket analysis. *Transactional Analysis Journal, 9,* 51-59.

Fairbairn, W. R. D. (1952). *An object-relations theory of the personality.* New York: Basic Books.

Fraiberg, S. (1983, Fall). Pathological defenses in infancy. *Dialogue: A Journal of Psychoanalytic Perspectives,* 65-75.

Freud, S. (1961). Beyond the pleasure principle. In J. Strachey (Ed. and Trans.), *The standard edition of the complete psychological works of Sigmund Freud* (Vol. 18, pp. 3-64). London: Hogarth Press. (Original work published 1923).

Friedman, L. (1969). The therapeutic alliance. *International Journal of Psychoanalysis, 50,* 139-159.

Goulding, M. M., & Goulding, R. L. (1979). *Changing lives through redecision therapy.* New York: Brunner/Mazel.

Greenson, R. (1967). *The techniques and practice of psychoanalysis.* New York: International Universities Press.

Guntrip, H. (1971). *Psychoanalytic theory, therapy and the self.* New York: Basic Books.

Kohut, H. (1971). *The analysis of the self.* New York: International Universities Press.

Kohut, H. (1977). *The restoration of the self: A systematic approach to the psychoanalytic treatment of narcissistic personality disorder.* New York: International Universities Press.

Langs, R. (1976). *The therapeutic intervention: Vol. II. A critical overview and synthesis.* New York: Jason Aronson.

Lipton, S. (1977). The advantages of Freud's technique as shown in his analysis of the rat man. *International Journal of Psychoanalysis, 58,* 255-273.

Loria, B. R. (1988). The parent ego state: Theoretical foundations and alterations. *Transactional Analysis Journal, 18,* 39-46.

Mahler, M. (1968). *On human symbiosis and the vicissitudes of individuation.* New York: International Universities Press.

Mahler, M., Pine, F., & Bergman, A. (1975). *The psychological birth of the human infant: Symbiosis and individuation.* New York: Basic Books.

McNeel, J. R. (1976). The parent interview. *Transactional Analysis Journal, 6,* 61-68.

Miller, J. B. (1986). *What do we mean by relationships?* Works in Progress (No. 22). Wellesley, MA: The Stone Center, Wellesley College.

Perls, F. S. (1944). *Ego, hunger and aggression: A revision of Freud's theory and method.* Durban, South Africa: Knox Publishing.

Perls, F .S., & Baumgardner, P. (1975). *Legacy from Fritz: Gifts from Lake Cowichan.* Palo Alto, CA: Science & Behavior Books.

Perls, F., Hefferline, R., & Goodman, P. (1951). *Gestalt therapy: Excitement and growth in the human personality.* New York: Julian Press.

Reich, W. (1945). *Character analysis.* New York: Farrar, Strauss & Giroux.

Rogers, C. R. (1951). *Client-centered therapy: Its current practice, implications, and theory.* Boston: Houghton Mifflin.

Slap, J. (1987). Implication for the structural model of Freud's assumptions about perception. *Journal of the American Psychoanalytic Association, 35,* 629-645.

Stern, D. (1985). *The interpersonal world of the infant: A view from psychoanalysis and developmental psychology.* New York: Basic Books.

Stolorow, R., & Atwood, G. (1989). The unconscious and unconscious fantasy: An intersubjective developmental perspective. *Psychoanalytic Inquiry, 9,* 364-374.

Stolorow, R., Brandchaft, B., & Atwood, G. (1987). *Psychoanalytic treatment: An intersubjective approach.* Hillsdale, NJ: The Analytic Press.

Sullivan, H. S. (1953). *The interpersonal theory of psychiatry* (H. S. Perry & M. L. Gawel, Eds.). New York: Norton.

Surrey, J. L. (1985). The "self-in-relation:" A theory of women's development. Works in Progress (No. 13). Wellesley, MA: The Stone Center, Wellesley College.

Winnicott, D. W. (1965). *The maturational processes and the facilitating environment: Studies in the theory of emotional development.* New York: International Universities Press.

This article was originally published in B. B. Loria (Ed.), The Boardwalk Papers: Selections from the 1993 Eastern Regional Transactional Analysis Conference *(pp. 1-26), Madison, WI: Omnipress, 1993.*

Part 2

The Structure of the Ego: Commentaries on Theory

Ego State Analysis:
A Comparative View

Rebecca L. Trautmann and Richard G. Erskine

In reading the transactional analysis literature on ego states one becomes quickly aware of a variety of definitions and interpretations. The purpose of this paper is to review the various understandings of ego states seen in the literature and synthesize them into four basic models, each of which is useful for different purposes. The intent is to provide the reader greater flexibility and precision in using ego state theory in his or her field of practice.

Conceptual Model

Berne's (1961) original conceptualization of ego states was defined in *Transactional Analysis in Psychotherapy* "phenomenologically as a coherent system of feelings related to a given subject, and operationally as a set of coherent behavior patterns; or pragmatically, as a system of feelings which motivates a related set of behavior patterns" (p. 17). He further described the ego states Parent, Adult, and Child as phenomenological *manifestations* of the psychic organs, exteropsyche, neopsyche, and archaeopsyche, whose function is to organize internal and external stimuli.

> A Parental ego state is a set of feelings, attitudes, and behavior patterns which resemble those of a parental figure. . . . The Adult ego state is characterized by an autonomous set of feelings, attitudes, and behavior patterns which are adapted to the current reality. . . . The Child ego state is a set of feelings, attitudes, and behavior patterns which are relics of the individual's own childhood. (pp. 75-77)

Berne (1961) in writing occasionally equated the psychic organs and their ego state manifestations, equating Parent with exteropsyche, Adult with neopsyche, and Child with archaeopsyche, yet theoretically viewed them as quite different. The first model of ego states, therefore, we call the Conceptual Model and diagram as in Figure 1.

Although it appears from this model that the psychic organ is equivalent to the ego state, Berne (1961) stressed that the effects of *all* psychic organs may be seen in *each* ego state (p. 240) (see Holloway 1977 for elaboration). The purpose of diagramming this model in such a way is to elucidate the concept of Parent as the attitudes, behaviors, and feelings incorporated (introjected) from significant others in a person's life; the Adult as those thoughts, feelings, and behaviors related to the here and now; and the Child as those thoughts, feelings, and behaviors that are remnants from childhood, the fixations from the past. This conceptualization of ego states is later seen reflected in the article on "Standard Structural Nomenclature" (Berne, 1969), in Stuntz's article "Second Order Structure of the Parent" (1972), Holloway (1977), Woollams and Brown's (1978) structure for transmission of Parent messages, and others. Other of Berne's diagrams that reflect the same conceptualization are shown in Figure 2.

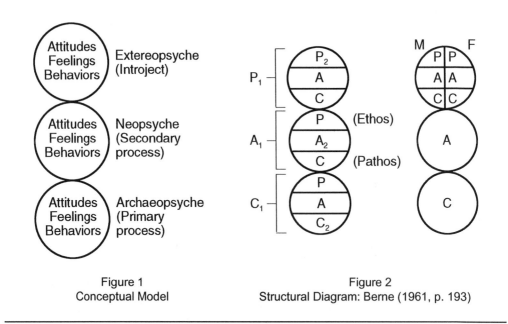

Figure 1
Conceptual Model

Figure 2
Structural Diagram: Berne (1961, p. 193)

Structural Model

Following the development of the conceptual model it appears in the writings of some transactional analysis theorists that these conceptualizations were consolidated into a form that was easier to communicate and to use. The following model, referred to by Joines (1976) as the structural model (Figure 3), is commonly used because of its simplicity for doing transactional analysis.

Although this is defined as the structural model, as Parent, Adult, and Child are described here they seem to reflect the phenomenological experience and are used in practice to describe the functions of each ego state, that is, retention of values and rules, problem solving, and feeling respectively; the psychobiological structure, as postulated by Berne, is seen more in the first diagram, specifically, the second-order structural diagram.

The process of consolidating the conceptual model into the structural model was begun by Berne (1961) when he wrote,

> The exteropsyche is judgmental in an imitative way, and seeks to enforce sets of borrowed standards. The neopsyche is principally concerned with transforming stimuli into pieces of information, and processing and filing that information on the basis of previous experience. The archaeopsyche tends to react more abruptly, on the basis of pre-logical thinking and poorly differentiated or distorted perceptions. In fact, each of these aspects perceives the environment differently, *in accordance with its functions* and hence is reacting to a different set of stimuli. (italics added) (p. 37)

The structural model is probably the most commonly used and is seen reflected in the works of such authors as Harris (1967), Schiff (1970), James and Jongeward (1971), and Berne (1972).

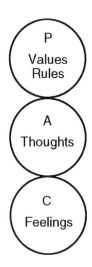

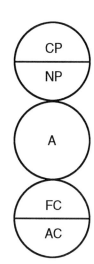

Figure 3
Structural (Phenomenological) Model

Figure 4
Functional (Behavioral) Model: Dusay (1977)

Functional Model

The third model, traditionally called the functional model (Joines, 1976) (Figure 4), describes the behavioral components of each ego state. These behaviors are referred to as "descriptive aspects" (Berne, 1972) of the Parent and Child ego states, that is, Controlling (Prejudicial, Critical) Parent, Nurturing (Natural) Parent, and Adapted Child and Natural (Free) Child.

The earlier functional diagram as used by Berne in *What Do You Say After You Say Hello?* (1972) is shown in Figure 5, although Dusay's (1977) diagram (Figure 4) seems currently to be more widely used.

> In describing these behavioral aspects of ego states Berne (1961) wrote:
> The *prejudicial* Parent is manifested as a set of seemingly arbitrary non-rational attitudes or parameters, usually prohibitive in nature which may be either syntonic or dystonic with the local culture. . . . The *nurturing* Parent is often manifested as sympathy for another individual, which again may be either culturally syntonic or culturally dystonic. . . . The *adapted* Child is manifested by behavior which is inferentially under the dominance of the Parental influence, such as compliance or withdrawal. The *natural* Child is manifested by autonomous forms of behavior such as rebelliousness or self-indulgence. It is differentiated from the autonomous Adult by the ascendency of archaic mental processes and the different kind of reality-testing. (pp. 76-78)

The behavioral aspect of the Adult in this model is problem solving, often described as "the computer."

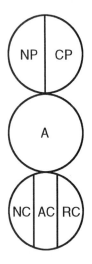

Figure 5
Functional Diagram:
Berne (1972); Joines (1976)

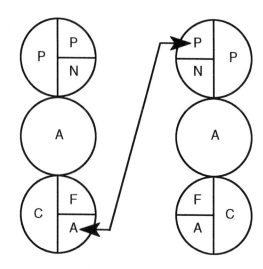

Figure 6
Karpman's Options Diagram (1971)

There are many variations of this model, generally reflecting an author's definition of ego states and the intended use of the model. In Karpman's (1971) article "Options," the model shown in Figure 6 is used to illustrate the behaviors related to each ego state and their effect in transactions.

Franklin Ernst (1973) and Robert Drye (1974) divide the Adapted Child into Compliant and Rebellious parts as in Figure 7.

A further variation is Kahler and Capers's (1974) in their article on the miniscript, in which they separated behaviors into OK and not-OK parts (Figure 8).

The functional (behavioral) model began as an outgrowth of the conceptual model when Berne (1961, 1964) described an *active* and *influencing* Parent ego state. He defined the Parent ego state (using the Conceptual Model) as active when a person behaved in the same way as the parental figures who have been introjected. These introjected or introjected behaviors can be broadly classified as *controlling* or *nurturing*, although the behavioral manifestations of an active Parent ego state are much more elaborate. The Parent ego state, when influencing, is not observable as Parent ego state behavior, but the individual responds intrapsychically as though the parental figures were actually directing the behavior, resulting in a Child ego state manifesting the influence. The Child ego state can respond either with *natural* behavior or *adapted* behavior in response to the internal influence of the Parent ego state just as when a child.

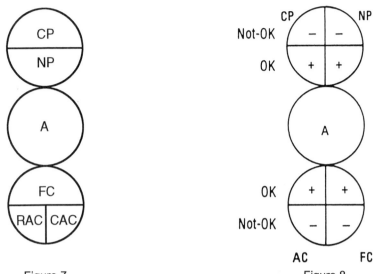

Figure 7
Functional Diagram: Ernst (1973), Drye (1974)

Figure 8
Functional Diagram: Kahler with Capers (1974)

Second-Order Structural Model

With the advancement of script theory and the interest in personality development, the fourth model of ego states was created, referred to as second-order structure (Figure 9).

This, again, is a variation on Berne's (1961) first model of second-order structure (Figure 10), which includes the breakdown of Adult and Parent. Note also that the numbering system was changed by the time Steiner (1971) developed the diagram shown in Figure 9.

The model in Figure 9 allows for the explanation of intrapsychic dynamics as they relate to the early development of an individual and is particularly useful in script theory where the focus is on the development of the individual in relation to external influences. Major authors who utilize this diagram are Steiner (1971), English (1972), Goulding (1974), and Schiff (1975).

Berne (1961) began describing second-order structure of the Child ego state in reference to a client's dream:

The Parental ego state he maintained when he was behaving *in loco parentis*; an Adult ego state which mediated his handling of blocks, games, and people, together with the emotional reactions appropriate to his age; and a Child ego state in which he regressed to previously abandoned forms of behavior. (p. 192)

In the above quotation Berne was referring to what is now commonly referred to as P_1, A_1, and C_1, all of which are contained within the Child ego state. He also suggested the possibility of third-, fourth-, *ad infinitum*-order structures for analyzing progressively younger Child ego states and similarly for the Parent, to represent previous generations

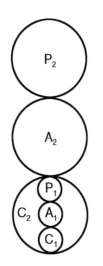

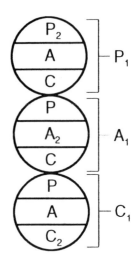

Figure 9
Second-Order Structural Model (Historical)

Figure 10
Second-Order Structure: Berne (1961)

of parental figures such as grandparents and great-grandparents, all incorporated into the Parent ego state.

Berne also consistently referred in the plural form to "Child ego states" in his early writings to indicate the various stages of child development within the Child.

Later P_0, A_0, and C_0 were defined as the state of the newborn with all the potentialities for developing a full Parent, Adult, and Child (Berne, 1969). Schiff (1975) extended this in describing C_0 as reflexive reactions to internal and external stimuli, A_0 as "preferences or avoidances that seem intrinsic to a particular experience" (p. 24), and P_0 as conditioned preferences or avoidances, all existing between birth and six to eight months.

The substructures of the Child ego state seem most prone to interpretation, and consequently we find a number of definitions and names related to these structures in the literature. Consider, for example, the various names of P_1: Ogre or Witch Mother (Steiner, 1971), electrode (Berne, 1972), Spooky (English, 1972), Witch Parent (Schiff, 1975), and Pig Parent (Steiner, 1979.) Each of these names for the Parent in the Child ego state reflects a different frame of reference which is clarified by understanding the model of ego states the author was using and the purpose in using that particular model.

For example, Schiff's use of the term Witch Parent described the process whereby a child who is not receiving adequate external structure can use a combination of fantasy and fear to force adaptation. Treatment, then, is directed toward providing adequate parenting and information, allowing the child to learn to adapt to external reality demands rather than internal fear resulting from fantasy. This definition of Parent in the Child is consistent with

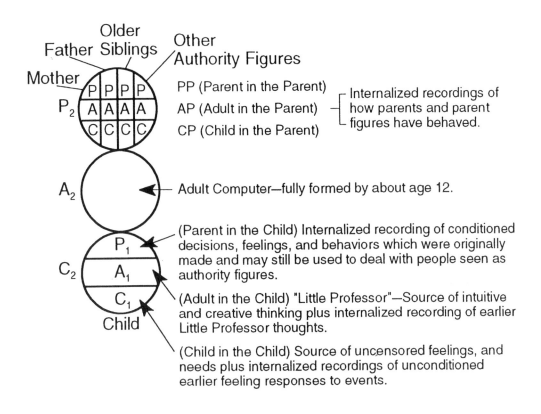

Figure 11
Second-Order Structure: Woollams (1977)

the structural model: that part of the personality that provides rules and values, that is, structure.

Woollams (1977) offered a second-order structural analysis diagram in which he combined the conceptual model to explain Parent and Child ego states and the structural model to explain Adult and Child ego states (Figure 11).

Ego State Pathology

The concepts of ego state contamination and exclusion change in definition depending on the model of ego states to which they are applied.

In the conceptual model, thoughts, feelings, and behaviors that were introjected from parental figures and that interfere with current functioning would constitute Parent contamination of the Adult. Child contamination of the Adult would exist when remnants

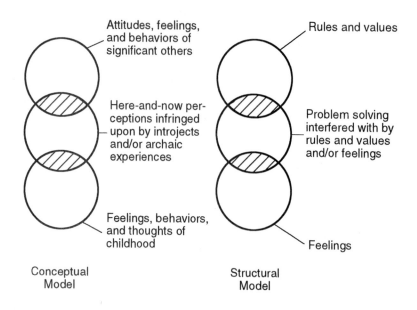

Figure 12
Contamination: Conceptual and Structural Models

of childhood experiences, in the form of thoughts, feelings, and behaviors, interfere with an adult's functioning in the here and now.

Using the structural model of ego states, Parent contamination of the Adult would occur when a preset system of rules, values, and attitudes interferes with a person's ability to problem solve in the present life context. Likewise, a Child contamination of the Adult would occur when feelings intrude on a person's thinking process.

In this model there is no differentiation as to whether the rules and values are incorporated or self-generated and whether feelings are archaic or emotions based on modeling (Figure 12).

Attempts have been made to illustrate contamination using the functional model and the second-order structural model but with little success. Berne (1961, p. 44) defined contamination as a structural pathology that is therefore theoretically inconsistent with a functional (behavioral) diagram. The functional model is a classification of sets of behaviors and each set of behaviors is discrete, making contamination impossible. Structurally, contamination involves the entire Child ego state, not a substructure of the Child, as in second-order structural analysis. Therefore, the use of the second-order structural model is theoretically not possible.

Exclusion, using the conceptual model, involves the withdrawal of psychic energy from those thoughts, feelings, and behaviors that are introjected (Parent ego state), or from those thoughts, feelings, and behaviors that are archaic (Child ego state), or from those thoughts, feelings, and behaviors that are in direct response to the here and now (Adult ego state). Exclusion of Parent in the structural model is generally seen as the absence of values and structures, while the exclusion of Child is the absence of identified feelings, wants, and needs. This would be somewhat consistent with the functional model, in which exclusion of Parent would be the absence of Critical and/or Nurturing behaviors; the exclusion of Child the absence of childlike behaviors, either Natural or Adapted; and exclusion of the Adult the absence of thinking related to problem solving.

Exclusion, using the second-order structural model, would be theoretically inconsistent or meaningless, given that each person has the existence of each of the ego state structures developmentally, although no psychic energy may be applied to one or two of the structures (as in the Schiff model of symbiosis [1975]).

Conclusion

Each of these models of ego states was developed and is used to meet different needs. The conceptual model was Berne's original conceptualization of the structure of the ego or aspect of the personality available to conscious awareness. It is a synthesis of the work of Federn, supported by Penfield's research, and includes Berne's unique development of the Parent ego state (Dusay, 1971; Ernst, 1971). This model is excellent for helping the practitioner to understand the aspects of personality that are the introjection of thoughts, feelings, and behaviors of significant other people, the remnants of archaic experiences, and the thoughts, feelings, and behaviors that are here-and-now responses to environmental and internal stimuli. The development of the structural model allows for these conceptualizations to be understood more easily by the layperson and is a simplification of the conceptual model, emphasizing how each ego state is experienced phenomenologically. The functional model is used to classify behaviors and to teach behavioral options in transactions. And finally, when the intent is to illustrate personality development or the scripting process, the second-order structural diagram is used.

REFERENCES

Berne, E. (1961). *Transactional analysis in psychotherapy: A systematic individual and social psychiatry*. New York: Grove Press.

Berne, E. (1964). *Games people play: The psychology of human relationships*. New York: Grove Press.

Berne, E. (1969). Standard structural nomenclature. *Transactional Analysis Bulletin, 8*(32), 111-112.

Berne, E. (1972). *What do you say after you say hello?: The psychology of human destiny.* New York: Grove Press.

Drye, R. (1974). Stroking the rebellious child: An aspect of managing resistance. *Transactional Analysis Journal, 4*(3), 23-26.

Dusay, J. M. (1971). Eric Berne's studies of intuition 1949-1962. *Transactional Analysis Journal, 1*(1), 34-44.

Dusay, J. M. (1977). *Egograms: How I see you and you see me*. New York: Harper & Row.

English, F. (1972). Sleepy, spunky and spooky. *Transactional Analysis Journal, 2*(2), 64-67.

Ernst, F. H., Jr. (1971). The diagrammed parent ego state—Eric Berne's most significant contribution. *Transactional Analysis Journal, 1*(1), 49-58.

Ernst, F. (1973). Psychological rackets in the OK corral. *Transactional Analysis Journal, 3*(2), 19-23.

Goulding, R. (1974). Thinking and feeling in transactional analysis: Three impasses. *Voices, 10,* 11-13.

Harris, T. (1967). *I'm OK—you're OK: A practical guide to transactional analysis*. New York: Harper & Row.

Holloway, W. H. (1977). Transactional analysis: An integrative view. In G. Barnes (Ed.), *Transactional analysis after Eric Berne: Teachings and practices of three TA schools* (pp. 169-221). New York: Harper's College Press.

James, M., & Jongeward, D. (1971). *Born to win: Transactional analysis with Gestalt experiments*. Reading, MA: Addison-Wesley.

Joines, V. (1976). Differentiating structural and functional. *Transactional Analysis Journal, 6*, 377-380.

Kahler, T., with Capers, H. (1974). The miniscript. *Transactional Analysis Journal, 4*(1), 26-42.

Karpman, S. (1971). Options. *Transactional Analysis Journal, 1*(1), 79-87.

Schiff, J., with Day, B. (1970). *All my children*. Philadelphia: M. Evans.

Schiff, J., with Schiff, A. W., Mellor, K. Schiff, E., Schiff, S., Richman, D., Fishman, J., Wolz, L., Fishman, C., & Momb, D. (1975). *Cathexis reader: Transactional analysis treatment of psychosis*. New York: Harper & Row.

Steiner, C. (1971). *Games alcoholics play: The analysis of life scripts*. New York: Grove Press.

Steiner, C. (1979). The pig parent. *Transactional Analysis Journal, 9*(1), 26-37. Note: The term Pig Parent was first used in by Hogie Wyckoff in C. Steiner (Ed.) (1977) *Problem solving groups for women. Readings in radical psychiatry*. New York: Grove Press.

Stuntz, E. (1972). Second order structure of the parent. *Transactional Analysis Journal, 2*(2), 59-61.

Woollams, S. (1977). From 21 to 43. In G. Barnes (Ed.) *Transactional analysis after Eric Berne: Teachings and practices of three TA schools* (pp. 351-379). New York: Harper's College Press.

Woollams, S., & Brown, M. (1978). *Transactional analysis*. Dexter: MI: Huron Valley Institute Press.

This article was originally published in the Transactional Analysis Journal, *Volume 11, Number 2, April 1981, pp. 178-185.*

Ego Structure, Intrapsychic Function, and Defense Mechanisms: A Commentary on Eric Berne's Original Theoretical Concepts

Richard G. Erskine

Eric Berne (1961) extended psychoanalytic thought with his elaboration and application of Paul Federn's (1953) concept of subdivisions of the ego. Berne's contribution to the theory of ego states produced the possibility for a dramatic change in the practice of psychotherapy and predated by several years the more recent psychoanalytic paradigm shift to "self psychology" (Kernberg, 1976; Kohut, 1971, 1977) and a developmental perspective that focuses on pre-Oedipal and infantile fixations (Mahler, 1968; Mahler, Pine, & Bergman, 1975; Masterson, 1976, 1981; Miller, 1981; Stern, 1985) as the cause of psychological dysfunction.

In the popularization of transactional analysis that has occurred in the past two decades, many of Eric Berne's original theoretical concepts have been misused or presented simplistically. Often Berne's examples and explanations have been used as definitions of ego states, or there has been a failure to correlate the four determinants of an ego state—phenomenological, historical, behavioral, and social—which is necessary for a full understanding of the intrapsychic and transactional functioning of the ego. As a result, ego states have been presented as a taxonomy of behavior or classifications of subjective experiences with a lack of emphasis on developmental phase fixation, introjection, and the mechanisms of defense.

The popularizing and simplifying of ego state theories has led to confusion regarding Berne's original concepts and a lack of understanding of intrapsychic phenomena in the minds of readers of post-Berne transactional analysis articles and books.

The Ego

In *Ego Psychology and the Psychoses* Federn (1953) described the ego as a real, experienced state of feeling and not simply a theoretical construct. The Latin word "ego," as used in the English translation of early psychoanalytic writings, replaced Freud's "Das Ich"—"the I." The ego is the identifying and alienating aspect of the self; it is our sense of "This is me" and "That is not me." The ego discriminates and segregates internal sensations from those originating outside the organism. The ego is our identity—the "I am hungry," "I am a psychotherapist," or "I am not a bus driver, although I can drive a bus."

Paul Federn observed that severely disturbed patients exhibit a current ego that both identifies with internal sensations and, at the same time, identifies with or discriminates from environmental stimuli. In addition, this ego manifests a feeling of identity and a response to the environment which is like that of a young child. He described these different manifestations as *states* of the ego, that is, different identities. In addition, he referred to the constant psychic presence of the parental figures in his psychotic patients (Weiss, 1950), although he did not go so far as to describe this phenomenon as a state of the ego. Rather, he continued to define it as related to the psychoanalytic concept of the superego.

In his personal analysis with Paul Federn, Eric Berne was greatly influenced by these theoretical ideas and interpretations regarding differing states of the ego. Throughout his analysis, first with Federn and later with Erik Erikson, Berne spent a decade and a half experimenting with intuition and ego image (Berne, 1949, 1955, 1957a). Based on these experiments and clinical observations, Berne made use of Erikson's 1950 developmental perspective to elaborate on Federn's 1953 theory and further refine the concept of ego states (Berne, 1957b, 1961).

States of the Ego

Berne assumed throughout his early writing (pre-1966) that the reader was familiar with a working definition of ego; he described a state of the ego "phenomenologically as a coherent system of feelings related to a given subject, and operationally as a set of coherent behavior patterns; or pragmatically, as a system of feelings which motivates a related set of behavior patterns" (Berne, 1961, p. 17).

Berne further used a colloquial description of ego state (Parent, Adult, and Child) to refer to phenomenological *manifestations* of the psychic organs (exteropsyche, neopsyche, and archaeopsyche), whose function it is to organize internal and external stimuli. Extero-psyche, archaeopsyche, and neopsyche refer to the aspect of the mind taken from an external source, the early mind from a previous developmental period and the current mind. Throughout *Transactional Analysis in Psychotherapy* (1961) Berne used the psychic organs terms interchangeably with the term "ego state" to "denote states of mind and their related patterns of behavior" (p. 30).

Berne (1961) stated, "The Adult ego state is characterized by an autonomous set of feelings, attitudes and behavior patterns which are adapted to the current reality" (p. 76). In this description Berne's use of the term "autonomous" refers to the neopsychic state of the ego functioning without intrapsychic control by an introjected or archaic ego. When in the Adult ego state a person is in full contact with what is occurring both inside and outside his or her organism in a manner appropriate to that developmental age. This neopsychic (current mind) function of the ego accounts for and integrates: (1) what is occurring moment-by-moment internally and externally, (2) past experiences and their resulting effects, and (3) the psychological influences and identifications with other significant people in one's life. This Adult ego state consists of current, age-related motor behavior; emotional, cognitive, and moral development; the ability to be creative; and the capacity for full, contactful engagement in meaningful relationships. Berne (1961, p. 195) emphasized these aspects through the use of the Greek terms Ethos and Pathos—to which this author adds Logos, the ability to use logic and abstract reasoning, and Technos, the ability to create—to describe the full neopsychic capacity of the Adult ego state to integrate values, process information, respond to emotions and sensations, and be creative and contactful.

This neopsychic state of the ego was contrasted by Berne with an archaic ego state that consists of fixations at earlier developmental stages. In Berne's (1961) words, "The Child ego state is a set of feelings, attitudes, and behavior patterns which are relics of the individual's own childhood" (p. 77). This Child ego state perceives the external world and internal needs and sensations as the person did in a earlier developmental stage. Although the person may appear to be relating to current reality, he or she is actually experiencing what is happening with the intellectual, social, and emotional capacities of a child at the developmental age of unresolved trauma or confusion, that is, fixation.

It should be noted that using the term Child ego state in the singular form is somewhat misleading. A child develops through a number of phases and stages (Erikson, 1950; Mahler, 1968; Mahler, Pine, & Berman, 1975; Piaget, 1936/1952), and repression and fixation may occur at any of them. Under the influence of one set of stressors, we may think, feel, and act much as we did when we were six years old; under another we may perceive ourselves or the world around us as we did as infants.

The archaeopsychic state of the ego is much more complex than implied by various writers who use simple examples of spontaneity, intuition, compliance, or emotive capacity to describe the Child ego states. The Child or archaic states of the ego are the *entire personality* of a person *as he or she was in a previous developmental period of time*. This includes the needs, desires, urges, and sensations; the defense mechanisms; and the thought processes, perceptions, feelings, and behaviors of the developmental phase at which fixation occurred.

The archaic state of the ego is the result of developmental arrest that occurred when critical early childhood needs for contact were not met. The child's defenses against the discomfort of the unmet needs became egotized—fixated; the experience cannot be fully integrated into the Adult ego state until these defense mechanisms are dissolved.

Berne (1961) also explored Federn's observations that in many of his clients there was a constant psychic presence of parental figures influencing their behavior. This parental influence is from real people who years before interacted with and had responsibility for this particular individual when he or she was a child. This parental presence is more tangible than the Freudian construct of "superego" *("Über-Ich")*. Through historical investigation it is possible to trace what was actually said or done, by whom, and at what time during the person's childhood. Through introjection (an unaware defensive identification and internalization) the child made the parental person part of the self, that is, ego.

Berne (1961) concluded that the introjected parents also become a state of the ego, which he defined as "a set of feelings, attitudes, and behavior patterns which resemble those of a parental figure" (p. 75). However, the phrase "resemble those of a parental figure" is somewhat misleading. From Berne's examples and descriptions in *Transactional Analysis in Psychotherapy* (1961) and from my own clinical observations it is apparent that the Parent ego state is an actual historical internalization of the personality of one's own parents or other significant parental figures as *perceived* by the child at the time of introjection.

Parent ego state contents are taken in, that is, introjected, from parenting figures in early childhood—and, to a lesser degree, throughout life—and, if not reexamined in the process of later development, remain unassimilated or not integrated into the neo-functioning ego. Since the child's perceptions of the caretaker's reactions, emotions, and thought processes will differ at various stages of development, so also will the actual content and intrapsychic function of the Parent ego state vary in relation to the developmental age when the introjection occurred. Introjection is a defense mechanism frequently used when there is a lack of full psychological contact between the child and the significant adult; the resulting conflict is internalized so that the conflict can seemingly be more easily managed (Perls, 1978). Introjected elements may remain as a kind of foreign body within the personality, often unaffected by later learning or development but continuing to influence behavior and perceptions. They constitute an alien chunk of personality, embedded within the ego and experienced phenomenologically as if they were one's own, but, in reality, they form a borrowed personality.

As long as the introjected elements are consistent or syntonic with Adult or Child ego state thoughts, feelings, and behaviors, the person is often unaware that there is any intrapsychic distress. However, when the introjects are inconsistent or dystonic with Adult or Child ego state experience they can lead to an uncomfortable sense of internal conflict.

Self-Generated Ego Images

In addition to the archaic (Child) ego states created and frozen out of early defensive reactions, decisions, and experiences, there is another process by which Child ego state contents can become fixated. The fixation may appear in later life as similar to an introjected Parent ego state, but its origin is in the fantasy of a young child. As a normal developmental process in the preschool and kindergarten years, children often create an image or being as a way to provide controls, structure, nurturing, or whatever was experienced as missing or inadequate in early life. Some children create their own personal "bogeyman," a frightening creature who threatens them with dire consequences for minor misdeeds. Investing this fantasy "parent" with all bad and scary aspects allows them to keep mother and father as perfectly good and loving. Others may create a fairy godmother sort of parent who loves and nurtures them even when their real parents are cold, absent, or abusive. This created image serves as a buffer between the actual parental figures and the desires, needs, or feelings of the young child.

In maturing to later developmental phases children often let go of these self-generated images. In families in which it is necessary to repress the awareness of needs, feelings, and memories in order to survive, the self-created image becomes fixated and is not integrated with later developmental learning. Whatever the characteristics of the self-created Child ego state image, over the years it comes to operate as an intrapsychic influence in a manner similar to the Parent ego state. However, the self-generated "parent" is often more demanding and less logical or reasonable than the actual parents were (after all, it had its origins in a small child's fantasy). These influencing images are comprised of an encapsulated, nonintegrated collection of thoughts, feelings, or behaviors to which the person responds as if they were actually introjections from the significant grown-ups of early childhood.

Defense Mechanisms and Ego State Functions

Up to this point the development and structure of ego states have been described. The function of ego states is the dynamic interaction of intrapsychic process and manifested activities. These include the fixated archaic behaviors and thought processes, the introjected behaviors and attitudes of significant others, and very importantly, the related defense mechanisms.

Berne assumed throughout his writing that the reader was familiar with the psychoanalytic defense mechanisms, and therefore he did not elaborate on their role in a functional analysis of ego states. Federn (1953) had previously gone into detail on defense mechanisms and ego states.

Knowledge of defense mechanisms is integral to understanding ego state functioning. It is because of the fixation of defense mechanisms that the archaic (Child) or introjected (Parent) aspects of the ego remain separate states and do not become integrated into neopsychic (Adult) awareness.

Adult ego state awareness of the needs, desires, memories, and external influences remain blocked through maintaining infant defenses of avoidance, freezing, and fighting (Fraiberg, 1983); the late oral defenses of splitting (Fairbairn, 1954) and transformation of affect (Fraiberg, 1983); and the early childhood defenses described by Anna Freud (1937).

As a result of the fixation of defense mechanisms, ego state function can be observed both *actively* and as an intrapsychic *influence*. We can observe the manifestation of the exteropsychic (Parent) ego state when a person actively feels, perceives the environment, or acts as parents did years before. When the exteropsychic ego state is intrapsychically influential "the individual manifests an attitude of child-like compliance" (Berne, 1961, p. 76). The archaeopsychic ego state is exhibited in one of two forms: The *adapted* Child is manifested by behavior that is inferentially under the dominance of the Parental influence, such as compliance or withdrawal. The *natural* Child is manifested by autonomous forms of behavior such as rebelliousness or self-indulgence" (Berne, 1961, pp. 75-76). In either case the Child ego state is archaic and manifests previously developmentally fixated defense mechanisms or is exhibiting a freedom from control and the archaic expression of that freedom.

Eric Berne used the terms *adapted* and *natural* Child in both *Transactional Analysis in Psychotherapy* (1961) and *Games People Play* (1964) as adjectives modifying the Child ego states and to refer to manifestations of intrapsychic dynamics. The terms "adapted" and "natural" are not used as nouns, that is, Adapted Child and Natural Child, nor were they meant to imply states of the ego; rather they were used to describe the interplay between a specific intrapsychic process and behavior.

The Integrated Adult Ego

Each person's identity of self—ego—may be comprised of all three states of the ego, and transactions with others can come from any one of the ego states, often without the awareness of which state is active. Psychological problems emerge when the introjected and/or archaic ideas, images, and emotions contaminate the here-and-now perceptions of the Adult ego state. When Adult ego state contaminations exist the phenomenological experience of the person is that of processing current stimuli, accounting for current sensations and feelings, and behaving appropriately to the situation, when in fact this is not so. The person is unaware that the introjected ideas and emotions and/or childhood decisions and feelings are infringing on present perceptions, often resulting in communication and relationship problems.

The healthy ego is one in which the Adult ego state, with full neopsychic functioning, is in charge and has integrated (assimilated) archaeopsychic and exteropsychic content and experiences. When earlier defense mechanisms remain fixated, as evidenced by the Adult ego state remaining syntonic with or contaminated by Parent and/or Child ego state experiences, or when the boundaries between ego states are too permeable or loosely defined, the Adult ego state cannot serve this healthy, integrative function.

Eric Berne's major contribution to the theory of psychotherapy was his elaboration and elucidation of the intrapsychic and manifested aspects of the ego in its various states and how these states of the ego determine our transactions with each other. Transactional analysis has the unique potential of contributing to the advancement of psychotherapy in the direction of both in-depth psychotherapy and cognitive-behavioral therapy by going beyond behavioral descriptions of ego states and emphasizing Eric Berne's contribution to our understanding of the structures of the ego, intrapsychic functioning, and interpersonal communication.

REFERENCES

Berne, E. (1949). The nature of intuition. *Psychiatric Quarterly, 23,* 203-226.
Berne, E. (1955). Intuition IV: Primal images and primal judgments. *Psychiatric Quarterly, 29,* 634-658.
Berne, E. (1957a). Intuition V: The ego image. *Psychiatric Quarterly, 31,* 611-627.
Berne, E. (1957b). Ego states in psychotherapy. *American Journal of Psychotherapy, 11,* 293-309.
Berne, E. (1961). *Transactional analysis in psychotherapy: A systematic individual and social psychiatry.* New York: Grove Press.
Berne, E. (1964). *Games people play: The psychology of human relationships.* New York: Grove Press.
Erikson, E. (1950). *Childhood and society.* New York: Norton & Co.
Fairbairn, W. R. D. (1954). *Psychoanalytic studies of the personality.* New York: Basic Books.
Federn, P. (1953). *Ego psychology and the psychoses.* London: Imago Publishers.
Fraiberg, S. (1983, Fall). Pathological defenses in infancy. *Dialogue: A Journal of Psychoanalytic Perspective,* 65-75.
Freud, A. (1937). *The ego and the mechanisms of defense.* London: The Hogarth Press and the Institute of Psycho-Analysis.
Kernberg, O. (1976). *Object relations theory and clinical psychoanalysis.* New York: Jason Aronson.
Kohut, H. (1971). *The analysis of the self.* New York: International Universities Press.
Kohut, H. (1977). *The restoration of the self: A systematic approach to the psychoanalytic treatment of narcissistic personality disorder.* New York: International Universities Press.
Mahler, M. (1968). *On human symbiosis and the vicissitudes of individuation.* New York: International Universities Press.
Mahler, M. S., Pine, F., & Bergman, A. (1975). *The psychological birth of the human infant: Symbiosis and individuation.* New York: Basic Books.
Masterson, J. F. (1976). *Psychotherapy of the borderline adult: A developmental approach.* New York: Brunner/Mazel.

Masterson, J. F. (1981). *The narcissistic and borderline disorders: An integrated developmental approach.* New York: Brunner/Mazel.

Miller, A. (1981). *The drama of the gifted child: The search for the true self* (R. Ward, Trans.). New York: Basic Books.

Perls, L. (1978, Winter). An oral history of Gestalt theory, Part I: A conversation with Laura Perls, by Edward Rosenfeld. *The Gestalt Journal*, 8-31.

Piaget, J. (1952). *The origins of intelligence in children* (M. Cook, Trans.). New York: International Universities Press. (Original French edition published 1936).

Stern, D. (1985). *The interpersonal world of the infant: A view from psychoanalysis and developmental psychology.* New York: Basic Books.

Weiss, E. (1950). *Principles of psychodynamics.* New York: Grune Stratton.

This article was originally published in the Transactional Analysis Journal, *Volume 18, Number 1, January 1988, pp. 15-19.*

Ego State Theory:
Definitions, Descriptions, and Points Of View

Richard G. Erskine, Petrūska Clarkson,
Robert L. Goulding, Martin G. Groder, and Carlo Moiso

Editor's Note: At the International Transactional Analysis Association's 25th Annual Summer Conference in Chicago, Illinois, July 29–August 2, 1987, a roundtable discussion was held to explore various topics in transactional analysis theory. Each participant selected articles from the others to read beforehand. These served as a springboard for a discussion of "Transactional Analysis Theory: Past, Present and Future." The following excerpts from the roundtable conversation were edited by Richard Erskine. In keeping with the theme of this issue of the Transactional Analysis Journal, *the content of these excerpts has been limited to the topic of ego states.*

RE: I want to begin by introducing Marty Groder, Bob Goulding, Petrūska Clarkson, Carlo Moiso, and I'm Richard Erskine. The empty chair is for Marilyn Zalcman, who is still sick with pneumonia and asked me to convey her disappointment at not being able to be part of this conversation today. To begin, I wonder if there is one question that each of you would like someone to ask you this morning.

MG: When I was reviewing the reading material again this morning, I realized that the major question I was asking myself, and therefore the question I would want to be asked, is, "What is reality?" One of the assumptions throughout most of the papers was that there is a process called reality testing, which presumes there is a reality to test, and this is a very questionable hypothesis.

RE: What was your personal reaction to that question?

MG: Well, in the many years I have been studying, as I jokingly put it, everything from anthropology to zoology, the question of what reality is has been a moot question. There are struggles within each discipline and between disciplines. At a theoretical level, which is what we are dealing with in this roundtable, the fact that no one even raised the issue about what they meant when they said, "The Adult does reality testing," or, "Is in the here and now," distressed me.

RE: You're assuming, then, that we just operate on assumptions.

MG: No, I'm assuming that you're operating on unstated assumptions—which is much worse.

BG: I think we operate on belief systems. Each of us has our own belief system, and I think that's okay. I think it's okay for me to believe something that you don't believe and okay for you to believe something I don't believe. You make your belief system work, and I make my belief system work.

MG: But we're not talking about working, Bob. We're talking about theory.

BG: Yeah, I know. But I don't have much theory.

CM: There might be a confusion here between reality description and the definition of reality. I think that all science and all arts attempt to describe reality, and we've mistakenly taken it as a definition of reality, as if there can be such a definition. Philosophers have been defining reality for two thousand years.

MG: The reason I believe that this is a pragmatic as well as theoretical question is that, in the fifties and sixties when Eric Berne and others evolved the transactional analysis theory that is now being so carefully rescrutinized, there was a consensus about what reality was, at least at a functioning, theoretical level. These days I find that many people I work with have already had successful therapy and cure in a number of senses, before they come to me. We're in a time of such transition about the nature of reality that the question about what reality is has become a pragmatic issue. I'm finding that I have to work with, "Now that I'm sane, where did the world go?" in which this sanity is supposed to be exercised. Why isn't sanity good enough?

PC: I think that is an important question, Marty, and I think for transactional analysis to be a coherent theory, we probably need to address it. I would go at it from the level of epistemology. How do we know what we know? How do we call what we call? And I agree that there is an assumption of consensual reality which we haven't really explicitly set out, and that doesn't allow for other phenomenological realities.

RE: I think that shows up in our theories in the inconsistent definitions that we have.

MG: Yes.

RE: It's as though each writer comes along and reinvents definitions. In my reading I find that when Berne laid down a definition of something, he then proceeded to give explanations of his definition. What I hear commonly used are those explanations or elaborations of the definition used as the definition.

BG: For example.

RE: The concept of ego states. He laid it down pretty clearly. He was talking about the ego and subdivisions of the ego: that the Parent is the introjection of the personality, the whole thoughts, feelings, behaviors, even the physiology and body sensations, of other significant people; that the Child is the full person in fixation at some other developmental period of time; and that the Adult represents the full developmental capacity to function now. Then he went on and explained that the Parent is *like* values, the Child is *like* feelings, the Adult is *like* thinking, and then that later illustration has been used by some people as a definition.

CM: It's a description.

RE: The description becomes the definition.

BG: Of course I don't see the Child as being fixated at points in time. Perhaps that's where we have a big difference. I see the Child as being a whole collection of fixations that flow from one to the other, and that it's always changeable.

RE: I agree with that. In fact, when Berne says Child ego states, he always says it in the plural.

PC: In the actual definition, in the first part of *Transactional Analysis in Psychotherapy* (1961) where he talks about ego states, he is not talking necessarily about fixations. He uses fixation as an example of Child ego state in the section in which he discusses developmental pathology. He doesn't necessarily define the Child ego state as always pathological or always fixated.

BG: That's true.

CM: What Richard describes as the definition and you are taking as a description shows that Berne wasn't perfect and was sometimes not clear. To me it isn't clear when he is giving a definition, a description, or a metaphor. For instance, when he said Adult is like thinking: To me that's a metaphor for the functioning of the neopsyche.

RE: He actually said it is like a computer. I think in the fifties when he wrote that what people were most impressed with was how rapidly a computer could analyze a tremendous amount of data. I think included in that data are all emotions, sensations, body functions, and perceptions.

CM: That's the content. When we say the Adult is the computer of the ego we put the metaphor into function. And I think that's a great mistake.

PC: That's making a symbol into something concrete.

CM: Exactly. And in rereading Berne's writing it's sometimes painstaking because of this process. What's definition? What's description? What's a metaphor?

BG: Of course we also have the advantage of seventeen years. Eric has been dead seventeen years, and we've all gone a long way beyond where he was when he died, in all kinds of ways, including changing some of the original definitions.

RE: Bob, what do you think were the major changes in those seventeen years?

BG: I think one major change is that Eric truly thought — maybe felt too — that changes came about by confronting the Adult and using Adult functioning to solve problems. I haven't believed that for twenty years. I've always thought of the Adult as essential in the process, but unless you get the Child to see, think, feel, and behave differently than the Child saw, thought, felt, and behaved in the old process, in the stuck place, then you aren't going to move, because any time a person makes a decision to change from his Adult, he is not taking into account where the Child is, what the Child believes in, and what the Child's behavior is based on. The Child's behavior is based on the fact that he made a successful decision for himself at some point to solve problems in the here and now, with these people, at this time, by behaving, thinking, and feeling a certain way. You can do all you want with Adult decision making, but unless you bring that Child along, he ain't got a chance in hell of changing. He'll sabotage everything you say.

CM: I think Eric Berne did not intend confrontation to be the major intervention. In reading *Principles of Group Treatment* (1966), the key intervention for cure was interpretation. Confrontation was one way to get to interpretation. Also, I think that we can infer from your book and from Berne's that pathology results from a protocol that is embedded in the Child ego state. The way to get to the Child ego state is different, but that's methodology, not theory.

BG: I know, but I'm more interested in results than I am in theory.

CM: Yes, but I don't think there's a big change in theory. The focus of the theory is the same. The Child ego state is being thwarted in a protocol situation. The way you go to the Child ego state is different, but I don't think that that's a change in the methodology (which is the theory of the pragmatics), but a change of the epistemology of transactional analysis or of ego states.

BG: I'm not sure I understand what you just said.

PC: I have a way of responding to that which may connect. It's that I continue to be delighted by the concept and the reality of ego states, and I think that's what transactional analysis is about—the fact that we have these chunks of psychic time that constitute our ego states. And that these are retrievable, that they can be cathected in treatment, and that we can find your Child and work with that ego state that has endured and do something about it. At the same time, we are creating new ego states, because what is happening now becomes a Child ego state or a historical Child ego state from yesterday.

BG: Sure.

RE: That's what I wanted to talk to you about, Petrūska. I like your term "chunks of psychic time." But in your rechilding article, you talk about creating new Child ego states after you have described the Child ego state using Berne's original term, the archaeopsyche. How do you account for that use of the term and what seems to be a major theoretical shift, because if you put it back in Berne's original terms, you cannot re-archaic someone.

BG: I don't see any contradiction. We just said that we see the Child as "chunks of time." And the Child as "chunks of time," for me, is as of this moment. Anything that happened yesterday, in terms of the theoretical understanding of Child, is in the Child ego state.

RE: I don't agree with that, Bob. I think anything that happened in a previous developmental phase, ten years ago and fixated, would be Child, not something that happened yesterday.

BG: Then where are you going to put yesterday?

RE: In the Adult. It is what occurred yesterday. It is the function of this developmental stage in life, and I would consider that a memory of what occurred yesterday.

BG: Then where do you draw the line between Child and Adult. At what age? Nineteen and a half?

RE: No. If at sixty, you're still functioning like you did at forty and fixated there, I would say that the forty year old is equivalent to archaeopsychic functioning.

BG: Okay.

PC: Okay.

RE: I see that all the time near the museum in New York on a Sunday. There are several eighty-year-old women who dress up like it's the 1930s, at a time when they were probably most beautiful, and they're still putting on the same clothes, the same style of make-up, and they are—their Child ego state is—thirty five years old.

CM: I have a comment on where we put yesterday. I think it is very difficult to put together time extension and psychic functioning. I think some of yesterday went in the Parent, some in the Child, and some in the Adult. I say that to be consistent with one of the properties of ego states defined by Berne, biological fluidity. Each ego state grows with time.

RE: I hope your Parent is not growing, but is really shrinking. And I hope your Child is not growing, and that it's also shrinking to the point where it's integrated within the Adult.

BG: I don't understand that at all. What's wrong with my Parent changing? I do an awful lot of my nurturing from my Parent ego state. You may think it's Adult!

RE: I hope it's Adult!

BG: I experience it as Parent, and I change my nurturers in my head.

RE: Why would you nurture according to the way your mother and father did?

BG: I don't. I nurture the way my Parent does, which involves my Uncle Harry, too. (Laughter)

RE: But why would you nurture like Uncle Harry did instead of according to the situation that's required right now?

BG: Now you're talking about something different, about me being aware of the situation as it is right now. I'm calling on some part of me which I don't see as my Adult to do the nurturing process.

RE: There's the difference in terms. You don't see it as Adult. And I think what you're describing is a here-and-now Adult function based on what you have internalized over the years, perhaps with some influence from other people, but you've made it part of yourself. If you're nurturing from Parent, then you are out of contact either with yourself or who's there.

MG: This is by definition, Bob.

PC: Yes.

MG: An alternative definition to the one you're using. It's not discussable in that form. (Laughter)

CM: I think it would be clearer, maybe, if we called what Bob is talking about neopsychic functioning. In neopsychic functioning, we can exhibit the kind of parental behavior that Berne would have put into ethos. It's parental, in a way, but it's still a neopsychic function. If when Richard said, "I hope your Parent shrinks," he actually said, "I hope your old, archaic Parent shrinks in order to foster a new and well-functioning ethos"—I agree with that. I think if we said it's a neopsychic parental exhibit, we would pull together (maybe stretching it a bit) a theory, because the Adult is a manifestation of the neopsyche. And again, is that a definition or a description? Sounds like a description to me.

RE: I think if it's an introject, by the definition of introjection, then there is no real contact. I think what you are describing is a parental role.

BG: All right.

RE: Or a parental-type behavior. But from what I've watched on your tapes and known about you over the years, Bob, I think it comes from Adult, a neopsychic functioning.

CM: Okay.

BG: I won't quarrel with that.

RE: Because I think if it is your Parent, if you are functioning from the Parent ego state, then you cannot be in contact with people with whom you are working.

BG: Well, we see it defined differently again, because I see the Parent also like I see the Child, as always capable of change. Not the original introject, that's unchangeable, but that doesn't mean that the things we all do stay fixed in that area, because we keep learning, we keep experiencing new kinds of parenting.

MG: I want to ask a question in reference to what is being discussed. In one of the other terminologies that's available, there's a notion called "the body ego." In terms of psychic functioning, where would you place that?

RE: Are you referring to Paul Federn's use of the term "body ego"?

MG: Well, there have been a bunch of uses of it, and I left it carefully undefined. I was interested in how you would place it.

BG: Your reaction first, Petrūska.

PC: Well, I am very interested in this because both Weiss and Fairbairn, I think, get involved with the body ego, and they differentiate between the mental ego and the body ego. I am actually thinking why I reacted, because that may be part of what would theoretically help explain how you can get people to regress to previous age levels in a neurophysiological sense, because then you can be talking about regression to an earlier bodily ego, which is separate from the mental ego of that time, or at least distinguishable.

MG: In terms of the way you are using the term, the Adult, as neopsychic functioning, how would you place the body ego?

PC: I would say that would be when the mental ego and the bodily ego are correspondent and congruent with the person's chronological and developmental age.

RE: Let me respond to that. I get up in the morning and see that I'm getting a pot belly. I accept it, it's there, I feel it. I would say that's neopsychic function. If I look in the mirror and still see a skinny kid, even though I'm not, then that's an archaic body ego. My sense of "I," my identity is still wrapped up with being a skinny kid. Or if I somehow see the image that my father had of his body, being a short, little guy even though I'm not, that means that my body ego is wrapped up or connected with the introjected image that he had of himself.

MG: These answers haven't satisfied me, so I'll share the comment I made in Harry Corsover's delightful talk a couple of days ago. I was hearing this kind of definition of the Adult ego state or neopsychic functioning as being a transformer, identical in its important components to the notion the new psychoanalytic thinking uses when they refer to the "real self." I can't see any difference in that.

RE: I think there are some similarities.

MG: Well, I'd like to hear what the differences are, not just in choice of language and so on, but in terms of a theoretical, functioning concept. If the Adult ego state or neopsychic functioning is identical to the "real self," that I could accept. But if that is what is going on, it ought to be stated in some way, because then the introjected Parental contents and the fixated and other contents from previous times in the Child ego state become the equivalent of the false self in those terminologies. Now, to return to the question I was asking about the body ego, I was talking with a friend who was learning how to be a pilot toward the end of the fourth decade of her life. She's qualified to take the pilot's exam, but she has been refusing to and was still struggling with it. I said to her, out of some inner knowing that surprised me as much as it did her, "Your problem is that you're a dancer." She said, "What does that mean, Marty?" I replied, "You were a dancer as a kid, and until you can dance the airplane, you're not going to get your pilot's license. When you can feel the plane in your bones and dance the plane, then you will be ready to get your license." She looked at me with tremendous relief and said, "Now I know what to tell my male instructors when they bug me about being not courageous enough. I know what it is I'm looking for." Now how would you describe that in the terms you are using?

PC: I think you're asking her to cathect to certain earlier, neurophysiological sets that she can use. So it is archaic in terms of a relic, but I read Berne to say clearly that the Child ego state is not necessarily fixations. So that would be using a relic in the service of the here-and-now neopsychic functioning.

BG: And furthermore, probably, although we don't have the whole history, to replace another relic, which is why she got stuck flying the airplane.

MG: So this would relate to what you call rechilding.

PC: Yes, that's the kind of thing I was thinking of.

RE: I think what you both described is what I would call integrating it into the Adult. You've taken that experience and made it fully conscious for the person to make use of now.

BG: It's not either/or. It's both. Furthermore, it's all three. Because you get a Child corrective experience—this was clearly a Child corrective experience—and you put that into Child operation. She gets a great anchor for it with the dancing. Her Adult is perceptive about what's going on and understands the process, while her Child is having a reflective experience, and I'm sure her parents would say, "Nice going, gal. Keep on up there flying."

PC: Berne and many other ego psychologists say we can have two ego states present at the same time, but one will be an executive, and I think Berne spent some time with that. I don't think that's integrated into the Adult because she's reliving an earlier stage, an earlier age of her life. It would be integrated into her Adult when she is no longer reliving that early, physiological-level experience.

MG: So, let me see if I'm hearing correctly. At the time that she can dance the airplane, to use my metaphor, then flying for her is part of her Adult ego state.

PC: Yes.

CM: I think of it another way. What you are addressing is the way her archaeopsyche functions in order to control the movement. Dancing and airplanes involve moving objects. So you've found a way to connect with the archaeopsychic neurological real functioning. It's embedded in her, through the archaeopsyche. You had her Adult look at the archaeopsychic function, but at the same time you hit the archaeopsyche. So, this archaeopsychic material is now available for neopsychic use. So you have two different things. What you hit and what you got. What you hit was archaeopsyche, and this archaeopsychic material will be transformed in neopsychic functioning.

BG: In Child corrective experiences people change their very guts in response to the same set of stressors. They don't respond to the stress in the bent coin, to think about Eric's pile of coins, but in a new, bright, shiny coin which is still often part of the Child experience, but transferred to another kind of stress.

PC: Sure. So I think in some ways, Child ego state is a misnomer. I would have been happier with historical or historical ego states, because that can imply that it has more to do with history, and it doesn't stop at some arbitrary point between childhood and adolescence.

RE: Carlo, when I asked each person what question they would like to be asked, we got off in this direction in response to Marty's question on reality. Do you want to come back to your question?

CM: Well, I want to comment on another problem. I think we are putting together two concepts that, for Berne, were different—psychic organ and ego states. Ego states are the phenomenological manifestation. And my question was, "Is methodology congruent with theory?"

RE: I want to respond to that, because I think one thing transactional analysis has that no other approach to psychotherapy has is the treatment of the Parent ego state. Bob, you commented before that you didn't think it was treatable. Am I quoting you right?

BG: I don't know, go ahead with the rest of the quote.

RE: Certainly Berne didn't think you could change the Parent ego state.

BG: The original introject.

RE: That's right. Stemming from articles by McNeel (1976), Dashiell (1978), and Mellor and Andrewartha (1980) on psychotherapy of the Parent ego state, I got stimulated and have done a lot of work in that area. I have watched people's personalities go through dramatic changes by treating the Parent ego state, particularly if I can take the Parent ego states into regression and do a redecision in the Parent ego states.

BG: I don't argue with that at all. I do a lot of stuff to change the Parent ego state. What I was saying was you can't change the original introject. That's there. But you can certainly add a hell of a lot more introjects to that.

RE: I think we should not be reintrojecting. If we are reintrojecting, we are doing the same damage. I think what we are doing in effective psychotherapy is bringing them face-to-face with the original introject. With the treatment of the Parent ego state, I explain, "That's Dad's feelings or that's Mom's reaction, and it doesn't have to be yours anymore." Or, "That was Dad's way of doing it, and it's a beneficial way, and now do you consciously want to make it your own?"

BG: Okay.

RE: That's the integration from Parent to Adult ego state.

BG: I hear what you're saying. Again, I don't think it's either/or. I think both are true, that we make lots of Adult decisions to not behave in old ways that we used to behave in because it was automatic. I think also over periods of time and constant reuse of the new introject, we begin to automatically do it, to parent in a new way. Not through thinking a process up, but by automatically responding.

CM: As I was saying yesterday, we don't need to eradicate the Parent, we need to decommission it. In order to decommission the Parent, which is the process which leads us to build new Parent, as Bob was saying, we need to go through the Child also, because it is dynamic. We cannot avoid working with the Child ego state, be it Gestalt-wise or in the relationship with the analyst. That's the only way to go to a new Parent, which is possible via the Child, because the whole introject is decommissioned but not annihilated.

RE: I think where we got off on this, Carlo, is your question about what is the transactional analysis methodology? I think what's evolved in the last decade is a methodology for cure of the Parent ego state, which Berne did not believe was possible.

MG: If you think of the Parental introject as being a thing, rather than a process which has various complicated loops to it, then it becomes possible to think about taking it out, putting it somewhere else, or putting something in its place, and then it becomes nonsense. What Richard said [is that it is possible to resolve the conflicts that originated in the parents and that were introjected by the child]. I have had the experience, both personally and professionally with patients, of seeing and experiencing Parent conflicts resolved in a later generation, inside that person's brain. And that's different than substituting some other introject. That really is a process of dynamic change in the original conflicted introject.

RE: And that's what I try to do in that Parent ego state therapy, make that a process change within the person. Let me respond to Carlo a bit about how I understand introjection. It is a defense mechanism. Introjection occurs when there is not full contact, so that to avoid the conflict that occurs because of a lack of contact, the Child takes the other person inside, where the conflict is seemingly more easy to manage. And so that introjection, by definition, is a defense against the lack of contact. Therefore, in psychotherapy I would not support a new introjection, but what I would focus on is the *quality of contact between us in the relationship so the person can find a sense of self* and not take me as a substitute self.

CM: That's your thinking.

PC: Introjection can also be a useful function. It is particularly useful for the child, so as the infant develops there is a lot of introjection that is not necessarily pathologically focused, but is a very useful way of learning.

RE: Sure. To memorize something is an introjection.

PC: No. To introject how someone feels, acts, and behaves in this particular situation. That kind of introjection.

MG: I think you are not differentiating between role modeling and introjection, and that's another area. I don't want to get off on that, because I want to come back to what Richard was saying. We can go then, perhaps, to the learning function of introjection as opposed to role modeling, which I see as a different . . .

RE: And identification.

MG: . . . and identification, which are different. In addition to the fearful defense that's involved in introjection, there is also a hopeful defense.

RE: Oh, yes.

MG: And one of the functions for the child of introjecting an unsolvable conflict in the Parent is the desire or hope that the conflict can be resolved at a later time.

RE: In the hopeful words of my clients, "If I take on and be Dad, then I will have all of his attributes at my disposal, including his power, language, and ability to get around in the world."

BG: I'm thinking of a patient who was very depressed, very suicidal, who when she was depressed and suicidal used all the rage of her original parent on herself, on her own Child. Her original parent was a very enraged person, well maybe persons, but I know one person. So what she suffered was that constant struggle with the original Parent. And in the process of the psychotherapy, we couldn't get her to make a redecision from her Child to survive, to live.

RE: Because of the Parent ego state influence being too strong?

BG: That's right. Well, I guess so. What we finally got her to do—and this goes along with what you said a little earlier—was to pretend that she was picking herself up off the nursery floor as the mother that she was to her own real children. Now she had children that she was very lovely with, while at the same time being harsh on herself. She began to nurture herself in the room, as her baby and as her own nurturing mother to her own children, in the same way that she nurtured her own children. Then she was able to say from this other Nurturing Parent of hers, I love you, I will not hurt you, I will never hurt you, I will never kill you.

RE: Other Nurturing Parent? Where would you put that structurally?

BG: Her own Nurturing Parent that she used to nurture her own children. Where she got that from, I don't know.

CM: Uncle Harry.

BG: Uncle Harry, yeah.

MG: Yes. (Laughter) Uncle Harry. I want to be an Uncle Harry.

CM: It wasn't a joke. I think she was suicidal and depressive because of the P_1 introject, and she was active because of "an Uncle Harry," which came much later.

RE: I want to draw this to a close at this point, and to invite the audience, which has been eavesdropping, to participate in our discussion with us.

HC: I'm Harry Corsover. I think this stuff about "What's the definition?" that may sometimes seem like nitpicking, gets to be really useful. We benefit from understanding: Is this an introject, is this in Parent ego state, is this in Child ego state, is this mom's little Kid, is it my little Kid—that differentiation really helps us get to what is going to help this person resolve this problem and get on with his or her life. When we have a theoretical structure that is not internally consistent, it becomes increasingly difficult to communicate effectively. And especially difficult to communicate to someone else our understanding of what happened.

PC: I want to respond. I value, applaud, and hope that I strive for consistency in theory. And at the same time I think it can become a prison for us. Most importantly, or equally important, we must remember that theory is not real and that we need to play with it. I think if we seek consistency, and we want to make it into concrete truths, that we lose the playful attitude. There is no psychological theory that is totally consistent, otherwise I'd be doing it. (Laughter)

BG: They are all belief systems.

HC: I think our task is twofold. I agree with you about the potential for it becoming a prison. Our task is to strive for greater consistency, without precluding new angles, new viewpoints. Perhaps in the meantime, until we reach such a utopia where we're all using all the words the same way, I think what we need to do is recognize that when somebody's saying Parent, Child, whatever, that it pays to take a few more seconds and find out what they mean by that, without assuming we know.

PC: I agree.

HC: Because we may all be transactional analysts, and we may all be using the three familiar words, but we should not assume that we're meaning the same thing until we've taken a little time to check out the other person's frame of reference.

PC: That's asking us to be clear about the terms we use, and I think that is extremely important. And the models we're using and the theoreticians we're using.

RE: I want to stop here. I think this has been a wonderful discussion to have on the twenty-fifth anniversary of ITAA's Summer Conference. Thank you, Carlo, Petrūska, Bob, and Marty.

CM: Thank you, Richard.

RE: Thanks to all of you for your participation.

BG: Thanks, Eric.

REFERENCES

Berne, E. (1961). *Transactional analysis in psychotherapy: A systematic individual and social psychiatry.* New York: Grove Press.
Berne, E. (1966). *Principles of group treatment.* New York: Grove Press.
Dashiell, S. (1978). The parent resolution process. *Transactional Analysis Journal, 8,* 289-295.
McNeel, J. (1976). The parent interview. *Transactional Analysis Journal, 6,* 61-68.
Mellor, K., & Andrewartha, G. (1980). Reparenting the parent in support of redecisions. *Transactional Analysis Journal, 10,* 197-203.

———————

This article was originally published in the Transactional Analysis Journal, *Volume 18, Number 1, January 1988, pp. 6-14.*

Transference and Transactions: Critique from an Intrapsychic and Integrative Perspective

Richard G. Erskine

In Eric Berne's writings there are two different explanations of psychological functioning: the ego, composed of separate states, with intrapsychic dynamics among the states; and ego state terminology applied to descriptive behavioral roles. Subsequently, throughout the transactional analysis literature, two views of transference and transactions exist that, when applied clinically, are at variance with each other.

One purpose of this article is to draw a distinction between Berne's two theories of ego states and to describe how each theoretical perspective creates a significantly different concept of transactions and transference. The practice of transactional analysis in psychotherapy is markedly different with each of these two theories.

A second purpose is to demonstrate that consistent use of Berne's developmental, relational, and intrapsychic theory of ego states in understanding the internal dynamics of transactions can lead to a sensitive and effective response to transactions and transference and to a comprehensive and integrative psychotherapy.

Transference within Psychoanalysis

Freud's (1905/1955) identification and specification of the transference dimension of the psychotherapeutic relationship is his most fundamental discovery (Langs, 1981). For the past 90 years psychotherapists have struggled with the problem of understanding patients' communications and clarifying the difference between transactions that are solely in response to the current situation and those that are an expression of archaic relationship conflicts.

In the case of Anna O., Breuer and Freud (1895/1955) discovered the phenomenon of transference when they tried to uncover childhood traumas that were the roots of hysterical symptoms. They first considered transference as resistance to the uncovering of repressed childhood traumas. However, by 1905 Freud described the importance of working with the transference and considered transference and resistance (defenses) as the two main elements of psychoanalysis.

Freud (1905/1955) described transference using the metaphor of new editions or facsimiles of old emotional experiences. In transference patients replace the emotional experience with an earlier person with a similar experience with the psychotherapist. Within psychoanalysis this description of transference remains the basis for treatment. It was echoed by Greenson (1967), who described transference as the emotional experience of a person that does not befit that person and which actually applies to another. A person in the present is inappropriately reacted to as though he or she were a person in the past.

Freud's hypothesis about the origin of transference was based on the assumption that each individual, through the combined operation of innate disposition and influences brought to bear during early years, acquired a somewhat fixed method or set of methods of living which were evident in all relationships. The patient in analytic treatment was seen as repeating these attitudes and reactions. Freud understood transference as the displacement of behavior and feelings onto the therapist, feelings that were originally experienced and directed toward significant figures from childhood (Freud, 1912/1958, 1915/1958). This early psychoanalytic concept of transference is the one most compatible with Berne's (1961) original writings on ego states and their application to a theory of transactions and transference.

In the 1910s and 1920s Freud shifted his focus away from a theory of relationship conflicts of early childhood, as represented in his original ideas (1905/1955), to a theory that emphasized innate biological drives. Anna Freud (1965), working within this drive theory model of psychoanalysis, described the defensive, projective aspects of transference as the externalization of instinctual drives. She wrote that many of the transference situations encountered in her work were because the person of the analyst is used to represent one or another aspect of the patient's personality. In this view, transference and projection are drive theory concepts that describe the defense against awareness of a specific biological drive.

For example, a patient may project a drive of aggression onto the therapist, thus subjectively attributing it to the therapist while experiencing the self as the object of aggression from the therapist. The patient then experiences the disowned and split off drives as being in the other person (Berg, 1977; Novik & Kelly, 1970). This drive theory concept of transference is not compatible with either Berne's (1961) intrapsychic or descriptive theories of transactional analysis.

Berne's (1961) descriptions of transference phenomena are more closely linked to those of psychoanalytic object relations theorists such as Bollas (1979), Fairbairn (1952), Guntrip (1971), Khan (1974), and Winnicott (1965). Spotnitz (1969) described the object relations theorists' view of transference as "the patient's attempt to reveal the basic maturational needs for objects that were not met in the course of his development" (p. 139).

Greenberg and Mitchell (1983) described in detail the bifurcation of current psychoanalytic theory between a relationship perspective and an instinctual drive perspective and the correspondingly differing views of transference. Anna Ornstein (1989) described transference as "current" resistance: "Transferences contain many elements of the past, but they are not only made of archaic reactions, they also contain a current reaction" to the therapist. When the transference is used to investigate the intersubjective field between patient and therapist, the behavior and unconscious intrapsychic processes of the therapist become an important source of information for use in understanding the patient. From this perspective, what looks like transference is at times a current reaction to the behavior and affect of the therapist (Stolorow, Brandchaft, & Atwood, 1987). Such insight into the meaning of the transference requires an empathic acceptance by therapists of their own childhood experiences and emotions (Brandchaft, 1989).

Kohut (1971) distinguished two types of transference: those based on instinctual drives and those representing early developmental needs such as approval, mirroring, and echoing. Kohut called the transactions that expressed fixated developmental needs "selfobject transferences" (p. 23) and ascribed to them a necessary reparation function within the therapeutic process. In Kohut's (1977) self psychology the therapeutic goal of working within the transference is the completion of interrupted developmental processes. This is a very different goal than the classical psychoanalytic interpretation of transference as an expression of instinctual drives.

Other psychoanalytic writers have explored the therapeutic relationship, questioning what distinguishes transference from nontransference. Some argue that transference pervades the therapeutic relationship (Brenner, 1979; Friedman, 1969; Langs, 1976), while others argue that there are neutral or rational relationships in therapy (Greenson, 1967; Lipton, 1977).

Baker (1982) described the crucial variable in psychotherapy as "the transference, which involves components of both the real relationship between patient and therapist and the more irrational components displaced, projected and externalized from the patient's history" (p. 196) of relationships with significant people and their internalized representations.

Greenson (1967) described two types of relationships in therapy that should not be equated with transference. Both the "working alliance" (p. 191) and the "real relationship" (p. 217) are nonarchaic and involve the patient's reasonable ego. The working alliance is the patient's cooperation in the therapeutic tasks and may be tinged with elements of archaic motivation (transference). There is, however, an observing ego that can stand back from the experience temporarily and reflect on it. The "real relationship is genuine and reality oriented or undistorted as contrasted to the term 'transference' which connotes unrealistic, distorted, and inappropriate" (p. 217). An example of the realistic relationship may be a patient's concern for or criticism of the therapist. Lipton (1977) used the term "cordial relationship" (p. 255) to describe the nontransference transactions between patient and therapist. In his 1961 theory of transactions Berne implied the ideas of both a transference and nontransference relationship between therapist and patient.

For the past two decades psychoanalysis has been undergoing a major reevaluation regarding practice and theory. Berne (1961) predated much of the current theoretical reframing of psychoanalysis when he dispensed with a theory based primarily on innate biological drives and instead viewed human functioning as based on relationships. Berne (1961, 1966) continued to acknowledge primary innate human motivations such as stimulus hunger—with its sublimation into recognition hunger, and later structure hunger—but each of these were manifestations of the need for human relationship. Berne's primary contribution to advancing knowledge of psychotherapy theory was his description of states of the ego and the use of these concepts to identify which transactions were transference and which were nontransference.

As reflected in *Transactional Analysis in Psychotherapy* (Berne, 1961), transactional analysis began as a reaction to and an advancement of psychoanalytic theory. Today there is much that transactional analysts can gain in theoretical perspective and clinical application by reexamining from an intrapsychic and integrative perspective both Berne's original theoretical conceptualizations and the current theoretical and methodological debate within psychoanalysis.

Berne's Original Concept of Ego

Berne's (1961) original conceptualization of ego states appears to this writer to be a logical and creative extension of psychoanalytic structural theory. He expanded on Federn's (1953/1977) concept of ego and elaborated the concept of the archaeopsychic and exteropsychic states of the ego. In so doing Berne paved the way for an explanation of *intrapsychic conflict that is relational and developmental* rather than relying on Freud's drive model of *intrapsychic instinctual-societal conflicts.* Berne (1961) eliminated the theoretical concepts of id (pp. 61, 194, 198) and superego (p. 32) by postulating that these psychological dynamics are functions of an ego composed of three states of psychic organization: fixations from childhood, introjections of elements of the personality of others, and an integrating state in full contact with what is currently occurring internally and externally. He hypothesized that "an ego state is the phenomenological and behavioral manifestation of the activity of a certain psychic organ, or organizer" (p. 24).

Based on the references and footnotes found in *Transactional Analysis in Psychotherapy* (Berne, 1961), one would deduce that Berne was building theoretically on the writings of psychoanalytic authors Breuer and Freud (1895/1955), Fairbairn (1952), Federn (1953/1977), Freud (1949), Klein (1949), and Weiss (1950) and the child developmentalists Piaget (1932, 1951, 1954) and Erikson (1950). Berne (1961) thought of ego function as, in part, composed of archaeopsychic states: "the ego state of the actual child" which "has organization, unified will, logic and, certainly, negation" (p. 198). These archaic ego states consist of fixations of earlier developmental stages. They are the entire personality of a person as he or she was in a previous developmental period of time (pp. 54-55, 192, 1964, p. 23). The archaic ego fixations occurred when critical childhood needs for contact were not met, and the child's use of defenses against the discomfort of the unmet needs became habitual (Erskine, 1980). These fixations became egotized or, in other words, formed separate ego units or states. The archaic or Child ego states (Berne, 1964, p. 23) are maintained in later life through the current use of defense mechanisms (Erskine & Moursund, 1988).

In Berne's (1961) words, "The Child ego state is a set of feelings, attitudes, and behavior patterns which are relics of the individual's own childhood" (p. 77). When functioning in the Child or archaic ego states the person perceives the internal needs and sensations and the external world as he did in a previous developmental age. Although the person may appear to be relating to current reality, he may actually be experiencing what is happening with the perceptual, emotional, intellectual, and social capacities of the child at the time of repression and fixation. It is this theoretical notion of the continuing fixation of Child ego states and the manifestation of a fixated Child ego that serves as one of the cornerstones for a transactional investigation of transferences.

Building on his own clinical observations, Berne extended Federn's (1953/1977) and Weiss's (1950) concept of the "psychic presence" (Berne, 1961, p. 19) of parental figures that influence an individual's current behavior. He postulated the existence of exteropsychic ego states. The exteropsyche or Parent ego states are the manifestations of introjections of the personality of actual people as perceived by the child at the time of introjection (Loria, 1988).

> Since the child's perceptions of the caretaker's reactions, emotions, and thought processes will differ at various stages of development, so also will the actual content and intrapsychic function of the Parent ego state vary in relation to the developmental age when the introjection occurred. (Erskine, 1988, p. 17)

Introjection is a defense mechanism (involving disavowal, denial, and repression) frequently used when there is a lack of full psychological contact between a child and the adults responsible for his or her psychological needs. The significant other is made part of the self (ego), and the conflict resulting from the lack of need fulfillment is internalized so the conflict can seemingly be managed more easily (Perls, 1978).

Introjected elements of another's personality may become egotized and theoretically form an exteropsychic ego state. Berne's theoretical premise of the existence of exteropsychic ego states is a second cornerstone in an intrapsychic and integrative understanding of transactions and transference.

Berne (1961) contrasted the exteropsychic and archaeopsychic ego states with a neopsychic ego state (Adult) that accounts for and integrates: (1) what is occurring moment-by-moment internally and externally, (2) past experiences and their resulting effects, and (3) the psychological influences and identifications with significant people in one's life. This Adult ego state consists of current, age-related motor behavior; emotional, cognitive, and moral development; the ability to be creative; and the capacity for full contactful engagement in meaningful relationships. This neopsychic state of the ego functions without intrapsychic control by an introjected or archaic ego.

Berne's original definitions of ego states provide the conceptual basis for an integrating psychotherapy (Clarkson & Gilbert, 1988; Erskine, 1977/1979, 1987, 1988; Erskine & Moursund, 1988; Loria, 1988; Massey, 1989; Moiso, 1985, 1988; Novellino, 1985; Trautmann & Erskine, 1981) that distinguishes nontransference transactions (neopsychic ego in origin) from possible transferential transactions. It is my understanding that *transferential transactions are externalized expressions of internal ego conflicts between exteropsychic and archaeopsychic ego states.*

Berne's Illustrations and Descriptions

In each of his writings Berne (1961, 1964, 1966, 1972) augmented his precise theoretical definitions of ego states and intrapsychic function with illustrations and behavioral examples. Evolving from these explanations was a distinctly different theory of ego states which he called "descriptive" (Berne, 1972, p. 13). Although his original definitions of ego states emerged from both clinical experience and an extrapolation of the ideas of psychoanalytic authors, his *descriptions* of ego states relied not on his theory of "states of mind," but on metaphors that tended to emphasize "their related patterns of behavior" (Berne, 1961, p. 30).

In providing illustrations of ego state theory in clinical practice, Berne shifted from a relational and developmental theory to a descriptive and behavioral understanding of ego states. He equated ego states with *roles* or specific behavior typical of those roles. For example, Berne (1961) used the phrasing "a Parental response" (p. 44) and "the parental role of comforting" (p. 95) to imply that the person was transacting from his or her Parent (exteropsychic) ego state. Another time the behavior "rational" (p. 132) was equated with the Adult ego state (p. 132). There are many other examples of ego states descriptively identified (pp. 128-135, 1964, p. 30, 1972, p. 14).

By shifting to a more descriptive and behavioral orientation, it seems that Berne greatly diminished his own creative extension of psychoanalytic theory. He lessened the impact of what his relational understanding of intrapsychic conflicts—as they are manifested in transferential transactions—had to offer. Berne (1972) changed perspectives and created an alternative set of theoretical analogies of ego states as roles and transactions as numerical probabilities of the roles (p. 19).

In articulating his theory Berne (1961) specified: "Ego states must be differentiated from 'roles' " (p. 233); and "Ego states are not roles but phenomena. Therefore ego states and roles have to be distinguished in a formal description" (Berne, 1964, pp. 53-54). Yet throughout his writings he both defined the theory of ego states from a developmental, intrapsychic perspective and also provided illustrations and descriptions of behavioral roles. At one point he acknowledged this theoretical inconsistency: "For the most part, the examples given have concerned the behavioral and social aspects of the Child" (Berne, 1961, p. 235).

Berne's writings contain several such theoretical inconsistencies as a result of his use of illustrative descriptions as definitions. Moiso (Erskine, Clarkson, Goulding, Groder, & Moiso, 1988) emphasized that Berne was not theoretically consistent: "It isn't clear when he is giving a definition, a description, or a metaphor" (p. 7). In referring to Berne's likening the Adult to a computer, Moiso added, "That's a metaphor for the functioning of the neopsyche" (p. 7).

Three examples of the use of metaphors as definitions follow:
   1. Berne (1961) described the Adult as working "deliberately and consciously" (p. 69) as if these two attributes were not possible in a Parent or Child ego state.
   2. "The Parent has two main functions. First, it enables the individual to act effectively as the parent of actual children" (Berne, 1964, p. 27). With this description of the function of Parent ego state Berne disregarded that it is the Adult ego state that is in contact now with those in the environment. "Automatic" parenting (Berne, 1961, p. 76), although conserving much time and energy, is not in contact with the child. Instead, it may often be an activation of an introjection related to some other person in another time and place. Effective parenting requires full contact in the present between parent and child.

3. "In the Child reside intuition, creativity and spontaneous drive and enjoyment" (Berne, 1964, p. 27). While this is true of many children, it is not a definition of the Child ego state. Two pages earlier Berne defined Child as "an archaic ego state" (p. 25), and elsewhere he said it was "a warped ego state which has become fixated" (Berne, 1961, p. 54). In cases where the child has been neglected and/or traumatized, the Child ego state of the adult may not be spontaneous or intuitive or joyous. The fixation of the archaic child may be depressed, inhibited, or defended. These symptoms are likely to emerge later in life in transactions with others and in the course of psychotherapy.

Many of Berne's descriptions sound as if he were reifying his theoretical ideas. His analogies have become specific entities. In his original developmental theory Berne (1961) used "*adapted* Child" and "*natural* Child" (p. 77) as adjectives to describe (1) the function of an archaeopsychic ego state under the oppressive internal influence of a Parent ego state and (2) the natural responsiveness of a child in the absence of such critical or controlling parenting. Berne's descriptive wanderings from his original theoretical definitions (1961) take their final form in his last writings. The adjectives used previously to describe intrapsychic functioning became the nouns, "Adapted Child" and "Natural Child" (Berne, 1972, p. 104).

A review of the *Transactional Analysis Journal* reveals that most authors have described ego states in behavioral or descriptive terms (Nurturing Parent, Critical Parent, Adapted Child, Natural Child, and Rebellious Child) or as a categorization of psychological processes (equating Parent ego state with values, Adult ego state with thinking, and Child ego state with feelings), or as a mix of these concepts.

When Berne shifted his illustrations of ego states to the descriptive, he ignored his own original definitions and the necessary four-part diagnosis (behavioral, social, historical, and phenomenological) that is required for complete identification of the state cathected (Berne, 1961, pp. 75-76, 225).

When psychotherapists and authors of articles about psychotherapy do not take into account the specific validating procedures that Berne (1961) outlined in his chapter on diagnosis (pp. 68-80), then the validity of Berne's original definitions and theory is not maintained. Transactional analysis theory loses both its internal and external consistency. Without such a four-part correlation and a consistent use of Berne's original developmental and relationship-based theoretical definition, ego state theory becomes merely a taxonomy of behaviors. A descriptive taxonomy of behaviors is very useful in a social control or behavioral therapy, but the elegance of Berne's logical and creative extension of psychoanalytic theory is lost. Transactional analysis becomes less a developmental, phenomenological, intrapsychic psychotherapy and more a therapy of behavioral adjustment. As a result, the meaning and purpose of analyzing transactions and the resolving of transference is uniquely different from the point of view of each of Berne's two theories of human functioning. Each theory and practical approach has a valid place in psychotherapy. And Berne's role/communication theory has application in nonpsychotherapy fields. An understanding and appreciation of Berne's early developmental and intrapsychic theory, however, allows for greater theoretical consistency and a more in-depth psychotherapy.

Loria (1988) highlighted these theoretical contradictions and the difficulties inherent in mixing concepts and in deviating from stated theoretical definitions without a supporting explanation of the new theoretical definitions. At the end of his writings Berne predicted the theoretical and methodological confusion inherent in mixing concepts. He recommended the use of "the Conceptual Grid" (Berne, 1972, pp. 409-413) so that theoretical discussions and treatment planning could remain within a given set of concepts and definitions. Berne concluded:

> If one takes a structural or biological approach to the Child ego state and another takes a functional and descriptive approach, it is impossible to reconcile the two. . . . One uses structural nouns, the other uses functional adjectives as modifiers, and the nouns and adjectives do not belong to the same framework or come from the same viewpoint. (pp. 411-412)

Ego State Determinants

In 1964 Berne stated that "transactional analysis is concerned with diagnosing which ego state implemented the transactional stimulus, and which executed the transactional response" (p. 29). In order to determine if a particular transaction is transferential or nontransferential, it is necessary to conduct a "careful and systematic analysis of the psychodynamics of . . . transactional stimuli and responses" (Berne, 1966, p. 154), of ego state cathexis and possible intrapsychic conflicts. Verification of which ego state is cathected is only possible with a four-part correlation of the behavioral, social, historical, and phenomenological determinants of ego states. "The complete diagnosis of an ego state requires that all four of these aspects be available for consideration, and *the final validity of such a diagnosis is not established until all four have been correlated"* [italics added] (Berne, 1961, p. 75).

Berne (1961, pp. 74-76) described the four diagnostic determinants of ego states in the order he saw them in psychotherapy: behavioral, social, historical, and phenomenological. From a perspective of facilitating an integration of the fragmentation of the ego, I have supplementally defined the identifying criteria and listed them in the following order of significance (Erskine & Moursund, 1988):

1. The identifying criterion of the phenomenological determinant is the subjective experience of the person. It includes the sensations, desires and needs, feelings, and beliefs that shape the person's perspective—the *how* and *what* it is like to live in his or her experience. Included in the phenomenological criteria are the physiological, emotional, and cognitive associations of significant life events and the times when elements of the personality of another were introjected. Also included is the subjective experience of the internal defense mechanisms fixated at times of neglect, traumatic experience, or cumulative devaluation.

2. The historical determinant is gleaned primarily from memories of the dynamic events between oneself and others, or the relationship between mother and father or other important family members. These can provide essential information regarding early conflicts. The *who* and *when* of early life may reveal memories of similar feelings and behavior in childhood or memories of the parental person who offered the prototype behavior. Included is an

inquiry into the distinction between the person's own fixated childhood defenses and the defense mechanisms possibly introjected from significant others.

3. The behavioral determinant involves a *developmental* focus (Berne, 1961, p. 154) on gestures, posture, vocabulary, tone of voice, or other mannerisms, and the content of what is communicated. The assessment of the person's current observable behavior is compared with information about human development regarding early mother-child interaction; motor and language development; emotional, cognitive, and social development; defense mechanisms; moral development; and adult life transitions. All of this comparative information provides a background of data to assist in determining the stage of development at which emotions, behaviors, or interactions have become fixated. Behavior that is not congruent with the current context may have been normal and appropriate for a child at a specific developmental age or may be an indication of how the patient defended himself or herself in a traumatic situation.

Childlike behavior may be an indication of the person's own active Child ego state, or just as likely, an indication of the Child ego state of an introjected parent. Interweaving the developmental assessment with the historical or phenomenological may be necessary to determine if a specific defensive reaction, behavioral pattern, or emotion is the manifestation of an exteropsychic ego state or of an archaeopsychic fixation.

4. The fourth determinant in verifying ego state cathexis is the social or *transactional*. The analysis of transactions provides data to indicate which ego state is active, the nature of the intrapsychic dynamics, and what stimulus from the psychotherapist served to trigger the cathexis. The intrapsychic dynamics include the influence of the introjected Parent ego state and the Child's need for a contactful relationship. Transactions between the person and psychotherapist, or, in group or family psychotherapy, between any two people, may reflect a transference either from an exteropsychic or archaeopsychic ego state. These transferences may take the form of "roles" such as childlike "compliance," "impertinence," or "rebelliousness"; adult-like roles of "problem solver" or information exchange; or parental roles of "comforting" or "controlling" (Berne, 1961, pp. 93-96). *It is essential in diagnosing ego state cathexis and intrapsychic conflict to evaluate these transactional roles or social entities within the context of a correlated phenomenological, historical, and developmental (behavioral) assessment.*

Transference transactions are an expression of the intrapsychic processes and ego state cathexis. To determine which transactions are nontransference and which are transference, it is necessary to validate which ego states are intrapsychically influential and which are active. "Transactional analysis consists of determining which ego state is active at a given moment in the exhibition of a transactional stimulus by the agent, and which ego state is active in the response given by the respondent" (Berne, 1966, p. 223). It is through the careful and systematic use of the four-part correlated diagnosis that it is possible to understand transference transactions and proceed with psychotherapeutic interventions.

An Intrapsychic and Integrative Perspective

An integrative intrapsychic approach to transactional analysis psychotherapy consists of deconfusing the archaeopsychic ego states and relaxing fixated archaic defenses, emending and/or decommissioning the exteropsychic ego states to resolve internal conflicts between archaeopsychic ego states and exteropsychic ego states, and facilitating the integration of one's life experiences into a neopsychic ego. "It is the process of making whole: taking disowned, unaware, unresolved aspects of the ego and making them part of a cohesive self" (Erskine & Moursund, 1988, p. 40).

This integrative perspective on psychotherapy is an extension and further refinement of Berne's (1961) original theoretical concepts of ego states, intrapsychic conflicts, and ensuing transferences. These concepts are augmented by the theoretical premise that *it is because of the continued fixation of defense mechanisms that the archaic or exteropsychic ego states remain separate states and do not become integrated into neopsychic awareness*. Neopsychic ego state awareness of needs, desires, memories, and external influences remains blocked through the fixation of childhood defenses.

Fixation refers to a relatively enduring *pattern of organization* of affect, behavior, or cognition from an earlier stage of development which persists into and may dominate later life. Defensive patterns of organization are often formed during an interpersonal conflict in which some psychological gain is achieved at the cost of the loss of others. The persistence of these childhood patterns of organization in later stages of development results in an inability to be spontaneous and flexible in problem solving and in relating to people (Erskine, 1980).

Intrapsychic conflict is the result of the cathexis of an influencing Parent ego state and an internal reaction by a Child ego state (Berne, 1961, pp. 32, 42, 75-78, 241, 1964, p. 26, 1966, pp. 222-223). For example, the *influencing* Parent ego state is sometimes phenomenologically experienced as a hallucinated voice, a compulsion, and/or an inhibition. It may be observable as a childlike adaptation, withdrawal, or dependency. In other situations the fixated Child ego state is defending against the intrapsychic influence of a Parent ego state. It may be phenomenologically experienced either as an overwhelming sense of need or as a lack of sensation and desires, an incapacity to think, or rage. It may also be observable as resistance, defiance, age regression, needy dependence, or a lack of full contact internally and externally. The observable behaviors may provide data for a partial hypothesis of an *adapted* Child ego state under the intrapsychic *influence* of a Parent ego state or states. The subjective or phenomenological experiences reported by the person may provide additional supporting data or lead to an alternate hypothesis.

The intrapsychic conflict is in part maintained by the child's needs for relationship (Fairbairn, 1952), attachment (Bowlby, 1969), or contact (Erskine, 1989) and the fixated archaeopsychic ego state's defense against full awareness of contact, attachment, and relationship needs. These needs may be manifested as psychological loyalty to the intrapsychically influencing Parent ego state.

Berne (1961) described the intrapsychic dynamics of ego states as representing "the relics of the infant who actually existed, in a struggle with the relics of the parents who once actually existed" for it "reduplicates the actual childhood fights for survival between real people, or at least that is the way the patient experiences it" (p. 66).

When the archaeopsychic ego state is active (either subjectively reportable or behaviorally observable), by theoretical inference the exteropsychic ego state is cathected and intrapsychically influencing (Berne, 1961, p. 42). I am suggesting that all transactions from an active *adapted* Child ego state—whether described as resistant, rebellious, compliant, or dependent—are aspects of transference. Transference transactions from a Child ego state are one way of obtaining relief from the intrapsychic conflict. Such transferences are theoretically assumed to be accompanied by a projection of elements of either an exteropsychic ego state or of a fantasy of a self-created parental figure (Erskine, 1988; Moiso, 1985). With projection, the intrapsychic conflict is once again externalized and then reacted to as though the stimulus were coming from outside the person. This provides some momentary relief of the intrapsychic conflict. With transference the intrapsychic conflict may once again be as it was in childhood, transactional between at least two people, with the hope of finally mastering the old interpersonal conflict. Projection also serves as a defense against awareness of the intrapsychic conflict and/or the actual historical conflict and the resulting effect on the child.

The active expression of a Parent ego state can also lead to relief from the intrapsychic conflict. *The active Parent ego state is a reaction to and expression of an intrapsychic representation of an internally contained historical transaction.* This is observable when the person manifests the thoughts, feelings, and behaviors of the introjected person and directs them toward another person. These *active* Parent ego state transactions are also defined as an aspect of transference.

An essential procedure in an integrative approach is the analysis of transactions to determine which are transferential and which are nontransferential. The purpose of analyzing transactions is to determine which ego states are active and which are intrapsychically influencing as well as to facilitate an amelioration of the fixations and intrapsychic conflicts. Many transactions in psychotherapy do not reflect a transference of early fixations or introjections. Nontransference transactions are an expression of full contact here and now between the patient and therapist or between any two people. Their conversations may include discussion of the life problems of mature adults, reactions to loss or change, existential dilemmas, spiritual searching, and the challenges faced by aware, responsive, and evolving persons.

Transference transactions are an expression of either an archaeopsychic or exteropsychic ego state and, by inference, reflect an intrapsychic conflict between two or more ego states. *Nontransference transactions are any expression of a neopsychic ego uncontaminated by fixations of either archaeopsychic or exteropsychic ego states.*

Berne's Analysis of Transactions

Eric Berne parted company with a classical psychoanalytic theory that regarded all transactions from patient to psychotherapist as transference of childhood conflicts or wishes. Berne's original theoretical concept of neopsychic ego made it possible to understand transactions as Adult-to-Adult—hence, *transactional analysis, and not only an analysis of transference.* Berne's diagrams of ego states also made it possible to graphically represent that which is transference and that which is nontransference.

Berne (1961) began his discussion of the analysis of transactions with a case presentation of "transference" (pp. 91-97) within a therapy group. He described an Adult-to-Adult ego state set of transactions between Camellia and Rosita, followed by Camellia's *misperception* of Rosita's questions, and a *shift* in Camellia to a Child ego state. Berne described this as a "crossed transaction" (p. 93)

> in which the stimulus is directed to the Adult while the response originates from the Child, . . . probably the most frequent cause of misunderstanding in marriages and work situations, as well as in social life. Clinically, it is typified by the classical transference reaction. (pp. 93-94)

In Berne's further writings he began each explanation of crossed transactions with an example of the "classical transference reaction of psychoanalysis" (1964, p. 30, 1966, p. 225, 1972, p. 14) that loosely fit his original theory of ego states. All his other examples of transactions were from a role theory perspective.

A review of Berne's (1961) group case presentations (pp. 91-96) shows that he parted company with his own intrapsychic theory (pp. 29-80, 191-210) and related interventions (pp. 224-231, 1966, pp. 233-258). His interventions in this case were "motivated by the ultimate aim of establishing social control" (1961, p. 95) and his assessment that the group members were not "ready to attempt a deconfusion of the Child or a resolution of underlying conflicts" (p. 95). His use of role analysis as an analogy and substitute for his original intrapsychic theory of ego states corresponded with his switch to behavioral therapy.

On the basis of this motivation Berne changed his theoretical concept of ego states and defined transference and transactions significantly differently from what his original ego state theory would have required for consistency. With his theoretical concepts of exteropsychic, neopsychic, and archaeopsychic ego states, the definitions of transactions and transferences would have had to be related to the expression of ego, ego fragmentation, and intrapsychic conflict. However, Berne's use of roles to describe ego states led to definitions of transactions that described communication from a behavioral perspective. An evaluation of Berne's role or descriptive theory reveals consistency between the analogy of ego states as roles and subsequent definitions of transactions. With role theory Berne developed a useful taxonomy of behavior and a theory of communication (1961, pp. 128-135) consistent with a social control therapy. Yet there remains a need for definitions of transactions and transferences that are consistent with Berne's original conceptualization of ego states.

Function of Defense Mechanisms

In describing the transactions between Camellia and Rosita, Berne (1961, pp. 91-97) unfortunately did not discuss two significant theoretical and clinical aspects of the transference reaction: what he referred to as the "misperception" and the "shift" (p. 93) in Camellia's ego states. Throughout his writings Berne seemed to assume that the reader was familiar with the dynamics of defense mechanisms. A missing link in Berne's concept of ego states is the lack of a definition of how defenses are related to ego state theory, such as in the case of Camellia's shift to her Child ego state.

An integrative perspective on transactional analysis assumes that it is because of the continued presence of active archaic defenses that Child and Parent ego states remain fixated and separate states of the ego that are not integrated into an Adult ego (Erskine, 1988). Any of the elements of the ego that are not integrated into the neopsychic ego may be denied; if intrapsychic stress increases, the nonintegrated elements are subject to projection. Projection reestablishes a shaky set of defenses, which were originally developed to keep the person somewhat comfortable in a very uncomfortable situation.

Also from an integrative intrapsychic perspective, it is with the dynamics of the misperception and shift that a phenomenological and historical evaluation is assumed to yield psychotherapeutically useful information about Camellia's ego states, intrapsychic processes, and the function of her misperception of Rosita (Erskine & Moursund, 1988). Berne (1961) only relied on a social role description—"the parental role of comforting and apologizing" (p. 95)—and an all too limited description of the developmental behavior. There is insufficient information with which to make an adequate correlated diagnosis to determine which ego states are involved in the transactions.

Berne did not elaborate on the significance of the misperception. Theoretically, it is a likely projection onto Rosita of elements of an introjected person (Parent ego state) in Camellia's life. This would provide a concomitant relief of the intrapsychic conflict and a parallel reexperiencing of an external conflict. Camellia can now enact the internal conflict with another person who can play the *role* of a "parental response" (Berne, 1961, p. 94), that is, one form of transference. The parental response does not require that the person be in the Parent ego state (exteropsychic ego state), but rather, only that she be a suitable projection screen (Joines, 1977; Moiso, 1985; Perls, 1944/1947).

Transference Analysis

Transference transactions of the type described above involve a denial of and *a projection of elements of exteropsychic ego states and a reaction from an active archaic ego state*. There also may be subsequent transactions from the Child ego state to the misperception of a parental response in the other person. It is also possible to have a transference that involves *projection of elements of exteropsychic ego states and a reaction or overt transaction from an exteropsychic ego state*.

These transferences from historical relationships provide defensive relief from the discomfort of the intrapsychic conflict. Memories are deflected of the original transactions, where the person(s) with whom the child needed a primary relationship, attachment, and contact were the ones who disappointed, neglected, or abused. In such a transference the interpersonal conflicts of childhood are once again experienced as originating with people in the environment and thus offer the opportunity for resolution.

Relief from intrapsychic conflict may also be achieved through a transference that involves denial of and *projection of elements of an archaeopsychic ego state*. To avoid the awareness of discomforting or painful feelings, needs, or experiences, the original denial or repression must be maintained. One way of accomplishing this, particularly when these feelings are stimulated, is by projecting elements of the repressed Child onto someone else. The transferential transactions may take two basic forms: (1) *projection of elements of archaeopsychic ego states and an overt transaction from an active exteropsychic ego state,* or (2) *projection of elements of archaeopsychic ego states and a reaction or overt transaction from an archaeopsychic ego state.*

A graphic example of Child ego state projection and transference transactions from an active Parent ego state occurs in some cases of multigenerational child abuse. The primary purpose is to diminish intrapsychic conflict: The painful experiences contained in the Child ego state are denied and projected onto a suitable screen, and the verbal or physical cruelty that was historically introjected into a Parent ego state is made externally active and directed at another person.

A second example illustrates the projection of elements of a Child ego state and a reaction by a Child ego state within the same person. In some clinical situations the patient may engage in primary process and magical thinking and project a fantasy onto the psychother-apist. The projection of an archaic fantasy provides an opportunity for the patient to express through the transference with the psychotherapist the Child ego state experiences of intrapsychic conflict. Such early childhood fantasies function as an intrapsychic protection and may be either terrifying and punitive or wonderful and nurturing, similar to Kohut's (1971, 1977) descriptions of idealizing transferences. Either fantasy serves both to maintain the denial of the caretakers' effects on the child and to express the need for protection from the intrapsychic conflict (Erskine, 1988). Psychotherapists who regularly confront, define as a game, or attempt to eliminate such a projection of either a terrorizing or idealizing transference inhibit an intrapsychic and integrative therapy process.

Another aspect of transference, the projection of elements of a Child ego state and an overt transaction from a Child ego state within the same person, is evident in those psychothera-pists who project their own childhood experiences onto patients. The overt transactions may be an expression of a benevolent, nurturing caretaker fantasy within a Child ego state that functions internally to protect against awareness of Parent ego state influence (Erskine, 1988; Erskine & Moursund, 1988; Moiso, 1985). As long as there is a suitable screen for the projection of a troubled child, the intrapsychic conflict can be transferred and the denial contained. This form of transference is commonly referred to as countertransference.

Ulterior transactions represent those transactions that are at the psychological level of motivation, outside of Adult ego state awareness, and that are a transferential expression of Parent or Child ego state elements (Berne, 1961, pp. 103-105). In 1964 Berne described ulterior transactions as the basis of games (p. 33), and earlier (1961) he defined games as
> segments of longer, more complex sets of transactions called *scripts*. Scripts belong in the realm of transference phenomena, that is they are derivatives, or more precisely, adaptations, of infantile reactions and experiences. But a script does not deal with a mere transference reaction or transference situation; it is an attempt to repeat in derivative form a whole transference drama, often split up into acts, exactly like the theatrical scripts which are intuitive artistic derivatives of these primal dramas of childhood. (p. 116)

Life script is the macro expression of transference; games are a subset of script, ulterior or psychological level transactions are the substance of games, and the analysis of transactions is dependent on the concept of the ego divided into states with ensuing intrapsychic dynamics.

> Transactional analysis is a theory of personality and social action, and a clinical method of psychotherapy, based on the analysis of all possible transactions between two or more people, on the basis of specifically defined ego states. . . . Any system or approach which is not based on the rigorous analysis of single transactions into their component specific ego states is not transactional analysis. (Berne, 1972, p. 20)

Psychotherapy of Transference

The psychotherapy of transference occurs in part when the therapist does not simply take the patient's words or behavior at face value but also looks for the unaware meaning of what patients are saying or not saying, doing or not doing through their affective communication and bodily gestures. The understanding of transference from an integrative intrapsychic perspective on transactional analysis requires a multifaceted focus. Transference can be viewed as:

1. the means whereby the patient can demonstrate his or her past, the developmental needs that have been thwarted, and the defenses that were erected to compensate;
2. the resistance to full remembering and, paradoxically, an unaware enactment of childhood experiences;
3. the expression of intrapsychic conflict and the desire to achieve intimacy in relationships; or
4. the expression of the universal psychological striving to organize experience and create meaning.

Novellino (1985) expanded on the importance of understanding the function of transference:

> In any psychotherapeutic relationship the unsatisfied childhood need will be projected onto the therapist who will be experienced by the patient as the source of the possible satisfaction of the need (positive pole of transference) as well as its frustration (negative pole of transference). In every case the transference will be characterized by the simultaneous presence of both poles. (p. 204)

Trautmann (1985), in a *Transactional Analysis Journal* editorial summarizing the transactional analysis literature on transference, said:

> Therapy is effective when the internal Parental influence or dialogue is externalized (transferred), allowing for the resolution of childhood impasses and traumas, and the emergence of a stronger, uncontaminated, more integrated Adult. The specific approach used to effect this resolution depends on the level of childhood fixation: the more symbiotic the Child, the more actively the therapist needs to take on the transference relationship. (p. 190)

Conclusion

Berne's (1972) application of the principle of "Occam's Razor" (p. 20) gave too close a shave to the theory of analysis of transactions. In his attempt at conceptual "simplicity" (Preface, p. xvi) and theoretical "economy" (p. 21), Berne cut the theoretical concepts to their most simplified explanation and in so doing, I believe, lost the significance and profundity within his own theory. No longer is there either internal or external theoretical consistency.

When Berne redirected the emphasis of ego state theory from the original definitions to behavioral descriptions, he created a fundamental change in the *analysis of transactions.* With the shift in the theoretical metaphor of ego states the focus of the psychotherapist moved to the effect of the communication (transaction) on the receiver and on the patient's options for changing behavior to produce more effective communication.

The methodology stemming from this change of theoretical emphasis often resulted in the patient's improving social skills, but the inherent meaning of the transactions, particularly those that are transferential, was lost. No longer was there a theoretical basis in the psychotherapist's mind for a sensitivity to the internal psychological message or the desperate communication in the unaware expression of the existential position (Berne, 1964) or script beliefs (Erskine & Zalcman, 1979). Berne's original theoretical postulates, which led to an understanding of intrapsychic functioning and psychological versus social levels of transacting, was diminished, and a form of transactional analysis as a behavioral therapy emerged. This shift defined the task of the transactional analyst as improving communication and social effectiveness rather than understanding and ameliorating the intrapsychic conflict that is communicated through transference.

Berne developed two distinctly different theories of ego states and transactions. Each has a specific and valuable clinical purpose, and Berne's descriptive theory has many applications in the social world of human behavior and communication. It has been my goal in this article to show that the use of Berne's developmental, relational, and intrapsychic theory of ego states and the consistent use of that theory in understanding the internal dynamics of transactions can lead to a sensitive and effective response to transactions and transference and to a comprehensive psychotherapy that results in the integration of ego state fragments.

REFERENCES

Baker, E. (1982). The management of transference phenomena in the treatment of primitive states. *Psychotherapy: Theory, Research and Practice, 19,* 194-197.

Berg, M. (1977). The externalizing transference. *International Journal of Psychoanalysis, 58,* 235-244.

Berne, E. (1961). *Transactional analysis in psychotherapy: A systematic individual and social psychiatry.* New York: Grove Press.

Berne, E. (1964). *Games people play: The psychology of human relationships.* New York: Grove Press.

Berne, E. (1966). *Principles of group treatment.* New York: Grove Press.

Berne, E. (1972). *What do you say after you say hello?: The psychology of human destiny.* New York: Grove Press.

Bollas, C. (1979). The transformational object. *International Journal of Psychoanalysis, 60,* 97-107.

Bowlby, J. (1969). *Attachment. Vol. 1 of Attachment and loss.* New York: Basic Books.

Brandchaft, B. (1989, October). *Countertransference in an intersubjective perspective: A case presentation.* Panel discussion, 12th annual conference on the psychology of the self, San Francisco.

Brenner, C. (1979). Working alliance, therapeutic alliance, and transference. *Journal of the American Psychoanalytic Association, 27,* 137-158.

Breuer, J., & Freud, S. (1955). Studies on hysteria. In J. Strachey (Ed. and Trans.), *The standard edition of the complete psychological works of Sigmund Freud* (Vol. 2, pp. 1-305). London: Hogarth Press. (Original work published 1895)

Clarkson, P., & Gilbert, M. (1988). Berne's original model of ego states: Some theoretical considerations. *Transactional Analysis Journal, 18,* 20-29.

Erikson, E. (1950). *Childhood and society.* New York: Norton.

Erskine, R. G. (1979). Fourth-degree impasse. In C. Moiso (Ed.), *T.A. in Europe: Contributions to EATA summer conference 1977/1978.* Geneva, Switzerland: European Association for Transactional Analysis. Workshop conducted at the European Association for Transactional Analysis Congress, Seefeld, Austria, July, 1977.

Erskine, R. G. (1980). Script cure: Behavioral, intrapsychic and physiological. *Transactional Analysis Journal, 10,* 102-106.

Erskine, R. G. (1987). A structural analysis of ego: Eric Berne's contribution to the theory of psychotherapy. In *Keynote speeches: Delivered at the EATA conference, July, 1986, Noordwijkerhout, The Netherlands.* Geneva, Switzerland: European Association for Transactional Analysis.

Erskine, R. G. (1988). Ego structure, intrapsychic function, and defense mechanisms: A commentary on Eric Berne's original theoretical concepts. *Transactional Analysis Journal, 18,* 15-19.

Erskine, R. G. (1989). A relationship therapy: Developmental perspectives. In B. R. Loria (Ed.), *Developmental theories and the clinical process: Conference proceedings of the Eastern Regional Transactional Analysis conference* (pp. 123-135). Madison, WI: Omnipress.

Erskine, R. G., Clarkson, P., Goulding, R. L., Groder, M. G., & Moiso, C. (1988). Ego state theory: Definitions, descriptions, and points of view. *Transactional Analysis Journal, 18,* 6-14.

Erskine, R. G., & Moursund, J. (1988). *Integrative psychotherapy in action.* Newbury Park, CA: Sage Publications.

Erskine, R. G., & Zalcman, M. (1979). The racket system: A model for racket analysis. *Transactional Analysis Journal, 9,* 51-59.

Fairbairn, W. R. D. (1952). *An object-relations theory of the personality.* New York: Basic Books.

Federn, P. (1977). *Ego personality and the psychoses.* London: Maresfield Reprints. (Original work published 1953)

Freud, A. (1965). *Normality and pathology in childhood: Assessments of development.* New York: International Universities Press.

Freud, S. (1949). *An outline of psychoanalysis.* New York: Norton.

Freud, S. (1955). Fragments of an analysis of a case of hysteria. In J. Strachey (Ed. and Trans.), *The standard edition of the complete psychological works of Sigmund Freud* (Vol. 7, pp. 1-122). London: Hogarth Press. (Original work published 1905)

Freud, S. (1958). The dynamics of transference. In J. Strachey (Ed. and Trans.), *The standard edition of the complete psychological works of Sigmund Freud* (Vol. 12, pp. 97-108). London: Hogarth Press. (Original work published 1912)

Freud, S. (1958). Observations on transference—love: Further recommendations on the technique of psychoanalysis, III. In J. Strachey (Ed. and Trans.), *The standard edition of the complete psychological works of Sigmund Freud* (Vol. 12, pp. 157-173). London: Hogarth Press. (Original work published 1915)

Friedman, L. (1969). The therapeutic alliance. *International Journal of Psychoanalysis, 50,* 139-159.

Greenberg, J. R., & Mitchell, S. A. (1983). *Object relations in psychoanalytic theory.* Cambridge, MA: Harvard University Press.

Greenson, R. R. (1967). *The technique and practice of psychoanalysis.* New York: International Universities Press.

Guntrip, H. (1971). *Psychoanalytic theory, therapy and the self.* New York: Basic Books.

Joines, V. (1977). An integrated systems perspective. In G. Barnes, (Ed.), *Transactional analysis after Eric Berne: Teaching and practice of three TA schools* (pp. 252-272). New York: Harper & Row.

Khan, M. M. R. (1974). *The privacy of the self.* London: Hogarth Press.

Klein, M. (1949). *The psychoanalysis of children.* London: Hogarth Press.

Kohut, H. (1971). *The analysis of the self.* New York: International Universities Press.

Kohut, H. (1977). *The restoration of the self: A systematic approach to the psychoanalytic treatment of narcissistic personality disorder.* New York: International Universities Press.

Langs, R. (1976). *The therapeutic intervention: Vol. II. A critical overview and synthesis.* New York: Jason Aronson.

Langs, R. (1981). *Classics in psychoanalytic techniques.* New York: Plenum.

Lipton, S. (1977). The advantages of Freud's technique as shown in his analysis of the rat man. *International Journal of Psychoanalysis, 58,* 255-273.

Loria, B. R. (1988). The parent ego state: Theoretical foundations and alterations. *Transactional Analysis Journal, 18,* 39-46.

Massey, R. (1989). Script theory synthesized systemically. *Transactional Analysis Journal, 19,* 14-25.

Moiso, C. (1985). Ego states and transference. *Transactional Analysis Journal, 15,* 194-201.

Moiso, C. (1988). Eric Berne memorial scientific award acceptance speech: Ego states, transference and the TA psychodynamic approach—an overview. *Transactional Analysis Journal, 18,* 4-5.

Novellino, M. (1985). Redecision analysis of transference: A TA approach to transference neurosis. *Transactional Analysis Journal, 15,* 202-206.

Novik, J., & Kelley, K. (1970). Projection and externalization. *Psychoanalytic Study of the Child, 25,* 69-95.

Ornstein, A. (1989, October). *Countertransference in an intersubjective perspective: A case presentation.* Panel discussion, 12th annual conference on the psychology of the self, San Francisco.

Perls, F. S. (1947). *Ego, hunger and aggression: The beginnings of Gestalt therapy.* New York: Vintage Books. (Original work published 1944 as *Ego, hunger and aggression: A revision of Freud's theory and method.* Durban: Knox Publishing)

Perls, L. (1978). An oral history of Gestalt therapy. Part I: A conversation with Laura Perls, by Edward Rosenfeld. *The Gestalt Journal, 1*(1), 8-31.

Piaget, J. (1932). *The moral judgment of the child.* New York: Harcourt Press.

Piaget, J. (1951). *Play, dreams and imitation in childhood.* New York: Norton.

Piaget, J. (1954). *The construction of reality in the child.* New York: Basic Books.

Spotnitz, H. (1969). *Modern psychoanalysis of the schizophrenic patient.* New York: Grune & Stratton.

Stolorow, R. D., Brandchaft, B., & Atwood, G. (1987). *Psychoanalytic treatment: An intersubjective approach.* Hillsdale, NJ: Analytic Press.

Trautmann, R. (1985). Letter from the editor. *Transactional Analysis Journal, 15,* 188-191.

Trautmann, R. L., & Erskine, R. G. (1981). Ego state analysis: A comparative view. *Transactional Analysis Journal, 11,* 178-185.

Weiss, E. (1950). *Principles of psychodynamics.* New York: Grune & Stratton.

Winnicott, D. W. (1965). *The maturational processes and the facilitating environment: Studies in the theory of emotional development.* New York: International Universities Press.

This article was originally published in the Transactional Analysis Journal, *Volume 21, Number 2, April 1991, pp. 63-76. The author wishes to gratefully acknowledge the members of the Professional Development Seminar of the Institute for Integrative Psychotherapy, New York, for their valuable suggestions in the formulation of this article.*

Fourth-Degree Impasse

Richard G. Erskine

Impasse simply means to be stuck. It is a term from Gestalt therapy that implies that a person is experiencing conflict and is having difficulty resolving the conflict. Robert Goulding (1974), in combining both transactional analysis and Gestalt therapy frames of reference, identified three major stuck places that seemed to be prevalent in the patients with whom he worked.

The first-degree impasse is a conflict between the introjected Parent messages and the needs of the Natural Child. It often takes the form of a You-Me dialogue. The person may say from his or her Parent ego state about himself or herself, "You should work hard," while his or her Child ego state says, "I don't want to work hard." This can be simply resolved through the use of two-chair work that allows for the dialogue between Parent and Child to emerge with the Adult making the decision to work a reasonable amount of time.

The second-degree impasse is a survival impasse. The conflict is between the introjected P_1 and the person's A_1. If the injunction was "Don't Be You," the result may be the person's shutting himself or herself down physiologically so that instead of being spontaneous and expansive he or she becomes tight and inhibited. Resolution can occur through the person affectively regressing to the early scene in which he or she decided to inhibit himself or herself and making a redecision to "Be myself," with all the emotional release of the original traumatic experience.

The third-degree impasse is an identity impasse. The conflict is between the Adapted Child, which is seen as Me, and the Natural Child, which is seen as Not Me. The Adapted Child may say "I can't have a career, I'm only a girl," while the Natural Child, which is experienced as Not Me, may say, "I can do anything I set my mind to." Through the use of two-chair dialogue the Natural Child becomes stronger and stronger and is eventually experienced as Me.

My contribution is the fourth-degree impasse. The fourth-degree impasse is an emotional conflict. The conflict occurs between the introjected emotions of the parents and the person's own affective response to the situation. According to Berne (1964), the Parent ego state is a consistent pattern of thoughts, *feelings,* and behaviors that we introject from our parents. If the parents are experiencing strong affect in a given situation the child will introject that affect as part of his or her Parent ego state. The impasse occurs between the introjected feelings in the Parent and the person's own feelings in Child. This impasse is at the affective level only and does not involve Parent messages as in the first-degree impasse. Resolution involves the distinction between one's own feeling and the introjected feelings from parents.

Author's Note: The ego state nomenclature Natural and Adapted Child (P_1 and A_1) used in describing the first three impasses follows Robert Goulding's usage in his article cited

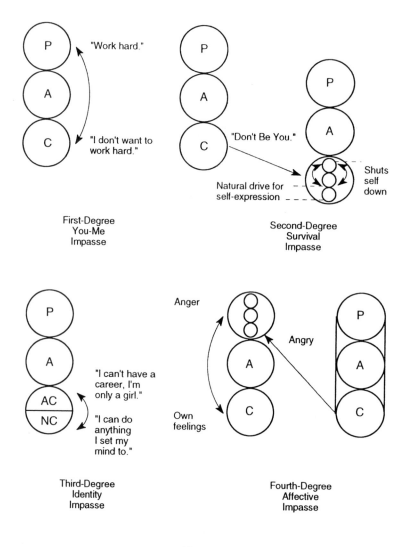

Figure 1
Impasses

in the following references. These impasses may also be explained through the use of Berne's original concept of ego states (see Erskine, 1988).

REFERENCES

Berne, E. (1964). *Games people play: The psychology of human relationships.* New York: Grove Press.

Erskine, R. G. (1988). Ego structure, intrapsychic function, and defense mechanisms: A commentary on Eric Berne's original theoretical concepts. *Transactional Analysis Journal, 18,* 15-19.

Goulding, R. (1974). Thinking and feeling in transactional analysis: Three impasses. *Voices, 10,* 11-13.

This article was originally published in C. Moiso (Ed.), Transactional Analysis in Europe *(pp. 33-35), Geneva, Switzerland: European Association for Transactional Analysis, 1978.*

Part 3

Life Scripts

Script Cure:
Behavioral, Intrapsychic, and Physiological

Richard G. Erskine

Transactional analysis, as a social psychiatry, has emphasized the behavioral change aspects of script cure. Within this framework cure is defined as the cessation of script syntonic behavior. Yet, for many people change in behavior alone is not sufficient to effect pervasive change of their life scripts. To achieve a total script cure change must occur at the intrapsychic level of the script as well, that is, change at the cognitive and affective levels of existence. In addition, I think that in every case of script formation, be it in response to introject, traumatic experiences, or the process of survival decisions, there is a corresponding physiological inhibiting reaction, and for many people change is also necessary at the physiological level of the script.

This integrative view of script cure implies that change needs to occur in three dimensions: behavioral, intrapsychic (affective and cognitive), and physiological.

Definition of Script

In understanding script cure I start with a definition of script as *a life plan based on decisions made at any developmental stage that inhibit spontaneity and limit flexibility in problem solving and in relating to people.* Such script decisions are usually made when the person is under pressure and awareness of alternative choice is limited. The script decisions emerge later in life as constricting script beliefs about one's self, others, or the quality of life. These script beliefs, along with the feelings repressed when the person was under pressure, are manifested in internal and external behavior and together with selected memories form a closed system of experiencing one's life. This closed system is the script.

Although many of the script beliefs on which we focus in therapy are decisions that have been made in early childhood before the child has any awareness of what his or her alternatives are for being in the world, this definition of script also includes those decisions that are made during any developmental period of a person's life when he or she is under pressures that restrict perception of options and alternatives for being and behaving. I think that at each of the passages in life, situations emerge wherein each of us must make choices. If restrictions are imposed on us that narrow our options for need fulfillment, it is likely that the decisions that are made, although they may seem to be the best possible choices under the circumstances to solve the immediate problem, will have the effect of limiting our spontaneity and flexibility in problem solving and in relating to people. In essence, any life plan made under pressure will most likely be growth inhibiting.

Within the parameters of this definition, script cure means that persons are free to contact people meaningfully and to respond to problem solving without preconceived ideas or plans that limit how they will interpret the situation and restrict behavioral choices. Cure is accomplished when each new experience is appreciated for its uniqueness and is perceived with an internalized sense, both viscerally and intellectually, as an opportunity to learn and grow.

Behavioral Cure

Script cure at the behavioral level means that the person is no longer engaging in script-related behaviors. For instance, if the script calls for being "not understood," therapeutic work aimed at the social control or behavioral level of cure may focus on encouraging the person to say what he or she is thinking and feeling and to shift ego states so that the listener has a clear understanding of the talker's internal experiences. The therapist's teaching of overt and ulterior transactions and the process of these in games is aimed at the person's using the knowledge to develop new behavior to be understood clearly in communications. Cure at this level means that the person in this example who believes "I'm not understood" would alter his or her behavior so that the listener has a thorough sense of understanding the talker. Specific change contracts are particularly relevant at the behavioral level of therapy.

When thinking of the behavioral level of script cure I also look for change in the fantasies and dreams of the person with whom I am working. I approach therapy with the concept that fantasy is an internalized behavior that occurs in the association area of the cortex without expression through the motor area. As psychotherapist I need to be aware of the content of a person's fantasies and dreams as a possible way in which he or she may act out the script in solitaire without ever engaging in observable or social behavior. For example, a person may have integrated new script-free behaviors at an overt or observable level when in awareness, but the script may emerge in nonconscious patterns during dream state or fantasy, producing reinforcement of "I'm not understood." Behavioral cure does not mean just the cessation of overt script actions, such as change in word usage, sentence patterns, expressions, or gestures, but also that the content and active processes of the dreams and fantasies are no longer determined by script beliefs or serve to reinforce the script.

Intrapsychic Cure

Since behavior is a manifestation of our intrapsychic processes I think that the therapist who is concerned with achieving script cure needs to focus on the cognitive and affective levels of script as well as the behavioral. The cognitive and affective aspects form the intrapsychic process of script through the continual nonconscious stimulation between feelings suppressed at the time of script decision (primal feelings) and the script beliefs resulting from those decisions. Therapeutic approaches that result in decontamination and deconfusion are designed for intrapsychic cure.

Cognitive-level script cure has occurred when a person is no longer contaminated by believing the script beliefs and by using them in a way that narrows his or her frame of reference. For example, the person would stop defining himself or herself as unlovable, or perceiving the world as a tragic place, or seeing people as untrustworthy, but rather the frame of reference would be unobstructed to allow each experience to be interpreted with a flexible view of self, others, and the quality of life. Cure at the affective level of script is the letting go of feelings that have been repressed since the time of script decision.

Script Development

To understand cure intrapsychically I look at the development of script within the young child. When the child has needs that are not met, either because of parental restrictions or environmental trauma, he or she experiences pressure or tension, and the organism responds to satisfy the need through the expression of emotions intended to draw attention to the unmet needs. If the emotions designed to meet the needs of the child are not expressed to need completion and the need remains unsatisfied, the result is an incomplete gestalt that demands closure. Once the child has reached the beginning of what Jean Piaget calls the concrete operational phase (preoperational stage) of development, closure of the incomplete gestalt occurs through a process of cognitive mediation in which the child symbolically replaces the unsatisfied need and concomitant feelings with a cognitive closure.

The cognitive closure is the child's explanation to himself or herself of why the need was never satisfied (i.e., "Something is wrong with me") and/or determines how to protect himself or herself (i.e., "I'll get hurt if I ask for what I want"). This cognitive explanation is the script decision, designed to protect the child through suppression of the need and related feelings from the discomfort of the unmet need. This explanation and any related physiological reaction still does not meet the need, but it does serve as a secondary closure of the needs and feelings—a fixed gestalten—and forms the intrapsychic core of the script. The child may also create an illusion that embellishes, justifies, and makes the script decision more acceptable. This illusion then is maintained later in life as fantasy.

Imagine a little child whose need at this point in time is for affection and who, for various reasons, has caretakers who are not providing it. If the environment lacks support for the child to express feelings all the way to need completion, the child may attempt to comfort himself or herself by suppressing the feelings and need and decide "Something is wrong with me" and "I won't get what I want." At the time when these script decisions are made they are probably the most effective response the child can make to protect himself or herself from the discomfort, but because these decisions do not satisfy the primary need, they form a fixed gestalt, a set of rigid beliefs that serve to limit the person's frame of reference years later. This limitation in perspective and the resulting behavioral restrictions constitute the life script.

Closing the Gestalt

Cure at the affective level is the release of the repressed emotions. When the repressed emotions are released and are no longer providing intrapsychic stimulation of the old script beliefs, the person then is free to experience feelings related to the current situation and to use the emotional sensations as an internal source of information and energy. This may be accomplished in therapy through redecision and disconnecting rubberbands by creating the environment in which the person can express the emotions that were inhibited in the original scripting situation all the way to need completion. Completion can be either in the reality of today's life or through granting in fantasy what was not provided in the original situation. The unmet need and related primal feelings (those feelings suppressed at the time of script decision) no longer dominate the foreground in internal perceptions; the gestalt is completed and new experiences come to foreground. As people express the repressed emotions and related needs they often become aware of what they decided about themselves, other people, or life and are still holding onto today as script beliefs—the cognitive level of the script. Recognizing that the script beliefs were decisions made a long time ago to protect themselves from the discomfort of the unmet needs is an important step in changing the cognitive level of the script. New decisions are made in light of today's realities, decision that enhance the views of self, others, or the quality of life beyond the perspective of the time when the person was under the scripting pressures. Cure at the cognitive level of script means that the person is no longer limited by the script beliefs.

Similarities may exist between script beliefs (i.e., I am *all alone*) and existential realities (i.e., I *am* all alone); however, the acceptance of existential realities is not limiting but provides a freedom to move beyond those realities, whereas script beliefs are inhibiting.

Body Scripts

Therapy aimed at the behavioral or intrapsychic levels does not account for the pervasive physiological aspects of script, and, since rigidity in the body represents a limitation in being, the somatic aspects of script need to be an important focus of script cure. Many of the script decisions described in the psychotherapy literature and those illustrated earlier in this paper are cognitive decisions that have been made or remade after the child has developed some use of language and has some understanding, at least symbolically, of cause and effect. Prior to this level of intellectual development I think that scripts are formed at a physiological level by the very young child, who in Piaget's framework is still operating within the sensorimotor period of development. When the child faces traumatic situations, responds to injunctions, or in some way has needs that are not being met, the child's body reacts in a self-protective way, and the scripting process takes place within the tissue of the body as a survival reaction.

This reaction of the body is a muscular and/or chemical defense against what the child experiences as threatening. It is a physiological closure of the unmet need for comfort, a shutting down or inhibition within the body that suppresses the unmet needs and unrelated emotions, and what Wilhelm Reich postulated as the basis for the development of "character armor."

This physiological reaction that is the primary basis of script in very early childhood also occurs to some degree in every scripting situation. Definitions of script imply inhibition in being, and with each scripting decision or script reaction I think there is always a corresponding physiological inhibition or restriction within the body. The younger the child or more severe the trauma, the greater the physiological reaction.

Physiological script reactions remain within the person much like conditioning and are the body script, the cause of many physical illnesses. Script cure at the physiological level is a letting go of the tensions, body armoring, and internal restrictions that inhibit the person from living life fully and easily within his or her own body. Changes in body script are often evident to an observer as a more relaxed appearance, freer movement, increased energy, and an established weight level that is appropriate for the person's frame. People report having a greater sense of vitality, an ease of movement, and an increased sense of well-being.

When I engage in body-script work the treatment goal is to energize the body tissue that was inhibited and rigidified in the repression of unmet needs and primal feelings. This may be the way into the intrapsychic level of therapy or may be a concluding step in the treatment of a specific script restriction. Interventions at the level of body script include those approaches that lead to somatic change, such as deep massage work, tension relaxation, proper diet, exercise, and recreational activities that enhance the flow of energy and movement of the body.

Recycling

The movement out of script may include some recycling back into script several times before the person is script free. This is the homeostatic or rubberband function of script drawing the person back to the old way of being whenever the pressures of life stimulate the unmet needs and feelings that were present at the time of script formation. Recycling may indicate that a level of script cure is still needing attention, such as emotional or body-script work that is undone even though the cognitive and/or physiological changes have occurred.

This integrative view of the intrapsychic, somatic, and behavioral levels of script cure implies that changes in a person's emotions and cognitive processes are determined by changes in behavior and/or in how the body functions and vice versa. The more levels of treatment the therapist can integrate the greater the likelihood of script cure.

Script Cure and Beyond

Therapy as a process of growth and development is unending. Therapy that focuses on script cure is complete when the behavioral, intrapsychic, and physiological restrictions that inhibit spontaneity and limit flexibility in problem solving and relating to people are removed. Beyond script is the realm of personal growth, which includes the successful movement through developmental passages, expanding creativity, understanding life purpose, and enhancing psychic and spiritual growth.

In my frame of reference script cure is equivalent to the definition I use of OKness: the belief and associated feeling of comfort that no matter what happens to me, no matter now bad the situation, I will learn and grow from the experience.

———————

This article was original published in the Transactional Analysis Journal, *Volume 10, Number 2, April 1980, pp. 102-106.*

The Racket System:
A Model for Racket Analysis

Richard G. Erskine and Marilyn J. Zalcman

When Eric Berne (1964) introduced the terms *racket* and *trading stamps*, he noted that his article was "only a bare outline, an introduction to what is . . . at the clinical level a highly elaborated subject" (p. 127). Berne (1966, pp. 308-309, 1970, pp. 157-158, 1972, pp. 137-147) later gave expanded descriptions of how people use rackets and trading stamps in games and script. He did not, however, fit the concepts of rackets and trading stamps into the general theoretical framework of transactional analysis.

Other transactional analysis authors have delineated the psychological development of rackets and their operation in social transactions. Currently, the literature on rackets and trading stamps presents the reader with contradictions that reflect the widely varying conceptualizations of several authors. The systematic theoretical development of rackets still remains far behind clinical usage.

The inconsistencies are immediately evident when one compares the definitions of a *racket:* (a) feelings used to manipulate or exploit others (Berne, 1964; Goulding, 1972, p. 116; Steiner, 1971, p. 16); (b) feelings experienced as payoffs in games and the reason for playing games (Berne, 1964; Steiner, 1971, p. 16); (c) feelings substituted for suppressed or prohibited feelings (English, 1971); (d) feelings that are outside the context of here and now (Goulding, 1972, p. 116); (e) transactional events or behavioral sequences, e.g., "racketeering" (English, 1976; Ernst, 1973); (f) the basic existential position (Steiner, 1971, p. 13); and (g) an underlying exploitative design for experiencing unpleasant feelings (Holloway, 1973a). Thus, in transactional analysis theory, rackets are like the diverse descriptions of an elephant given by four blind men positioned at the elephant's truck, leg, side, and tail. Each one experiences only a part of the elephant and does not conceptualize the whole elephant. While transactional analysis authors identify the phenomena they are describing as rackets, they seem to be describing different or related aspects of the same phenomena and arriving at very different conclusions about exactly what is a racket.

In our experience, the different approaches to rackets are all valid and quite applicable to clinical situations; however, several phenomena observed are not adequately explained by existing theories. (1) Individuals frequently use a variety of feelings to engage in rackety manipulation rather than a single "favorite feeling." (2) For some individuals there appears to be a hierarchy of substitute feelings rather than a direct substitution of one feeling for another. For example, in the process of dealing with scared feelings a client may switch to angry feelings, only to discover that it was sad feelings that were most strongly suppressed in childhood. (3) Whereas rackets have been primarily limited to feelings, "thinking rackets" are sometimes observed. For example, guilt, inadequacy, and confusion rackets would be more accurately described as "thinking rackets" accompanied by feelings and physical responses. (4) Equating rackets and trading stamps as the same "favorite feeling" does not always apply. This is especially true for clients experiencing depression. In many instances depressed clients use sad feelings as a manipulative racket and save angry feelings as their trading stamps to justify suicide or a trip to the hospital.

An additional problem is that rackets have not been sufficiently integrated with other concepts of transactional analysis theory. In addition to its definition as a separate construct, the idea of rackets has been classified as types of transactions (English, 1976; Ernst, 1973; Steiner, 1971, p. 16) and as internal games (Berne, 1970, p. 163; Goulding, 1976). And while rackets have been related to games, especially game payoffs (Berne, 1964; Steiner, 1971, p. 16), rackets and games have not been clearly differentiated (English, Erskine, Goulding, Karpman, Mellor, Zalcman, 1976; Karpman & D'Angelo, 1976).

Furthermore, the interrelationships that exist between rackets and scripts lack specific theoretical clarity. While identified as an element in the early decision (Holloway, 1973b) and related operationally to scripting, rackets and their specific relationships to scripting and elements of the script have not been explained.

In this article we propose two advances in transactional analysis theory:
1. The addition of racket analysis to the four major divisions of transactional analysis theory and phases of treatment; and
2. The use of the racket system as a model for identifying, explaining, and dealing with the phenomena related to rackets and trading stamps.

Racket Analysis

Structural analysis, transactional analysis proper, game analysis, and script analysis were developed to constitute a complete system of theory sufficient for describing all human behavior and dynamics relevant to social psychiatry (Berne, 1961, p. 11).

Limiting consideration to ego states, transactions, games, and script omits the intrapsychic or intrapersonal processes involved in human behavior. In his terminological grid, Berne (1972, pp. 409-413) limited transactional terms to ego states, transactions, games, and script. In our opinion, these four areas alone do not meet the requirements for a complete system of transactional analysis theory and therapy. To effect change at a script level is highly unlikely without focusing on the intrapsychic processes in transactional analysis treatment; furthermore, much of the therapeutic work of transactional analysis clinicians does not fit into any of the established four categories, particularly when the therapeutic emphasis is on decontamination and deconfusion.

As a major division of transactional analysis theory, racket analysis will precede script analysis and will include analysis of:
1. the intrapsychic (intrapersonal) processes of thinking, feeling, and physical responses that occur as intervening variables in social transactions and through which individuals structure their perceptions and interpretations of experience; and

2. the behavioral phenomena that are directly related to these intrapsychic processes and that may occur as separate events or as a part of transactional sequences.

This definition of racket analysis includes both the intrapsychic processes and associated behaviors related to script and provides theoretical grounding for research and clinical practice. That is, results of studies, such as the left-brain, right-brain research (Sample, 1975), describing how neurological development and processes influence perception and interpretation of experience would be as appropriate for consideration in racket analysis as clinical studies describing how individuals distort experiences to maintain, elaborate on, and advance the script.

As an area of transactional analysis theory, racket analysis would include phenomena that: (a) may be explained in terms of ego states (this meets requirements Berne sets forth as necessary for transactional analysis theory); (b) may occur in the absence of social transactions (and, therefore, not a method of structuring time); (c) are not transactions, games, or scripts but may influence or be operating as a part of these phenomena; and (d) can be related to structural analysis, transactional analysis proper, game analysis, and script analysis. As a phase of transactional analysis treatment, racket analysis would include the identification of these phenomena and the therapeutic operations designed to effect changes in them.

Theoretical Constructs and Definitions

The *racket system* is defined as a *self-reinforcing, distorted system of feelings, thoughts, and actions maintained by script-bound individuals*. The racket system has three interrelated and interdependent components: the *script beliefs and feelings*, the *rackety displays,* and the *reinforcing memories* (see Figure 1).

The script beliefs and feelings are all the Parent and Child contaminations of the Adult based on and supporting script decisions. (The term script beliefs is used to describe contamination of the Adult, which results from script and, therefore, is not the same as frame of reference [Schiff et al., 1975, p. 49], which includes all the ideas about self, others, and the world.) They begin developing when a child is under pressure either from parental programming (injunctions, counterinjunctions, attributions) or environmental trauma, and his or her expression of feelings does not result in needs being met. The child's suppression of feelings and concomitant failure to satisfy needs produce an incomplete emotional experience. If closure (a completed or dynamic gestalt) does not occur, the contained energy goes into either a physiological or cognitive attempt at closure (a secondary or fixed gestalt). Through the process of cognitive mediation, the child attempts to make sense of the experiences and produces fixed gestalten—survival conclusions or script decisions, which remain as the core script beliefs or the basic decisions about self, others, and the quality of life (personal destiny). For the sake of clarity we are describing the early script decision or survival conclusion and the adoption of core script beliefs as though they occur at a particular time in a child's life. It is important to keep in mind that these may occur over a period of time and may be the result of fantasy as well as of an actual occurrence. Script beliefs are synonymous with script decisions or survival conclusions except that the latter two refer to what the child may have decided early in life, and script beliefs refer to how the person is maintaining those decisions or conclusions as beliefs and associated feelings as an adult. These core script beliefs are usually expressed in concrete terms consistent with the thinking levels of which young children are capable (Piaget, 1952). Once adopted, the core script beliefs influence what experiences are attended to, how they are interpreted, and whether or not they are regarded as significant by the individual. The child then begins to add *supporting script beliefs* that reaffirm and elaborate on the core script beliefs.

Years later when the person experiences feelings similar to those felt at the time of script decision, the script beliefs may be stimulated. Or, when the person is actively believing a script belief, the old feelings may be stimulated. As long as the script beliefs and feelings remain contaminations of the Adult, they are not available for updating with new information and experiences. For example, if the script decision included the belief, "I'm unlovable," and the feeling present at the time was sadness, there will be a continual recycling of the script belief ("I'm unlovable") and feeling (sadness) on the intrapsychic level, which reinforces and maintains the script. And, when this intrapsychic process occurs, the person is likely to engage in *rackety displays*.

The rackety displays consist of all the overt and internal behaviors that are manifestations of the script beliefs/feelings. Included are the *observable behaviors,* such as words, sentence patterns, tone of voice, displays of emotion, gestures, and body movements a person makes that are a direct result of the intrapsychic process. A person may either act the way defined by the script beliefs, that is, saying "I don't know" when believing "I'm stupid," or attempt to defend against the script beliefs, that is, being very quiet and nice when believing "I'm bad." During childhood a whole range of behaviors is tested (English, 1971, 1972; Holloway, 1973b) to elicit strokes while maintaining compatibility with the script beliefs. The child experiments to find which behaviors will elicit responses in others that will confirm what he or she is believing. Parents and other significant figures also influence the child's choice of behaviors through instructions ("Boys don't cry"); prohibitions ("Don't you ever do that again"); stroking ("You're so cute when you pout"); attributions ("He's the toughest kid in the neighborhood"); and modeling (Dad's temper tantrum always gets everyone's attention). The child's interpretations of the outcomes of his or her own or others' behaviors result from symbolic and egocentric thinking (Piaget, 1952) in which magical powers may be attached to certain behaviors with the expectation that engaging in them will either ward off or fulfill the script belief. Eventually, the child settles on a specific group of behaviors, including displays of emotion, and uses them repeatedly and especially in situations that may challenge the script beliefs. These behaviors may be labeled rackety displays since they are repetitive and stylized and are a manifestation of the script beliefs/feelings. In adolescence and in adulthood individuals may continue to use the rackety displays learned in early childhood. They may, also, decrease or increase their repertoire of behavior after contact with the world outside the family.

An individual may have a body reaction to the intrapsychic process in addition to or in place of the overt behaviors. These *reported internal experiences* are the behaviors that are not readily observable but on which the person can give a self-report, such as fluttering in the stomach, changes in perceived body temperature, increased muscular tension, headaches, colitis, and all the somatic responses to the script beliefs/feelings. These internal behaviors are a manifestation of the script beliefs/feelings and also maintain the script.

Rackety displays also include *fantasies* in which the individual imagines behavior, both his or her own or someone else's, that lends support to the script beliefs. During the time of script decision a child may symbolize behavior (Piaget, 1951) to either confirm or deny his or her experience. In the absence of one's own overt or somatic behavior, or when no other person is present, an individual may fantasize or hallucinate behaviors of himself or herself or others that are syntonic with script beliefs. These fantasied behaviors function as effectively in reinforcing script beliefs/feelings and, in some instances, even more effectively than the overt behaviors.

Each of the various ways of engaging in rackety displays can result in the collection of *reinforcing memories*. Reinforcing memories are the recall of selected events during the person's lifetime. They are a collection of emotional memories of transactions, either real or imagined; recall of internal bodily experiences; or the retained remnants of fantasy, dreams, or hallucinations. Each memory has an emotional or feeling component associated with the experience. In some instances people may forget the factual aspects of an event but will retain the emotional components of the memory. Berne (1964) termed this feeling component "trading stamps" (p. 127).

Reinforcing memories serve as feedback to the script beliefs. Each reinforcing memory has the capacity either to reinforce or to negate the script beliefs. Since script beliefs function as a contamination of the Adult, only those memories that support the script

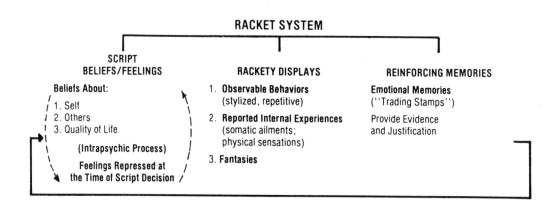

Figure 1
The Racket System

belief are readily accepted and are used as reinforcement of the beliefs. Those memories that negate the script beliefs are often rejected or forgotten since they would challenge the prejudice and serve to decontaminate the Adult. They may also be distorted through fantasy to create script-syntonic memories that serve to support the script beliefs. For example, a person may have a script belief, "No one likes me," and when the therapist says to the person, "I like you," he or she may attempt to maintain the belief and associated feeling of sadness by saying, "You didn't really mean it because you didn't say it with much feeling." Grossly misinterpreted or fantasized experiences are sometimes called "counterfeit strokes" and are seen as distortions of the intended stroke (Bruce & Erskine, 1974; James & Jongeward, 1971).

When memories that are syntonic with script beliefs are recalled, they serve to reinforce and strengthen the script beliefs, which then stimulate the feelings present at the time of script decision. Those feelings in turn stimulate the script belief, and the intrapsychic process serves to reinforce continually the contamination. When a memory is dystonic with a specific script belief the person may, instead of distorting the memory, simply negate it by switching to another script belief. In the aforementioned example the person distorted the memory of "I like you" by saying that the therapist's statement lacked feeling; the person could also switch to another script belief, "People cannot be trusted." In switching, the memory that challenges the script belief is negated and the person continues to be sad and thinking remains contaminated and is in script.

Case Example of a Racket System

The following example of the racket system illustrates how the client maintained script through script beliefs/feelings, rackety displays, and reinforcing memories (see Figure 2).

Beginning with the birth of her first sibling, Louise made a decision, based on the care her sick sibling received and her being "pushed off," that she was not important. At this time her mother was under great emotional pressure and was psychologically unavailable while father was frequently away. The early decision, "I'm not important," was reinforced with each successive sibling and in every traumatic home situation where, being oldest, Louise's needs were ignored. Louise reported in therapy that she often experienced her parents' nonverbal attitude as an injunction, "Don't be important." At an early age the client discovered that one solution to the problem of not being important was to take care of others—siblings and parents—which would make it possible for some of her needs to be met.

In adult life this decision was observable in her choice of a helping profession. Her general demeanor was quiet and withdrawn, deferring to others. The social response from others was that she was ignored and often did not get what she wanted, thereby reinforcing her belief that she was not important, was unwanted, and that others were more important. Her affective behavior was one of sadness, leading to periods of depression and/or severe headaches.

Her fantasy life often centered around the counterscript decision that if she were good enough to someone else they would love her and take care of her. To support this decision she also occasionally fantasized ending up alone, poor, and unloved.

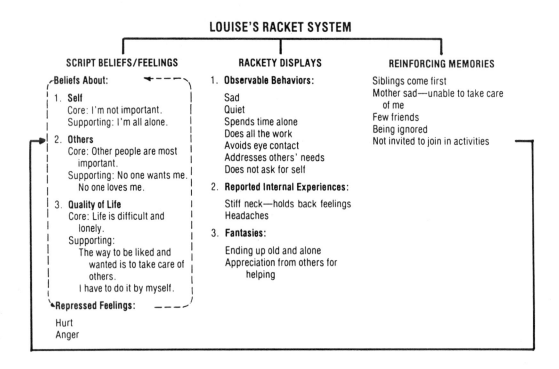

Figure 2
Louise's Racket System

The course of treatment involved: (1) reexperiencing a series of old traumas in which the original and reinforcing decisions were made and making new decisions about self, others, and the quality of life; (2) expressing the underlying anger at not being taken care of; (3) beginning to identify and ask for needs to be met; (4) behaving in a more social manner to experience positive responses from people; (5) changing fantasies from being alone to being loved for being joyful, spontaneous, and intimate; and (6) massage work on neck muscles where inhibition of self was reflected.

Therapeutic Interventions

Another common example is the person who has a belief about self, "I'm helpless," and about others, "No one can understand me." Behaviorally the person will often act helpless or confused, say "I don't know," sigh, and shrug his or her shoulders. This presents a double bind for the therapist. If the therapist helps, the memory of the helping therapist will be used as evidence to prove "I'm helpless"; if the therapist suggests that a person is not helpless and can do it himself or herself then the belief that "No one understands me" is reinforced. We have found it quite effective to draw the racket system (see Figure 3) for the client, pointing out that we do understand—in fact, we understand that *he or she* believes that no one understands him or her and that he or she is helpless. Once the racket system is drawn out, the person may act helpless and seem not to know what is on the board. At that point we record the request for help under the observable behavior and tell the client that we are risking reinforcing "I'm helpless" but will do so this time to explain. Each subsequent request for help is listed in writing along with switches to supporting beliefs. The process often elicits a strong emotional reaction, which can be used to disconnect the rubberband (Erskine, 1974) to the script feeling.

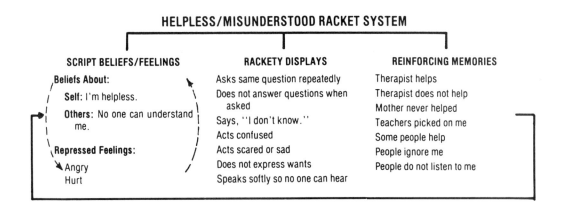

HELPLESS/MISUNDERSTOOD RACKET SYSTEM

SCRIPT BELIEFS/FEELINGS	RACKETY DISPLAYS	REINFORCING MEMORIES
Beliefs About:	Asks same question repeatedly	Therapist helps
Self: I'm helpless.	Does not answer questions when asked	Therapist does not help
Others: No one can understand me.	Says, "I don't know."	Mother never helped
	Acts confused	Teachers picked on me
Repressed Feelings:	Acts scared or sad	Some people help
Angry	Does not express wants	People ignore me
Hurt	Speaks softly so no one can hear	People do not listen to me

Figure 3
Helpless/Misunderstood Racket System

Any therapeutic intervention that interrupts the flow in the racket system will be an effective step in the person's changing his or her racket system and therefore his or her script. Contracts that focus on changing the overt behavior in the rackety display will result in different social responses from other people and hence a change in the reinforcing memories. It is possible for someone to change his or her overt behaviors and still maintain the racket system by imagining script-related behavior and collecting reinforcing memories as a result of fantasy. For some clients it is important, therefore, for the therapist to check if the script is being lived out in fantasy; this is most often apparent in dreams.

In Louise's case the stiff neck and headaches produced memory traces that reinforced the belief, "Life is difficult." In therapy the somatic level of the rackety display can be dealt with through techniques designed to change the body or physiological level of script. Such approaches may include deep muscle massage, biofeedback, bioenergetics, meditation and yoga, or physical exercise such as expressive dancing.

Reinforcing memories will no longer have an effective role in maintaining the system when people live in the "here and now" and do not dwell on old memories or fantasied memories of events that are yet to come, that is, when they let go of all of their trading stamps. A specific therapeutic intervention may involve the confrontation of discrepancies between what the client remembers and what actually occurred and the meaning of what occurred.

The script beliefs themselves can be challenged directly through various decontamination operations (Berne, 1966, pp. 233-247). Based on how the client describes himself or herself we will often hypothesize what the script beliefs might be, write them on the board, and then check whether the hypothesized beliefs are operational for the person, particularly in stressful situations. A direct question, "Is this belief really true in your life today?" frequently produces the insight that he or she is operating from old perceptions or misconceptions and has been living life based on script beliefs that originated in early childhood. For some clients the only thing needed at this point is an invitation to drop the script beliefs and to live with an awareness of all the possible options that are available.

Where trauma has played a significant part in forming the script, clients have made major changes in their racket systems when the therapeutic work has been focused on the unexpressed affect that was present and suppressed at the moment of script decision. The release of repressed emotion through cathecting to an early age, Gestalt work, or the expression of primal feelings often leads to a redecision and disconnecting the rubberband. The therapeutic focus may then become cognitive and/or behavioral as the person decides to change his or her script beliefs. The racket system concepts may be taught to clients so they have a conceptual tool for understanding how they have maintained script, and contracts for new behavior may be negotiated to support their decision to change their beliefs about self, others, and the quality of life.

However the therapist decides to intervene—at the level of script beliefs, the repressed script feelings, the various rackety displays, or the reinforcing memories—any change that stops the flow in the racket system can stop the script. The more aspects of the racket system on which the therapist focuses, thereby dealing with the behavioral, cognitive, and affective levels, the greater the probability that the client will maintain a script-free life.

Conclusion

As a whole, the racket system is maintained through selective awareness and perceptions that are based on the requirements of the script and involve discounting as a mechanism. The racket system operates only when a person is living in script and may be viewed as *a cross section of the script.* That is, the racket system in operation is a demonstration of how the person is supporting and carrying out the script decisions in day-to-day life. The script beliefs provide a distorted framework for viewing self, others, and quality of life. Since these are paired Parent and Child contaminations of the Adult, the views are not available for updating, and any contradictory information will be ignored. Rackety displays are stimulated by the script beliefs and are designed to confirm or get others to confirm the contaminations and to avoid or reexperience the script feelings. In order to engage in a rackety display individuals must discount other options and frequently will maintain that their behavior is the "natural" or "only" way they can respond. When used in social transactions, rackety displays are likely to produce reinforcing memories, especially as game payoffs. Reinforcing memories, in turn, are governed by and contribute to the reinforcement of the script beliefs and rackety displays, as well as the elaboration and advancement of the script. Thus, the racket system is distorted and self-reinforcing through the operation of its three interrelated and interdependent subsystems: script beliefs/feelings, rackety displays, and reinforcing memories.

The racket system has been proposed here as a theoretical and clinical model for racket analysis. It specifies those phenomena appropriately fitting in this area of transactional analysis theory and therapy and offers criteria for selecting therapeutic interventions. The diverse definitions and descriptions of rackets and trading stamps in the transactional analysis literature have been integrated in the racket system. Discrepancies noted between theory and clinical observations have been taken into account. The racket system is also offered as a framework for further theoretical developments in racket analysis, for the integration of other psychotherapy concepts, and for research.

REFERENCES
Berne, E. (1961). *Transactional analysis in psychotherapy: A systematic individual and social psychiatry.* New York: Grove Press.
Berne, E. (1964). Trading stamps. *Transactional Analysis Bulletin, 3*(10), 127.
Berne, E. (1966). *Principles of group treatment.* New York: Oxford University Press.
Berne, E. (1970). *Sex in human loving.* New York: Pocket Books.
Berne, E. (1972). *What do you say after you say hello?: The psychology of human destiny.* New York: Grove Press.
Bruce, T. T., & Erskine, R. G. (1974). Counterfeit strokes. *Transactional Analysis Journal, 4*(2), 18-19.
English, F. (1971). The substitution factor: Rackets and real feelings, Part I. *Transactional analysis Journal, 1*(4), 27-32.
English, F. (1972). Rackets and real feelings, Part II. *Transactional Analysis Journal, 2*(1), 23-25.
English, F. (1976). Racketeering. *Transactional Analysis Journal, 6,* 78-81.
English, F., Erskine, R., Goulding, M., Karpman, S., Mellor, K., & Zalcman, M. (1976, August). *Rackets and games.* Panel presented at the International Transactional Analysis Association conference, San Francisco.
Ernst, F. H., Jr. (1973). Psychological rackets in the OK corral. *Transactional Analysis Journal, 3*(1), 19-23.
Erskine, R. G. (1974). Therapeutic intervention: Disconnecting rubberbands. *Transactional Analysis Journal, 4*(1), 7-8.
Goulding, M. (1976). Rackets as stereotyped feelings. In S. B. Karpman & A. D'Angelo (Eds.), Feeling rackets: Notes from state of the art, winter congress, January 1976. *Transactional Analysis Journal, 6,* 344.
Goulding, R. (1972). New directions in transactional analysis: Creating an environment for redecision and change. In C. J. Sager & H. S. Kaplan (Eds.), *Progress in group and family therapy* (pp. 105-134). New York: Brunner/Mazel.
Holloway, W. H. (1973a). Rackets—an up-dated view. Monograph VI, mimeographed. Medina, Ohio: Midwest Institute for Human Understanding.
Holloway, W. H. (1973b). Shut the escape hatch. Monograph IV, mimeographed. Medina, Ohio: Midwest Institute for Human Understanding.
James, M., & Jongeward, D. (1971). *Born to win: Transactional analysis with Gestalt experiments.* Reading, MA: Addison-Wesley.
Piaget, J. (1951). *Play, dreams and imitation in childhood* (C. Gattegno & F. M. Hodgson, Trans.). New York: Norton.
Piaget, J. (1952). *The origins of intelligence in children* (M. Cook, Trans.). New York: International Universities Press.
Sample, R. E. (1975). Learning with the whole brain. *Human Behavior,* 16-23.
Schiff, J. L., with Schiff, A. W., Mellor, K., Schiff, E., Schiff, S., Richman, D., Fishman, J., Wolz, L., Fishman, C., & Momb, D. (1975). *Cathexis reader: Transactional analysis treatment of psychosis.* New York: Harper & Row.
Steiner, C. (1971). *Games alcoholics play: The analysis of life scripts.* New York: Grove Press.

This article was originally published in the Transactional Analysis Journal, *Volume 9, Number 1, January 1979, pp. 51-59.*

The Ultimate Psychological Concern: Nuclear War

Richard G. Erskine, PhD
Acceptance Speech, Eric Berne Memorial Scientific Award
International Transactional Analysis Association

Receiving the Eric Berne Memorial Scientific Award for "The Racket System: A Model for Racket Analysis" (1979) fills me with joy and a sense of gratitude to all of you who found the concepts valuable in your work with people. I would like to thank Eric Berne, Fanita English, Franklin Ernst, Robert and Mary Goulding, Bill Holloway, Claude Steiner, and numerous other authors for their writings, which were a stimulus in developing the concept of racket analysis. And thanks to my clients and trainees who taught me invaluable lessons about life scripts. I have a particular appreciation for Marilyn Zalcman, without whom these ideas would not be as you now know them.

I want to take this opportunity to talk to you heart-to-heart about a concern I have had for a long time. I am concerned about our culturally shared suicidal-homicidal racket system, the result of which may be nuclear war. I am alarmed that several nations of this world are preparing nuclear weapons, and that suspicion and distrust between governments is growing at a rate that a war that could annihilate all human life on this planet is indeed a possibility. There are now enough nuclear bombs that the world could be destroyed several times over. Every day three to five new nuclear weapons are added to the 50,000 that currently exist worldwide. Nuclear war means the end of all life—self-extermination.

Each of us in various ways supports a cultural script or racket system that could mean the destruction of humankind. Like people who are caught in their individual life scripts, as a society we perpetuate, without awareness, commonly held societal beliefs, such as, "There is not enough . . ." and "We will lose if we share," which lead to hoarding behaviors, not giving to others, and a drive to get more, more, more. Often these beliefs are reinforced by memories of past losses or a fantasy of not having needs satisfied. A system such as this, when mindlessly shared by large numbers of people, can escalate to war, the function of which is to decrease threat by stealing, enslaving, and killing others. The war escalations of nations represent the repression of infantile rage along with the repressed fear that our group—I—will be annihilated.

A core belief, "We must be in control," produces a block to communication, a lack of trust, and dishonest behavior. Our elected leaders support the belief that it is possible to win a nuclear war. Such outrageous delusions perpetuate the mass obsession with control, yet every new bomb manufactured really means that each of us has less control over our own life.

To deny the loss of control and suppress the related scare we fantasize that through creating more nuclear weapons or faster delivery systems we, as nations, can increase our control over the world. Each increase only escalates the scare of other nations, which in turn deny their scare and create even more lethal weapons. This increase in weapons stimulates other nations to increase even faster. The result is a vicious cycle of escalated scare, denial, and an increased likelihood of nuclear war. The psychological effect of this cycle is a loss of vitality for life.

As the stockpile of nuclear weapons increases in the world so does the sense of alienation from life; each person's ability to be in charge of his or her own life is decreased. The response of many people is, "I'm helpless," "There's nothing I can do," and the suicidal belief, "What's the use?" These beliefs are displayed through passivity and psychic numbing. The joy and enthusiasm for life is suppressed when we suppress our knowledge and feelings, and all that remains is a dull existence—a loss of motivation and involvement in something greater than our own lives. There is no commitment to the survival of humanity, but only a giving up on life—a prime condition for nuclear destruction. "What's the use?" is the acquiescence to mass suicide and murder.

We ignore the irrefutable scientific evidence regarding the potential for ultimate total destruction of all life forms on our planet when we perpetuate a lie to each other that "We can survive a nuclear war." I am convinced that nuclear war is not just a threat to a few million Russians and Americans; the potential radiation is such that it will destroy all water supplies and the vital ozone layer surrounding the earth, bringing an end to all life. To avoid confronting the illusion that we can survive the lethal effects of nuclear war, we, like the proverbial ostrich that buries its head in the face of threat, bury our heads in day-to-day activities that structure our time rather than talking to each other about our hidden scare and working together to create cooperative, peaceful approaches to conflict resolution.

August 6, 1945, the day the atomic bomb was dropped on Hiroshima, marks a turning point in the history of humankind. No longer do we each only face the prospect of our own individual death; we are now confronted with the potential extermination of all forms of life. Albert Einstein is reported to have said,

> We must never relax our efforts to arouse in the people of the world, and especially in their governments, an awareness of the unprecedented disaster which they are absolutely certain to bring on themselves unless there is a fundamental change in their attitude toward one another as well as in their concept of the future. The unleased power of the atom has changed everything *except our way of thinking*.

Psychotherapists and those who work in the human service fields can have a significant impact in changing what people believe, in elevating every person's concept of what it means to be alive. Through understanding the causes and function of psychic numbing we can act as catalysts to help people overcome the societal inertia of complacency about the stockpiling of atomic weapons and the potential for nuclear war.

Transactional analysis has a long history as a social psychology. The time has come to take a stand, to be involved in nuclear disarmament and the creation of peace. We have a theory and the methodology to bring about lasting change in people's lives and to end the craziness that permeates our society.

Each of us who takes responsibility for our own thoughts and actions can have a positive impact on the future of the world. Our words and behaviors have the power to reinforce destructiveness or to impart health. What we say and do does have an impact.

As transactional analysts we have an ethical responsibility that goes beyond simply helping people adapt to a society that functions under the possibility of nuclear devastation. Our role is to help people be aware of their feelings and attitudes and to empower them so that they are free to say "No" to the possibility of war and instead to develop a lasting peace, to create a safe and sane world.

My hope is that each of you will join with me in a common goal for the future: the elimination of all nuclear weapons and a commitment to peaceful conflict resolutions, not just for ourselves, but for all life—the life of our children and grandchildren and their grandchildren.

This speech was originally published in the Transactional Analysis Journal, *Volume 13, Number 1, January 1983, pp. 7-9.*

Identification and Cure of Stroke Rip-Off

Richard G. Erskine

Many people who come to therapy do not know how to ask for strokes and go about living their lives in a relatively strokeless existence. Their presenting problems often include listlessness and a lack of interest in activities, low productivity, psychosomatic complaints, and/or depression. Through the use of permission and stroking exercises many transactional analysis therapists have focused their attention on teaching people how to get their stroking needs met.

A subgroup of those who come for treatment actively engage in stroking exchanges with people and yet report many of the same presenting problems as those who receive few strokes. In addition, they often report having continuous low-level conflicts on the job or with acquaintances, a lack of "available" friends with whom to engage in activities, and, if single, difficulty in attracting or maintaining people to date. This second group of people may be getting their strokes by ripping them off. The identification and cure of stroke rip-off may be important in the treatment of those people who are avid stroke seekers and who also have difficulty maintaining interpersonal relationships.

A stroke rip-off involves the taking of strokes from other people without the other person willingly giving the stroke of his or her own choice. It is a way of getting attention from another person whether or not that person freely wants to give the attention. Some of the ways people rip off strokes include butting in on conversations or answering questions addressed to others, telling of events or personal accomplishments in a way that makes them seem more important than they actually are, counterfeiting positive strokes (Bruce & Erskine, 1974), or explaining what happened more than once. Many stroke rip-off artists talk on and on without the awareness of whether the other person is interested in listening. In essence they are social schlemiels, and the listener is faced with the recourse of either going away (ignoring) or asking the speaker to stop talking. In other cases the person ripping off strokes may be getting his or her strokes by taking care of other people in a rescuing way or by talking either so loudly or softly that the listener has to increase his or her energy level to avoid hearing or to understand what is being said. In a more subtle way, stroke rip-offs may occur when people begin sentences with "Guess what!" or a Child ego state exclamation followed by a factual statement, such as, "Wow! It's time to begin the meeting." In almost every case the ripping off of strokes involves a discount of the situation or the other person.

People who rip off strokes often appear gregarious and outgoing at first, but once people get to know them they tire quickly of their company. On the surface they look as though they have a lot of Free Child energy, but in essence they are relating as an Adapted Child. Often persons engaged in getting strokes in this way claim to have many acquaintances but report having few enduring friendships. Other people often experience the person ripping off strokes as an energy drain; this is most frequently due to the urgency experienced in getting all their strokes *right now* as if the source might dry up. The

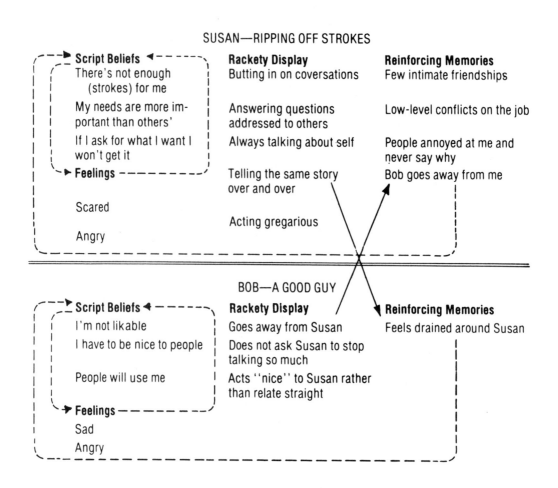

Figure 1
Interlocking Racket System

problem that the person who is ripping off strokes reports is that people become annoyed at him or her and don't state why. Since they are often unaware of their need for strokes and that they are stealing strokes they may continually search for reasons as to why people avoid them (see Figure 1).

At the social level many stroke rip-off artists look as though their basic life position is "I'm OK—You're not-OK" while their psychological position may more accurately be "I'm not-OK—You're OK." Their racket system (Erskine and Zalcman, 1979) often includes the script beliefs, "There's not enough (strokes) to go around; I'll take whatever I can get" or "My needs are more important than others'." The resulting dynamics in social situations are that they attempt to get close to people and, as a result of their demanding to be stroked, push people away.

The person engaged in ripping off strokes often elicits angry responses in others through the mechanism of projecting their own anger onto others. This anger in many clients is related to unmet early childhood stroking needs and an associated fear that his or her stroking needs will never be met. The elicited anger of the other person, interpreted as rejection, then reinforces the belief that there are not enough strokes available or a secondary script belief, "If I ask for what I want I won't get it." The resultant process of stealing strokes is thus reinforced.

A counterpoint to stroke rip-off exists with the person who allows himself or herself to be ripped off. Often the person being ripped off is operating as a "Good Guy" or "Sweetheart" (Harris, 1972) and will continue to stroke the person who is ripping him or her off. Such individuals often discount their own discomfort in the social interaction and later may avoid or blemish the person who was ripping them off. Several clinical examples have revealed a consistent pattern of script beliefs and related behavior: "I'm not likeable" with the supporting belief, "I have to be nice to people" and/or "People will use me." The behavior involves being nice to people, not saying what one is feeling and thinking, then collecting the memory of being ripped off, and avoiding the person who is stealing their attention. Each person ends up with the script reinforced through their interlocking racket systems (Erskine, 1976; Holtby, 1979).

The initial step in therapy for those who rip off strokes is to identify the need for strokes, teach the concept of stroke rip-offs, and work with the person to identify the various behaviors involved in getting strokes. Confronting the actual rip-off behaviors in a caring social setting brings into immediate awareness his or her effect on other people. Specific contracts for behavioral change can be made that emphasize awareness of what is happening in each transaction, taking into account what others are experiencing, and asking for strokes in a straight way.

Further treatment is done affectively and cognitively through disconnecting the rubberband feelings of rejection (Erskine, 1974) and giving up the script beliefs through the process of redecision (Goulding & Goulding, 1978). If necessary, the therapist can provide the setting in which the person can cathect an early age and experience having early unmet stroking needs met.

REFERENCES

Bruce, T., & Erskine, R. (1974). Counterfeit strokes. *Transactional Analysis Journal, 4*(2), 18-19.
Erskine, R. (1974). Therapeutic intervention: Disconnecting rubberbands. *Transactional Analysis Journal, 4*(1), 7-8.
Erskine, R. (1976, October). *Racket analysis: Theoretical perspectives and clinical applications.* Workshop presented at the Midwest Transactional Analysis conference, Minneapolis, Minnesota.
Erskine, R., & Zalcman, M. (1979). The racket system: A model for racket analysis. *Transactional Analysis Journal, 9*, 51-59.
Goulding, M., & Goulding, R. (1978). Redecision: Some examples. *Transactional Analysis Journal, 8*, 132-135.
Harris, A. (1972). Good guys and sweethearts. *Transactional Analysis Journal, 2*(1), 13-18.
Holtby, M. (1979). Interlocking racket systems. *Transactional Analysis Journal, 9*, 131-135.

This article was first published in the Transactional Analysis Journal, *Volume 10, Number 1, January 1980, pp. 74-76.*

Therapeutic Intervention: Disconnecting Rubberbands

Richard G. Erskine

Kupfer and Haimowitz (1971) have described how the "rubberband" (p. 10) is used to relate past feelings to current situations. Past unresolved feelings can remain and affect our current transactions. An extension of the use of rubberbands is an effective way for patients to accept responsibility for their feelings and to change their behavior.

Disconnecting the rubberbands involves the patient in: reexperiencing past feelings that are the same as the current ones; receiving permission and protection to feel and express those feelings that are not expressed in the original situation; taking control of the situation and owning the related not-OK decisions; recognizing how early decisions have and are still affecting life; and finally, making a new OK decision.

A clinical example follows.

Mitch, a 25-year-old male, who has had numerous conflicts with the police and has spent the last two years in prison, entered therapy complaining of having difficulty with authority figures.

In past therapy sessions, Mitch complained that the therapist was operating like a Critical Parent, although group members and the therapist perceived the transactions as coming from the therapist's Adult ego state. Mitch would alternately become angry or depressed on these occasions. He often used the incident as an excuse to leave the group; he also used it as a pretext to overadapt, trying to please the therapist but not working on his problem.

The disconnecting of the rubberband began with Mitch's complaint that he had been depressed all week because of his boss's treatment of him. With the use of the empty chair technique (Perls, 1969), Mitch told his boss about his angry feelings. He tightened his arms across his stomach and drew up his knees until he was in a hunched position.

Therapist: I have a hunch someone is hitting you in the gut. Talk to that person.
Patient (angrily): I don't want you near me. I don't want to have anything to do with you.
Therapist: It's OK to tell him what you feel.
Patient: I'm hurt that you never write to me. You used to pick on me. . . . I hurt because you always hit me. (Mitch then began to cry and beg his father not to hit him. He continued to weep for several minutes.)
Therapist: Tell your father to stop hitting you.
Patient: Don't hit me. I don't want you to hurt me. Don't hit me. Stop it.
Therapist: Tell your father what you want from him.
Patient: I want you to love me and hold me. I want you to include me as part of the family.

Therapist: Tell your father what it means when he hits you.

Patient: When you hit me I feel that I am bad and rotten inside, that I'm not worth loving because I'm so bad.

Therapist: Tell your father how you've been using this all of your life (hooking the patient's Little Professor).

Patient: I'm scared that authorities will hurt me the way you did. I do bad things to get punished.

Therapist: Tell your father what decisions you are now making.

Patient: I'm grown up now, and you can't ever hit me in the stomach again, Dad. I won't be scared and get sick to my stomach when I deal with my boss or others. I am OK and I will not use you as an excuse to be not-OK.

The therapist's prescription to reinforce the new decision: When you have a transaction with an authority figure, take a deep breath and say to yourself, "You're not my Dad. I'm OK, you're OK."

The therapeutic reason for this kind of intervention is that it speeds the patient's differentiation between inappropriate (rubberband) feelings and appropriate (now-related) feelings. The patient is aware that the current feeling is an extension of a past feeling related to a not-OK decision about himself. Reexperiencing those old feelings appears to be a way to get final closure on the event. The awareness of how the old decision has affected his life and a redecision to change is the patient's active taking of responsibility and commitment to change (Erskine, 1973).

REFERENCES

Erskine, R. G. (1973). Six stages of treatment. *Transactional Analysis Journal, 3*(3), 17-18.

Kupfer, D., & Haimowitz, M. (1971). Therapeutic interventions: Part I, rubberbands, now. *Transactional Analysis Journal, 1*(2), 10-16.

Perls, F. (1969). *Gestalt therapy verbatim.* New York: Bantam Books.

This article was originally published in the Transactional Analysis Journal, *Volume 4, Number 1, January 1974, pp. 7-8.*

Transactional Analysis and Family Therapy

Richard G. Erskine

Definition

The family is a group of two or more persons who have a commitment to one another over time and who share resources, responsibility for decisions, values, and goals. It is the unit of persons one "comes home to," regardless of the biological or legal ties, adoption, or marriage. The basis for the life of a family is the communication and interaction that occur between individuals in the family. Clear communication contributes to the family's well-being and growth, while faulty communication is a hazard to the psychological and physiological health of each member of the family.

Transactional analysis is a theory of personality that focuses on communication. This model of personality describes each personality as being composed of three ego states. Each ego state organizes external and internal stimuli in a specific way, resulting in uniquely different communication. The analysis of the transactional patterns that appear using this model provides a tool to understand and to change interpersonal and intrapersonal dynamics that may block effective communication.

The tendency of a person to favor any one ego state as a basis for communication is determined in part by the life script. A script is a life plan decided on in childhood as a way to fit into the family. It is formulated out of what the child hears, experiences, and perceives as possible options.

Transactional analysis provides family members with a cognitive understanding of the dynamics of family scripts, the functions of personality, and transactional patterns. The counseling methodology encourages each person to take responsibility for himself or herself consistent with his or her developmental age, to express the emotions that are often held back or are ineffectively communicated, and to focus on specific behavioral changes that can improve family life.

The work of the transactional analysis therapist is to provide the environment and means whereby persons are free to make meaningful contact with others and to respond to problem solving without preconceived ideas or plans that limit interpretation of the situation and restrict behavior choices.

Historical Development of the Model

Beginnings

Transactional analysis began with the San Francisco Social Psychiatry Seminar in the late 1950s. Eric Berne, a leader of the seminar, was interested in the social aspects of psychiatric problems. He believed that if the client's problem could be resolved at the social level it would lead to more rapid and effective intrapsychic cure. He encouraged his clients to work in a group setting, facing each other in a circle of chairs, and to engage in communication. He focused on the transactions between the people in the group and provided them with an understanding of their behavior and an opportunity to experiment with behaving differently.

Tenets of the Model

In the early 1950s Berne wrote a series of papers on intuition (Berne, 1949, 1952, 1953, 1955, 1957, 1962) and communication wherein he developed a model of personality that provided a structure for understanding an enormous variety of human behavior. The theory was aimed at extracting a simple set of concepts for people at all levels of development based on developmental psychology and Freudian theory.

Basic to this model was Paul Federn's (1952) concept that psychological reality was based on unique and discrete ego states. Eduardo Weiss (1950) also detailed evidence on the existence of ego states. Federn and Weiss both maintained that hypnosis, dreams, and psychosis prove that ego configurations of earlier age levels remain in potential existence throughout life (Dusay, 1971).

These theoretical concepts were supported experimentally in the work of Wilder Penfield (1952), a neurosurgeon who used an electronic probe to stimulate the temporal cortex of epileptic patients. The electrical stimulation awakened in the person not only the memory of past events, but the total reexperiencing of all sensing and feeling associated with past experiences. At the same time, the patient was aware of being on the operating table undergoing a procedure.

Ego states. Drawing from the theoretical work of Federn and Weiss, Berne postulated that in Penfield's patients there was a sense of self (an ego state) that was conscious as an observer and a separate archaic ego state that was reexperienced. He began to realize the similarities between this idea and the observation that many of his clients, who were reporting difficulty in interpersonal relations, were at times relating to people as rational adults and at other times feeling and behaving just the way they had when they were young children; in essence, they were functioning from two different ego states (Berne, 1957).

In his initial model, Berne identified two ego states that had a separate system of feelings related to a set of thoughts and corresponding behaviors. The archaic aspects of the personality became the *Child* ego state, distinguished by relics of beliefs, behavioral patterns, and feelings carried over from childhood. The Child ego state is not just the thoughts, feelings, and behavior patterns that resemble children, but are from childhood. They are *fixations* of an earlier developmental period. Berne called the observant, rational sense of self the *Adult* ego state, composed of thoughts, actions, and feelings that are self-developed responses to the current situation.

In later psychotherapeutic group work, Berne began to realize that people have not only an ego state that is an observer and participant in current reality and an archaic ego state, but also an ego state that feels, thinks, and behaves much like their parents. This introjected or exteropsychic aspect of the personality was described as the *Parent* ego state.

The Parent ego state is not what resembles parental behavior but is an actual historical *incorporation* of the feelings, attitudes, and behavior patterns of one's own parents or other significant parental figures. Each personality has all three aspects of "self," colloquially referred to as Parent, Adult, and Child.

Berne (1961) used the term ego state to describe a state of mind with a coherent system of internal feelings and thoughts and a corresponding system of postures, facial expressions, speech patterns, voice tones, and other external behaviors. The two together, the behaviors and the state of mind, form the active ego state.

It is from these active ego states that people communicate. Sometimes people talk to others from their Parent with all the feelings, attitudes, and expressions that their mother or father used years before; at other times they may react as a little child, perceiving the situation as they did when they were only 5 or 6 years old. They may then switch to the Adult ego state and react to the communication with the emotions, ideas, and behaviors that are situationally and developmentally appropriate and unencumbered with that which is borrowed from parents or a fixation from childhood.

Ego states are not related to the psychoanalytic concepts of id and superego but only with the concept of ego—defined here as the self that is knowable. Each person's identity of self is comprised of all three states of the ego, and transactions with others can come from any one of the three ego states, often without the awareness of which state of the ego is active.

Phenomenologically, the Parent ego state is experienced as a structure for living, a set of values and rules, and is manifested as controlling or nurturing behavior. The Adult

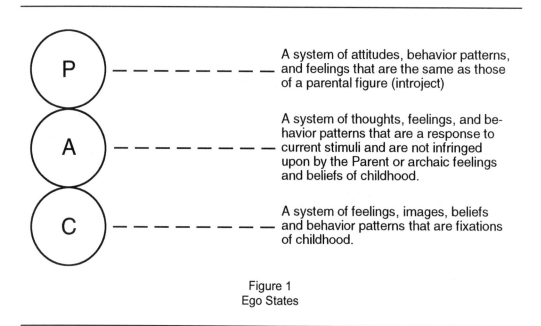

P — — — — — — — — A system of attitudes, behavior patterns, and feelings that are the same as those of a parental figure (introject)

A — — — — — — — — A system of thoughts, feelings, and behavior patterns that are a response to current stimuli and are not infringed upon by the Parent or archaic feelings and beliefs of childhood.

C — — — — — — — — A system of feelings, images, beliefs and behavior patterns that are fixations of childhood.

Figure 1
Ego States

ego state is experienced as the here-and-now integration of perceptions, thoughts, and feelings and is evidenced behaviorally as problem solving appropriate to the person's developmental stage. The Child ego state is experienced as a state of feelings, needs, wants, and fantasies and is manifested as either adapted behavior or spontaneous, natural behaviors from previous developmental periods.

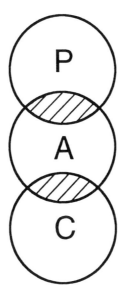

Figure 2
Contaminations

Dysfunctions. Psychological problems emerge when the introjected and/or archaic ideas, images and emotions contaminate the here-and-now perceptions of the Adult ego state. When Adult ego state *contamination* exists, the phenomenological experience of the person is that they are processing current stimuli, accounting for current sensations and feelings, and behaving appropriately to the situation, when, in fact, this is not so. The person is unaware that the introjected ideas and emotions and/or the childhood decisions and feelings are infringing on present perceptions. These contaminations function as a delusion or prejudice in processing current thoughts, feelings, and perceptions. An example of contamination is Bob's statement, "We don't have any problems" (see transcript, transaction #48, for transaction to which this refers). His Parent view that the role of a father was to work hard distorted his ability to process information about his relationships with his wife and children.

Transactions. When two people contact each other the unit of social intercourse is called a *transaction.* Each of us has the potential to transact with another person from one of three ego states.

Complementary transaction

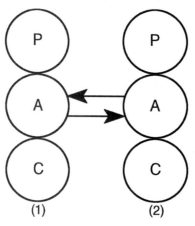

1. Did you take the garbage out?
2. I took it out after dinner.

Crossed transactions

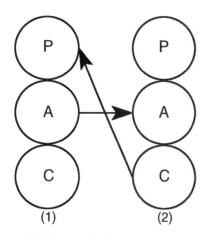

1. Did you take the garbage out?
2. You're always picking on me!

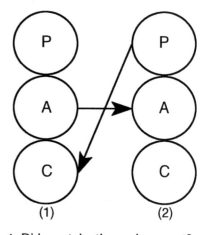

1. Did you take the garbage out?
2. You should have done it yourself.

Figure 3
Transactions

Complementary transactions occur when one addresses an ego state in another person and the response is from the same ego state. As long as transactions are complementary, communication can continue indefinitely with the response of each person serving as the stimulus for the next transaction. When transactions are crossed, that is, a different ego state than that addressed responds, communication stops or the subject changes. The most common crossed transactions involve an Adult-to-Adult stimulus and a Child-to-Parent response or a Parent-to-Child response. Transactional analysis involves analyzing which ego states are used to communicate and to which ego states they are directed and then teaching the client how to choose the most effective way of transacting.

Sometimes a stimulus is directed at more than one ego state, in which case an ulterior transaction exists, as in Jean's communication with her husband where, at the social level, she says, "I would like to go away for a weekend" (transcript #51, 55). Simultaneously, she shrugs her shoulders and laughs, directing a message at the ulterior or psychological level that implies, "I won't get what I want." Bob responds socially with "I have to work in the store" and ulteriorally, "Work is more important than your wants" (transcript #85).

When there is an ulterior message it is the psychological level of communication that determines the outcome of that communication. People often think that their communication is at the social or content level and are unaware of the ulterior level of transaction. In doing family therapy the function of the therapist is to make the ulterior messages explicit, allowing the psychological message to be dealt with openly.

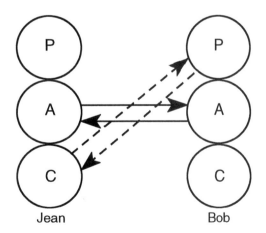

Jean: I would like to go away for a weekend.
   Psychological: I won't get what I want.

Bob: I have to work in the store.
   Psychological: My work is more important than your wants.

Figure 4
Ulterior Transaction

Strokes. A transaction consists of a series of *strokes* or units of recognition. A stroke can be a verbal or nonverbal indication of recognizing another's existence: a hello, a smile, a pat on the back, a letter in the mail. The psychological strokes are an outgrowth of what each person needs in infancy in the form of physical stroking; such stroking is an important component in the survival of all infants. In addition, the way in which an infant is stroked often affects the view that that child will have of the world—gentle, rough, reliable, unpredictable. As children grow they develop preferences for different kinds of strokes, preferences that are generally present throughout life. Sometimes these preferences are based on the kinds of strokes available. For a child who lives in a family in which the predominant kind of strokes is negative, the learned preference may be for negative strokes, resulting in the child acting out, agitating, or being disruptive. Negative strokes are better than none at all and provide at least some stimulation for survival! Besides being positive or negative, strokes are either conditional or unconditional, that is, recognition for specific behaviors or lack of behaviors or recognition for being.

A major focus in family therapy is understanding and, if necessary, changing the stroking patterns of a family. In some families members have to compete for strokes by out-performing each other or by having the greatest need, such as through sickness, accidents, or getting in trouble. In other families, strokes are given only indirectly through a third person, as when mother strokes Billy by telling the neighbors how well he did in school. Some families stroke only through giving objects such as food or gifts; in other families a parent gives strokes only when he has been drinking alcohol or is high on drugs.

In all of these cases what the therapist looks for are patterns of who strokes whom, when, under what conditions, how, and the kinds of strokes exchanged. A family with an enuretic child experienced significant change by giving the child a back rub every night before sleep. This provided an opportunity for the child to get physical strokes, to have 15 minutes alone with one parent, and to have an opportunity to discharge tensions left from the day by talking to that parent.

Games. A specific series of transactions that serves to provide negative strokes and maintain the script is called a *game*. A game is a series of complementary ulterior transactions leading to a well-defined payoff (Berne, 1964). The ulterior or psychological level of these transactions is always out of awareness, while the overt communication is experienced as real and ego syntonic. The underlying attempt in each of these games is to meet some need. For example, a child who habitually plays a game where he ends up getting some form of negative recognition, referred to in Berne's (1964) catalog of games as "Kick Me," is probably attempting to fill a need for strokes and possibly to resolve an earlier developmental need to be accepted in spite of negative behavior.

There are many colloquial names ascribed to the various games to make them easier to identify with and to assist people in being able to smile at their own foibles. Examples of games are, "Now I've Got You, You SOB," "Courtroom," "Why Don't You, Yes But," and "Ain't It Awful."

The family therapist will often identify the dominant family games, look for what need is attempting to be met, and teach the family new ways of asking for and responding to needs so that they can be satisfied without collecting bad feelings in the process and thereby reinforce script beliefs and behaviors.

A way of looking at games is through the social roles of Persecutor, Rescuer, and Victim (Karpman, 1968). When functioning from the limitations of script, people have a tendency to transact socially from one of the three positions. These positions behaviorally either defend against or support the script beliefs. Victims habitually see themselves as helpless in the world and will go in search of Rescuers to help them. Often in the process Victims will stimulate a response in others to persecute as a way of defending against their own sense of helplessness.

An important element in games is the switch in social roles, which leads to the negative payoff. A mother who starts the day giving and giving to her family without taking for herself (Rescuer) may be in tears by nighttime, accusing her family of not loving or appreciating her (Victim). She ends up feeling mistreated and sad, and the family members may end up feeling annoyed or guilty.

Current Status and Other Systems

Script

Much of the current work of transactional analysis focuses on life *script*. Script is a life plan formulated from what one experiences as a child and decisions made under stress. A script limits spontaneity and flexibility in problem solving and in relating to people because the story, including the ending and all the major events, is already written in early childhood. In essence, the script answers the question, "What does a person like me do in a family like this with people like you?"

The script can be established in either of two ways. One, a child may *introject* implicit or explicit messages and behavioral patterns from parents in order to be accepted and loved by them (Steiner, 1971, 1974). For example, mother may say to the child, "You don't need anything" and the child may accept it literally, developing a life plan of denying wants and needs. Or the message can be inferred, as when a boy whose father continually ignored him concluded that father was saying to him, "Don't exist."

A second way in which a script is formed is through the child's *decisions* about life, which are based on perceptions of which options are open. These decisions may be about the child, other people, and the quality of life. When these decisions are made by a person under pressure, they emerge later in life as beliefs that inhibit personal relationships, communication, and problem solving.

These script beliefs begin developing when a child is under pressure from parental programming (Berne, 1972; Steiner, 1974) or from environmental trauma where expressing feelings does not result in needs being met (Erskine, 1980). Through the process of cognitive mediation the child attempts to explain the experiences and the unmet needs through decisions about self, others, and the quality of life. These script beliefs are usually expressed in concrete terms consistent with the thinking levels of which young children are capable (Piaget, 1952).

Mary was extremely quiet and uncommunicative to others about her wants and needs. In therapy she reexperienced having to suppress her joy and enthusiasm for life as a young child living in a home with a bedridden grandmother who spent several years in pain. Mary's noise often awakened the grandmother, so she decided as a young child, "My wants will hurt people." She continued to live out this decision years later with her own husband, children, and friends.

The early script decision (script belief) is described as though it occurs at one particular time in a child's life. It is important to keep in mind that these may occur over a period of time and may be the result of fantasy as well as of an actual occurrence.

To the child, the decisions that are made seem to be the best possible choice in the circumstances to solve the immediate problem. Once adopted, the script beliefs influence what experiences are attended to, how they are interpreted, and whether or not they are regarded as significant by the individual.

The life script is maintained as the person grows older in order not to reexperience the unmet need and the feelings suppressed at the time of script decision and to provide a predictive model of life and interpersonal relationships. Although the script is often personally destructive it does provide psychological homeostasis. Any disruption in this predictive model produces anxiety (Epstein, 1972); therefore, perceptions and experiences will be organized to maintain the script beliefs.

During childhood a whole range of behaviors is tested to elicit strokes while maintaining compatibility with the script beliefs. The child experiments to find which behaviors will elicit responses in others that will confirm what he or she is believing. Parents and other significant figures also influence the child's choice of behaviors through instructions ("Be Good"); prohibitions ("Don't cry"); stroking ("You're so cute when you pout"); attributions ("He's the toughest kid in the neighborhood"), and modeling (Dad's temper tantrum always gets everyone's attention). Eventually the child settles on a specific group of behaviors, including displays of emotion, and uses them repeatedly, especially in situations that may confront the script beliefs.

As a child Jean decided, "I won't get what I want," and learned to laugh rather than feel the discomfort of not getting what she wanted. As an adult, Jean seldom asks for what she wants and, whenever she does ask, covers it with a laugh (see transcript, transaction #55).

Racket System
Script refers to a longitudinal life plan. A way in which the script is lived out day by day is detailed in the "The Racket System" (Erskine & Zalcman, 1979). It describes a one-act scene demonstrating how the script plot is reinforced and how others are manipulated into the roles the script requires. Identifying a client's racket system provides useful guideposts for therapeutic intervention.

The racket system is defined as a self-reinforcing, distorted system of feelings, thoughts, and actions maintained by individuals who are functioning in script. The racket system has three interrelated and interdependent components: the script beliefs and feelings, the rackety display, and the reinforcing experiences.

When needs are not met in life today the script beliefs and related feelings will be stimulated as they were at the time the script was written in early childhood. The person is then likely to engage in behaviors that will verify the script decision, referred to as the *rackety display*. This may include *observable behaviors* (choice of words, sentence patterns, tone of voice, displays of emotion, gestures, and body movements) that are a direct manifestation of the script beliefs and feelings (the intrapsychic process). A person may either act in a way defined by the script beliefs, that is, saying "I don't know" when believing "I'm stupid"; or he or she may act in a way that socially defends against the script beliefs, that is, excelling in school and acquiring numerous degrees.

An individual may also have a physiological reaction in addition to or in place of the overt behaviors. These *reported internal experiences* are the behaviors that are not readily observable but on which the person can give a self-report, such as fluttering in the stomach, muscular tension, headaches, colitis, and all the somatic responses to the script beliefs/feelings. Persons who have many somatic complaints or illnesses frequently believe, "Something is wrong with me," and use the physical symptoms to reinforce the belief.

Rackety display also includes *fantasies* in which the individual imagines behaviors, either his or her own or someone else's, that lend support to the script beliefs. These fantasied behaviors function as effectively in reinforcing script beliefs/feelings and, in some instances, even more effectively than the overt behaviors.

When the other 8- and 9-year-old children were not playing with Karen she imagined them having fun together and laughing at her for not being like them. She used the fantasy to reinforce her beliefs that "I don't belong" and "No one likes me" (see transcript #14).

Any rackety display can result in the collection of *reinforcing experiences*, which are the recall of selected events during a person's lifetime. Reinforcing experiences are a collection of emotional memories of transactions and the reactions, either real or imagined, of other people; recall of internal bodily experiences; or the retained remnants of fantasies, dreams, or hallucinations. Reinforcing experiences serve as a feedback mechanism to reinforce the script beliefs.

Since script beliefs function to maintain psychological homeostasis, only those memories that support the script belief are readily accepted and used as reinforcement. Those memories that negate the script beliefs are often rejected or forgotten since they would challenge the prejudice. They may also be distorted through fantasy to create script-syntonic memories. A memory or response that is dystonic may be negated by switching to another script belief. This is identical to the function of contamination of ego states where the Parent's beliefs or the Child's perceptions interfere with Adult processing of information.

Bob's script beliefs were, "Life is hard and difficult" and "No one understands me." When the therapist suggested that he ease the pressure on himself by picking a date for a weekend alone with his wife, his response was, "Life doesn't work that way, unfortunately. That's too easy" (transcript #89). This maintained his belief about life and indirectly also reinforced that, again, no one understands him.

The following example of the racket system illustrates how the client maintained script through script beliefs/feelings, rackety displays, and reinforcing experiences.

Beginning with the birth of her first sibling, Louise made a decision, based on the care her sick sibling received and her being "pushed off," that she was not important. At this time her mother was under great emotional pressure and was psychologically unavailable while father was frequently away. The early decision, "I'm not important," was reinforced with each successive sibling and in every traumatic home situation where, being oldest, Louise's needs were ignored. Louise reported in therapy that she often experienced her parents' nonverbal attitude as an injunction, "Don't be important." At an early age the client discovered that one solution to the problem of not being important was to take care of others—siblings and parents—which would make it possible for some of her needs to be met.

In adult life this decision was observable in her choice of a helping profession. Her general demeanor was quiet and withdrawn, deferring to others. The social response from others was that she was ignored and often did not get what she wanted, thereby reinforcing her belief that she was not important, was unwanted, and that others were more important. Her affective behavior was one of sadness, with periods of depression and/or severe headaches.

Her fantasy life often centered around the belief that if she were good enough to someone else they would love her and take care of her. To support this belief she also occasionally fantasized ending up alone, poor, and unloved.

The model of the racket system describes how Louise lived out her old script decisions day by day. Within a family context the behavior of other family members is used either to reinforce or to extinguish script beliefs. When a family system is dysfunctional family members are in script and are reinforcing each other.

Interlocking racket system. In a dysfunctional family, awareness of each person's needs and desires is avoided or concealed and family problems are met with rigidity and manipulation. The dynamics of a dysfunctional family are illustrated in the *interlocking racket system* as various family members attempt to live out their scripts.

The model of the interlocking racket system describes how the script of each family member is intricately woven into a family pattern. Each person influences and is influenced by the behavior of others in the family who provide reinforcing experiences that confirm the script beliefs. In family therapy, the therapist will watch for the transactions (or lack of appropriate transactions) that are script reinforcing for someone in the family.

In the example used earlier of Louise, her behavior often consisted of long periods of silence, often without initiating contact with her husband, and spending time alone reading. Louise's husband, Bill, in wanting contact with Louise, would use Louise's behavior as a reinforcing experience to confirm his script belief, "There is something wrong with me." During the periods of Louise's silence Bill would fantasize a variety of things that he might have done wrong to lead Louise to avoid him. In each fantasy he would collect further evidence to support the script belief. He then would defend against the belief by angrily telling his wife and son all that they had done wrong. Louise would then use the memory of Bill's angry criticism to reinforce "I'm not important" and would withdraw, providing further evidence for Bill's script belief. While Louise was at work she would repeatedly remember Bill's criticism of the night before, each memory serving to stimulate her childhood sadness and anger and old script decisions. To repress the old feelings she would work harder to please Bill, anticipating all the things she could do to please him.

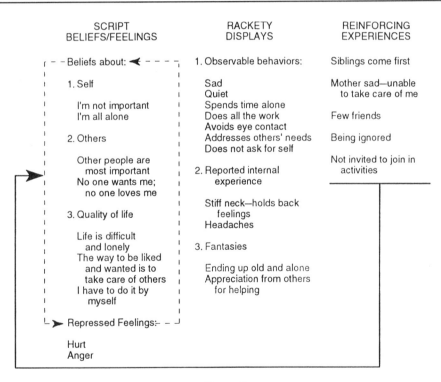

Figure 5
Louise's Racket System

In response to father's criticisms, Ron, who is 10 years old, came to the conclusion as a younger child that "Something is wrong with me." Each angry criticism of Bill would serve to reinforce Ron's script belief. His pattern of behavior included doing poorly in school, breaking neighbors' windows, stealing, and getting into trouble with grown-ups. Each problem behavior proved to him that there was something wrong with him. Bill, in turn, would use Ron's behavior to reinforce that something was wrong with him as a father and would then give his son even more negative strokes. Louise would use Ron's discipline problem to reinforce her beliefs that she was unimportant and could not make an impact on her son to control his behavior. The behaviors of each family member interlocked with the others' racket systems to maintain each person's script.

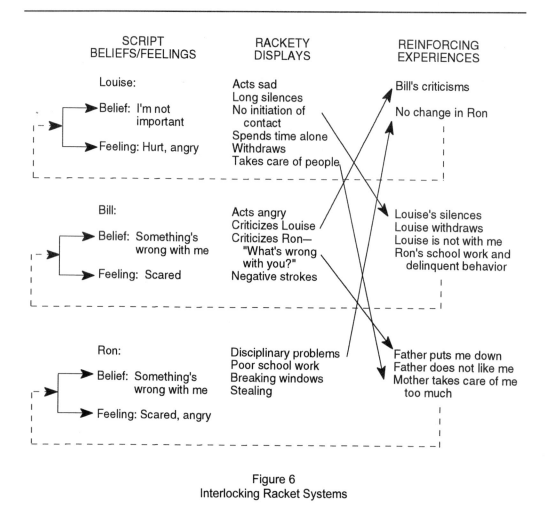

Figure 6
Interlocking Racket Systems

The interlocking racket system demonstrates in operation how each family member supports and helps others to carry out his or her own script decisions in day-to-day life and describes both the interpersonal and intrapersonal dynamics of a dysfunctional family. Each person's script beliefs provide a distorted framework for viewing self, others, and the quality of life. In order to engage in a rackety display individuals must discount other options and frequently will maintain that their behavior is the "natural" or "only" way they can respond. When used in social transactions rackety displays are likely to produce reinforcing experiences that, in turn, are governed by and contribute to the reinforcement of the script beliefs and rackety displays. Thus, each person's racket system is distorted and self-reinforcing through the operation of its three interrelated and interdependent subsystems: script beliefs/feelings, rackety displays, and reinforcing experiences.

Application

Clients for Whom the Model is Especially Effective

Transactional analysis is a psychotherapy that has been used in a broad range of cultures and socioeconomic groups. The client populations to which transactional analysis has been applied have varied from people seeking personal growth to people requiring treatment for severe pathologies. Clinical transactional analysis has been effective in the treatment of schizophrenia (Schiff with Day, 1970), alcoholism (Steiner, 1971), drug addiction (Windes, 1973), and with inmate populations in prisons (Corsover, 1979; Groder, 1977). Elementary and high schools have used transactional analysis to improve student behavior and self-concept (Erskine & Maisenbacher, 1975).

When used in family therapy transactional analysis provides the tools for understanding the interpersonal and individual dynamics and the methodologies for effective intervention (Bader, 1980).

The personality adaptation of each individual will determine to a large degree how they will respond to psychotherapy. Under psychological stress and/or in response to unmet needs people foster personality adaptations to protect against what they experience internally as vulnerable. Some people will present themselves to the world in an intellectualizing way, others will be emotive, and still others will be highly active. In order to be effective with various personality adaptations that can be present in family therapy, the theoretical concepts and methodology of the psychotherapy need to address the cognitive, affective, or behavioral levels of personality adaptations of each person as well as provide a protective means to reach the person where they experience vulnerability.

For the person who presents himself or herself as highly intellectual the therapeutic goal may be the comfortable expression of feelings. However, to press for feelings too quickly may be very threatening. In understanding the client's personality adaptation the therapist would make contact with him or her first at the level he or she was most comfortable, moving towards making behavioral changes and finally dealing with the threat of emotional display after the therapeutic alliance is strong and positive results have been experienced in the therapy.

A particular advantage of transactional analysis in family therapy is that it is flexible to adjust to a wide variety of problem areas clients present. It provides therapeutic options for working with people affectively, behaviorally, and cognitively (Erskine, 1975). Some clients may be resistant to behavioral changes until they first receive cognitive information that explains the problem or their psychodynamics. Others may need to express pent-up emotions before they can process information about their dynamics, and still others may need to change behavior first and then later cognitively process their effect on other family members. Some transactional analysis therapists also include a focus on physical stroking and body constrictions as an important area of therapy (Cassius, 1975; Erskine, 1980).

Goals of Therapeutic Process

The aim of family therapy is to meet the contracts for change that each family makes with the therapist. In most cases the aim of the contract is to create a functional, interdependent family structure. This is accomplished through creating changes in the communication patterns and the interrelationships of family members so that needs are met in a cooperative way. For families who decide not to live together the contract may be to make the separation process nontraumatic and to provide for the optimal welfare of each person involved.

Dependence. Three types of family relationships are identified. The first type is one of dependency where boundaries between individuals or between family roles may be distorted or undefined. For example, one person may function in a problem-solving capacity while the other person may continually focus on personal feelings and needs to the exclusion of others. This symbiotic relationship is dramatically expressed in the hard-working wife and the alcoholic husband. There is often a shift of feelings and responsibility for behavior from one person to the other, exemplified by the statement, "She made me do it." For a symbiotic family the goal in therapy is to help each individual to function independently consistent with his or her developmental level. The aim is for each person to take responsibility for his or her own thoughts, feelings, and behaviors.

Independence. In the process of family therapy independence can be a phase between dependence and a final goal of interdependence. However, some families come to therapy with relationships that are so rigid and independent that they cannot rely on each other for meaningful contact and mutual need fulfillment. The final therapeutic goal for both types of family is the establishment of interdependence.

Interdependence. In a functional, interdependent family there is an acknowledgment that each person has an impact on the other. In order to live comfortably and cooperatively together individual feelings and needs have to be accounted for and responded to in some meaningful way. Interdependence is a combination of the autonomy of independence and the acknowledgment of the responsibility and dependency each person experiences in relation to others with whom he or she is living for the satisfaction of some emotional and physical needs. The aim is to have family members actively ask for and negotiate to get what they want while also learning to give without resentment and hidden "You Owe Me's."

Learning. An early treatment goal in this change process is to teach family members a framework for understanding themselves and a simple language to describe their internal experiences and the dynamics that occur in the family relationships. An additional goal is to teach individuals to identify needs and to make a distinction between thoughts, feelings, and behaviors so that they can develop effective ways of communicating and problem solving. In some families a goal may be for parents to learn about developmental needs of children and to identify ways of meeting those needs, either directly or by helping the child develop internal or other external resources.

Intrapsychic therapy. Once family members have an understanding of their own ego states, transactional patterns, and their effects on others in the family the goal may then be in-depth intrapsychic therapy. This process may include examining, exploring, or reexperiencing early life experiences that have led to present-day problems. In the reexperiencing of old scenes, the goal is to release repressed emotions, identify the decisions that were made at that time, and make redecisions that disconnect the old beliefs and feelings from their current situation (Erskine, 1974; Goulding & Goulding, 1979).

Script redecision work may be useful for adults or older children where script patterns have already been established. This level of therapy may be done in individual or couple sessions or within an ongoing therapy group as well as within the context of the family sessions. For younger children it is often sufficient to provide information, develop options, and give permissions that will lead to a change in script beliefs and enable them to get what they need. In a situation where a 7-year-old girl was in a symbiotic relationship with mother, evidenced by school phobia, the child was frequently given permission by the therapist (and later in therapy by the mother also) to have her own feelings, which may be different from Mom's. The mother was encouraged in the session to talk to the child about what she was feeling and to provide information to the child that she would be home and available at specific after-school hours.

Integration. A final treatment goal is to integrate each individual's personal changes into a healthy family structure. This includes supporting changes in script beliefs, developing options for new behavior patterns, and maintaining family dynamics that allow for joyful, spontaneous, intimate, and creative living.

Client's Responsibility

Transactional analysis is based on a contractual model of therapy in which the client is responsible for identifying personal goals and investing the energy necessary to accomplish those goals. Goals are frequently formulated in clearly defined behavioral terms so that the client can experience success and the active participation in his or her own growth. The contractual model also allows a balancing of power between the therapist and clients so that all are equally responsible for the progress of therapy.

In family therapy clients are asked to take responsibility for being open to confrontation and feedback and to respond to others with their thoughts and feelings honestly and with care for themselves and others.

Members of the family are also asked to take responsibility for their own behavior and how their behavior contributes to the well-being of the family or causes conflict. This is particularly important for parent figures who by their behavior may be contributing to the formation of script in a child. It becomes the parents' responsibility to identify the needs of their children and what they can do to effect the satisfaction of those needs. For example, for the child whose security needs are unsatisfied the therapist may encourage the parents to make more physical contact with the child—holding on their laps, cuddling before bedtime—or to find ways to share more information, like having short talks before going to school each day. They are also taught to recognize the clues in the child that he or she is experiencing this need in order to respond to it effectively. In some situations the parents' responsibility may be to teach children to care for themselves.

The members of the family are also equally responsible for identifying the completion of the contract and either establishing a new contract or terminating the therapy.

Therapist's Role and Function

Resource. The role of the transactional analysis therapist is primarily to provide a resource for the family to help solve its communication difficulties and for each member of the family to resolve his or her intrapsychic problems which contribute to dysfunctionality within the family.

Safety. Often the first task of the therapist is to provide safety for each person. In families where physical violence or sexual abuse exists, protection needs to be established so that each person can express himself or herself freely in the therapy process. This may involve specific contracts with the abusive person that he or she will not engage in such behavior or even the threat of the behavior. In one case where the mother continually inflicted beatings on a 7-year-old girl the therapist assumed a child advocate position and informed the parents that they would be reported to legal authorities if the child was beaten again. Several months later the mother reported to the therapist that the strong child advocate position of the therapist was what she had needed as a child to protect her from her parents, and although she had been angry at the therapist for taking "the kid's side and not mine," she did honor the contract not to hit the child. At first the contract was made out of fear, and after doing some regressive therapy, the contract was from awareness of her daughter's needs for security and affection.

In families that are verbally abusive the therapy needs to work to establish a contract that what is said in the therapy session will not be used in a hurtful way outside. This level of protection to be free to express what one is thinking and feeling is necessary before the therapist can begin to work with the family on meaningful contact and any individual therapy.

Contact. An important early role of the therapist is to make contact with each family member and then to use the contact between each person and the therapist to open communication between family members. This is often done early in therapy by having the family members talk about themselves and by not focusing on the identified "problem" person. When the focus is on the family dynamics, family members have to communicate with each other and can no longer use the "problem" person as a refuge from relating to each other.

Contract. It is the responsibility of the therapist to have clear contracts as to his or her role in the therapy process. This includes a clear statement of involvement in solving the dynamic problems of the family as well as the type of investment in working individually with each person. This may begin with a role of helping participants clarify what they want from the therapy. Often families come for therapy out of desperation or by referral and have very little idea of what possibilities for change lie ahead. Other times members of the family come reluctantly because they were brought by someone else. The therapist needs to establish a straightforward relationship with each family member and to help each person identify the changes he or she wants.

In addition to the therapy contracts the therapist is responsible for clear administrative contracts regarding appointment procedures, fees, availability in crisis situations, and other procedural matters related to the therapy.

Termination. An important function of the therapist is to help families determine when they have gotten the maximum from the therapy and to plan a goal for termination. This may include getting a commitment from each member that he or she will not quit before the specified therapy work is finished.

Skills. The responsibility in the ongoing work of the therapist is to use the training and skills in opening the communication process within the family and in providing direct feedback so that family members can step out of their internal frame of reference and see themselves from a new perspective. Since a transactional analysis approach to family therapy often involves a great deal of investment on the part of the therapist in the dynamics of the family, the responsibility of the therapist includes a commitment to seek supervision and/or peer feedback on the therapy approach and the nature of the therapist's involvement in the therapy process.

Primary Techniques Used in the Treatment Process

The primary techniques in the transactional analysis approach to family therapy vary with the stage of family therapy. Ruth McClendon (1977) has identified three stages of therapeutic work with a family. The first stage involves identifying the dynamics of how the whole family relates. The second stage consists of therapy with each individual, and the third stage is a reintegration of the whole family with a focus on creating healthy family dynamics.

In the initial stage the therapist encourages family members to talk about the family, why they came to therapy, and the goal they wish to accomplish. The object of this stage is for the therapist and the family to gain an understanding of the transactional dynamics that make life within the family uncomfortable for some members. For the therapist this is accomplished by taking these observations of the behavior of each family member and relating it to the theories of ego states, the concepts of transactions, and the dynamics of interlocking scripts to develop hypotheses in formulating specific treatment interventions. A premise of the transactional analysis approach to therapy is that awareness is an important first step and support for change. In the early process of family therapy many of the techniques are aimed at increasing the family members' awareness of the problems and options for change.

Having gathered an essential amount of information, each family member may develop a contract with the therapist for what he or wants to accomplish. Change for any person is dependent on the goals that person sets and on his or her willingness to make and follow through on decisions necessary to accomplish the goals. Contracts may be for generalized changes or for specific, observable behavioral changes.

As some members begin to initiate changes the therapist needs to be particularly aware of how other family members react to these changes and the subtle invitations back to the homeostasis of the old structure. At this point it may be important for the therapist to share information about why people do what they do, pointing out transactional patterns and how communication can be more effective and, specifically, about the racket systems of each individual and how they connect with each other, forming the structure of the family.

Stage One: The family dynamics. During this first stage of therapy the focus of the interventions is on the stroking patterns and transactions of the whole family and not specifically with the "problem member." This is intended to get each family member involved in identifying his or her respective role in the dynamics of the *family's* problem.

Therapeutic operations. In the process of collecting information and effecting change the therapist makes use of several therapeutic operations (Berne, 1966). *Interrogation* involves the gathering of information from each member in the family. This may be done by asking questions about how each one experiences himself or herself and transactions within the family or by having the family discuss among themselves how they handled a particular situation (see beginning of the transcript and transactions #116, 130, 139, 177b). *Specification* is a statement or question designed to elicit more detailed information and to provide the family with certain sets of information that may be significant. The therapist may make comments that describe the dynamics among family members, such as, "When father talks, mother crosses her arms and legs and Susan looks the other way." Specification may also involve questioning other family members in order to verify information about one member's perceptions or beliefs (#73, 98, 120, 128). *Explanation* is the sharing of information with either the whole family or an individual regarding his or her behavior and how it may be affecting others in the family. This usually involves some teaching about transactional analysis concepts. Examples are used that have already occurred in the therapy to explain ego states, crossed or ulterior transactions, or games. Together with the clients, the therapist will explore options for behaving differently. Homework assignments, which may include popular reading on transactional analysis (Babcock & Keepers, 1976; Harris, 1967; James & Jongeward, 1971) may be given to increase a person's understanding (#56a, 78, 132, 177, 183). *Illustration* is the therapist's use of a story or metaphor that describes the family dynamics or change possibilities. It is used particularly effectively with young children or where members of the family are resistant to explanation (#92). *Direction* is a statement or permission by the therapist that guides individuals to behavior that they are not initiating on their own. It should only be used after a good therapeutic relationship is established (#56b, 107, 143, 164). *Confrontation* is a statement or question used by the therapist to bring into the client's awareness a discrepancy in his or her perceptions and behaviors or between beliefs and actual events. Confrontation can be of two types: (1) for awareness, so the person gains greater insight into his or her discrepancies, which may lay the groundwork for later change (#52, 80, 82, 96, 105); or (2) to effect immediate behavioral change (#86, 90, 94, 118, 154). Family therapy involves a continual balance between confrontation and support—alternately intervening into the dynamics and supporting each individual in his or her change process.

Specific interventions. There is a wide range of specific interventions that the transactional analysis therapist may use. These may include having each speaker state the psychological level of communication overtly, as in the expression of expectations and resentments.

Once resentments are expressed the therapist may have the person contract not to bring them up again, particularly if resentments are used either to distance or punish another or to reinforce internally the script beliefs. The therapist will usually interrupt blaming anger such as, "You never . . ." and direct the person to express the anger in a problem-solving way, such as, "I want. . . ." (#148).

The therapeutic procedures are aimed at making explicit what is implicit through identifying how the family members are adapting or not adapting to each other and the possible advantages and disadvantages (#177a, 183). The assumptions of one member may not be known by another. When one member is expressing what he or she is thinking and feeling the therapist will encourage other family members to respond with their internal response.

Much of the work involves showing people how to ask directly for what they want. This may involve explaining about the need for physical and unconditional strokes and teaching people to be sensitive to others' stroking needs. Initial work with stroking problems usually begins by directing people to look at the person to whom they are talking and to talk directly to that person rather than about him or her to someone else. The therapist may also direct the person to express the appreciations that are unexpressed. When appreciations are not stated openly often only the negative thoughts and feelings about the other get communicated. This is a beginning step in changing a negative stroke or nonstroking family pattern to a positive pattern.

Another approach may involve having people specify their different frames of reference. For example, when someone in the family says he or she wants another member to be close, the therapist may ask the person to describe specifically what "close" means so that others will know exactly what is wanted.

Stage Two: Therapy with each individual. Many of the approaches used in the initial stage of therapy are used in the second stage except that the focus of the second stage is on individual intrapsychic and script dynamics. In this intrapersonal stage the therapist may do individual work with each person within the context of the family, may work with one person in extensive individual therapy, may have another member attend a therapy group, or work conjointly with the couple. The division between stages is not discrete but is thought of by the therapist primarily for treatment planning. In practice there is some shuttling back and forth between stages one and two. In stage two work, as one family member makes a change it may reveal family dynamics that had not emerged earlier, and the therapist may again focus on the whole family.

Racket system therapy. In working with each individual, any therapeutic intervention that interrupts the flow in the racket system will be an effective step in the changing of script and therefore the family dynamics. Contracts to change the overt behavior related to the rackety display will most likely result in different social responses from other family members, hence a change in either one's own or someone else's reinforcing memories.

Even when overt behaviors are changed the racket system may be maintained by imagining script-related behaviors and collecting reinforcing memories as a result of fantasy. For some clients it is important, therefore, for the therapist to check if the script is being lived out in fantasy. This is often apparent in dreams. One man maintained continual anger and a belief in rejection by imagining his wife having sex with each man she met. When he changed his fantasies by intentionally creating images of building a new house he related to his wife with much less anger and more joy.

In therapy the somatic level of the rackety display can be dealt with through techniques designed to change the body or physiological level of script. Such approaches may include deep muscle massage, biofeedback, bioenergetics, meditation and yoga, or physical exercise such as expressive dancing.

Reinforcing experiences will no longer have an effective role in maintaining the system when people live in the "here and now" and do not dwell on old memories or fantasied memories of events that are yet to come. A specific therapeutic intervention may involve the confrontation of discrepancies between what the client remembers and what actually occurred and the meaning of what occurred, as well as what was anticipated to happen in the future.

The script beliefs themselves can be challenged directly, sometimes through a question such as, "Is this belief really true in your life today?" This frequently produces the insight that he or she is operating from old perceptions or misconceptions and has been living life based on script beliefs that originated in early childhood. For some clients the only thing needed at this point is an invitation to drop the script beliefs and to live with an awareness of other possible options that are available.

Where trauma has played a significant part in forming the script, clients have made major changes by focusing on the unexpressed affect that was present and suppressed at the time of script decision. The release of repressed emotion through cathecting to an early age and the expression of primal feelings often leads to a redecision about one's self, others, or life (Erskine, 1974; Goulding & Goulding, 1979).

The therapeutic focus may then become cognitive and/or behavioral as the person decides to change his or her script beliefs. The racket system concepts may be taught to clients so they have a conceptual tool for understanding how they have maintained script, and contracts for new behavior may be negotiated to support their decision to change their beliefs.

However the therapist decides to intervene—at the level of script beliefs, the repressed script feelings, the various rackety displays, or the reinforcing experiences—any change that stops the flow in the system can stop the script. The more aspects of the racket system on which the therapist focuses, thereby dealing with the behavioral, cognitive, and affective levels, the greater the probability that the client will create functional and healthy family dynamics.

Stage Three: Developing a functional family. The final stage of family therapy is a reintegration process aimed at developing a family structure in which each person will have needs met and live in supportive harmony that will provide for maximum personal development of each family member.

The therapist may make use of the techniques of direction, explanation, or illustration to guide a family in developing interdependence. This is the acknowledgment that each person has an impact on the other, and in order to live comfortably and cooperatively together, individual feelings and needs have to be accounted for and responded to in some effective way. In this stage family members actively ask for and negotiate to get what they each want while also learning to give freely.

Case Example

Mrs. Brown initially made an appointment by phone stating the school psychologist had referred the 8-year-old adopted daughter, Karen, and the family for therapy. Karen was doing poorly in school, was not paying attention in class, and had no friends among the other school children and in the neighborhood. The appointment had to be rearranged three different times because father was unable to find time to get away from the store he owns.

The initial session began with the therapist asking the members of the family to introduce themselves and to state why they had come for family therapy. The family consisted of the father, Bob, age 36, and mother, Jean, age 33, who has been married to Bob for 10½ years. There are four children: Roberta, the 15-year-old daughter by the father's first marriage, who lived with her mother after the parents' separation from age 3 to 8 and then came to live with Jean and Bob, who report that they took her because her mother was neglecting her. Karen, 8 years, is a child Jean and Bob adopted when she was 2 years old after they had been married four years and were unsuccessful in having a child of their own. They then had two daughters, Denise, 4, and Tina, 14 months, who are at home all day with mother.

Father described the problem as Jean and the two older children not getting along and that he was being called at work by Jean who was always upset with the children. Roberta reported that there really were no problems in the family except that her stepmother always bossed her around, but that that wasn't much of a problem. During this time mother held the two youngest children, attempting to entertain them both. In order to free mother to talk the therapist invited four-year-old Denise to play with crayons and paper. Mother described the family problem with laughter, as an overwhelming one, and with two older children not cooperating. She said that Karen often would not talk. When Karen was asked why she had come to family therapy she answered, "I don't know." Several additional questions elicited the same response. A large portion of this session was spent in having the family talk among themselves about what they wanted to accomplish by coming for family therapy. Bob, Jean, and Roberta discussed chores not being accomplished while Karen remained quiet and uninvolved in the conversation. The therapist then asked the two adults to develop a contract that would establish the goal of this therapy session as well as forthcoming therapy. Bob and Jean set an overall contract to lessen the stress in the family and to enjoy being together. They each agreed to do whatever personal therapy was needed. Although this aspect of the contract seemed to be an adaptation to the therapist on their part, the therapist accepted it as a tentative statement of willingness. Both parents then stated that their goal for this session was for the therapist to work directly with Karen to resolve the problems she was having.

Transcript of Family Therapy Session

The therapist addressed the mother:

Therapist: When you and I first talked on the phone you told me that Karen was having problems in school and that's why you wanted family therapy. Will you tell me more about that? Transaction #1

Mother: Well, the teachers and school psychologist say she daydreams in school all day and that she doesn't play with or get along with the other kids. She does the same thing after school—she won't play with anyone, except she bothers her sister Roberta while she's doing her homework. #2

Therapist: (turns to Karen) Will you tell me what you think about what your mother has just said? #3

Karen (8 years): I don't know. #4

Therapist: If I really listen to you . . . and if you really think about school, what do you feel when you're there? #5

Karen: The kids just don't want to play with me . . . just leave me alone. They don't like me that much. #6

Therapist: And what do you do? #7

Karen: I just stay away from them. #8

Therapist: And what do they do? #9

Karen: They just ignore me and take other kids to play with. #10

Therapist: And what do you do when they play with someone else? #11

Karen: I go away from them. (pause) And I keep thinking about them and how they all like each other and not me. #12

Therapist: And what else? #13

Karen: I think about them having fun playing together and laughing at me for not being like them. #14

Therapist: What do you feel inside then? #15

Karen: I feel hurt. #16

Therapist: And then? (long pause) #17

Karen: Roberta pushes me out of her room too. (Begins to tear, but no audible cry) #18

Therapist: And what do you feel? #19

Karen: I don't belong with her either. #20

Therapist: Is that like with the other kids? #21

Karen: I don't know. #22

Therapist: (softly) Well, your tears look like they know. What do you feel? #23

Karen: I just don't belong—I just go away from them. #24

Therapist: And what do you feel inside when you believe you don't belong? #25

Karen: Well, I usually go upstairs and cry or something. #26

Mother: (to therapist) She usually gets in a bad mood, then Roberta gets upset 'cause she pesters her, then I get upset 'cause there's more for me to do, then Dad gets upset because I don't have things ready the way he wants them, then we're all in a bad mood all night. #27

Therapist: (to Karen) Would you like me to explain how this problem works so you can change it? #28

Karen: (nods, yes) #29

Therapist: Come over here to this pad of paper and I'll draw a little diagram to show you what I think is happening. (Both go to a large pad on the floor) What do you say to yourself when you think of the kids? #30

Karen: There's no one who likes me. #31

Therapist: So one of the things you believe is that "no one likes me?" (Karen nods) And what do you feel when you believe this? #32

Karen: I'm in a bad mood. #33

Therapist: What does that mean? (pause) Is a bad mood like feeling mad or sad or scared? #34

Karen: I don't know—I think I'm sad. Sometimes when I come home I don't want to do anything. #35

Therapist: Is that when you go to Roberta's room? #36

Karen: Yes, but she tells me to get out. #37

Therapist: And then what do you feel? (while drawing the racket system) #38

Karen: That I don't belong anywhere. #39

Therapist: And then what do you do? #40

Karen: Mom tells me to do something but I just go watch TV or say the opposite of anything anyone says to me, but mostly I just watch TV. #41

Therapist: And what do you feel inside? #42

Karen: I'm sad—'cause the only reason she wants me is to boss me around. #43

Therapist: And what do you think about then? #44

Karen: No one likes me (begins to cry hard). #45

Therapist: And what else? #46

Karen: I don't belong in this family. #47

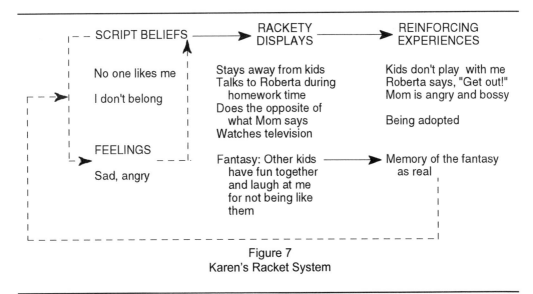

Figure 7
Karen's Racket System

The therapist explains each item of the racket system to Karen and continually checks for her understanding of each element and how they fit together.

After explaining the racket system the therapist asked Karen what she wanted to change and together they identified several behaviors that Karen made a contract to do differently and to report on the following week. These behavioral change contracts were more specific than the general overall contract at the beginning of the therapy. At one point Karen said that she did not know how to get attention from her sister, so the therapist worked with Karen and Roberta to arrange ways to spend time together. Roberta made a contract to spend 20 minutes of play time with Karen each day.

The therapist then worked with Bob regarding his lack of contact with each of the children in the family. He explained the importance of physical stroking as a psychological message of security to children and supported Karen in asking Bob to hold her. Four-year-old Denise also curled up in father's lap while Jean continued to hold the sleeping 14-month-old, Tina. The session ended with Jean and Bob agreeing to read *Born to Win* (James & Jongeward, 1971) before the next session.

In the initial session just described the therapist worked with the identified "problem" member of the family in regard to her internal beliefs and feelings related to not belonging, resulting in the relationship problems at school and at home. Change in the family dynamics was initiated by encouraging immediate changes in Karen's transactional and stroking patterns with Roberta and with father and by facilitating Karen's receiving direct information from her parents about their wanting to adopt her and that she belongs in the family.

In the second session Karen reported that she and Roberta were spending time together and that she had brought a friend home from school one day. Jean interrupted to add that on Sunday Karen was back in the old pattern but that the rest of the time there had been a definite improvement.

Father: You are all good kids—you won't grow up drinking and smoking dope. (To therapist) We don't have much problems. Just the problem that's solved with Karen and friends and school. We are the kind of family they put on TV. (To the kids) You are all working well now. #48

Mother: (To Bob) But it's not working. (To therapist) He's just away all day and doesn't see it. I am involved with the problems, and as great as the girls are, we have a lot of problems. #49

Therapist: Talk directly to Bob. #50

Mother: You're never home to see—I have to handle it all. You're never really involved. (Turns to therapist) He won't even go away with me (laughs). #51

Therapist: In your laughter, Jean, there seems to be a lot of pain behind it. #52

Mother: I'm dead serious, though. He won't take me away even for one day. #53

Therapist: Look at Bob and tell him what you want. #54

Mother: I have—he knows. I'm very serious. I would like to go away—without the kids, though (laughs). #55

Therapist: Stop there for a moment. That's a family pattern—"He knows," "They know" (a dynamic that occurred frequently in the first session). Will you assume each time that the other person does not know? Every time that you use "He knows" and tell it to me, it is a distancing process. #56a Will you start over again and assume he doesn't know and tell him this time so he really hears you? #56b

Mother: You promised me (laughs) that you would take me (laughs) away for a weekend without the kids (laughs). (Long pause) I still want to go! (said seriously) #57

Father: Yes, I promised. #58

Mother: . . . and I still want to go (pleadingly). #59

Father: Yes, I did (curtly). #60

Mother: . . . without the kids. #61

Father: Yes, I will (5-second pause) . . . in due time. #62

Karen: Where are you going to put us? #63

Mother: (simultaneously with Bob) I don't care! (angrily) #64

Father: (simultaneously with Jean) In a home. #65

Mother: I really don't care! (angrily) #66

Roberta (15 years): I want to know what due time is. #67

Mother: This summer! That's what I call due time. (Date of session is early May) (crying) I give only till this summer. #68

Therapist: What do you mean, Bob, by "due time?" #69

Father: I will say within the calendar year. #70

Roberta: (Gasps for breath) (Long pause) #71

Mother: (Looks down, then up with a smile) #72

Therapist: Jean, right now I suspect you are angry inside and are covering it up with a big smile. Are you? #73

Mother: I'm really not angry. I just know that if we don't go in the summer, we don't go. (Pause) So if we don't go by the end of summer, I know I'm not going—and so does he. (Turns to Bob) Right? #74

Father: Not necessarily. #75

Mother: Yes! (angry tone) That's how it is. #76

Father: OK. That's your opinion . . . you're entitled to it. (Pause) #77

Therapist: If you continue like this, what will happen is that you will get further and further away from each other. #78

Mother: We have been at it (laughs) a long time. (Laughs) This is just a continuation. #79

Therapist: And what I observe you doing right now, Jean, is to laugh and shrug your shoulders. The implication is that there will be no change. #80

Father: (to therapist) She is entitled to her opinion. I don't want to sit her and stamp on her and say "Shut up." #81

Therapist: No, but you can give her a date. #82

Father: Oh, well. . . . (Roberta and Karen pull together on the couch) #83

Mother: You could give me . . . #84

Father: . . . no offense, but that's easy for you to say, but not easy for me to pick a date. Impossible for me to pick a date, because I have people that work for me. I have schedules. I have a manager that's out. I work many days I'm not supposed to. Because when you are the guy that owns the joint you are the last guy on the list. You are meaner and lousier and worse and harder on yourself that on *any* of all the other people that work for you! #85

Therapist: It doesn't have to be that way. #86

Father: (pause) Well, I have to agree with you on that. Which is one of the reasons I would like to change my business, but . . . #87

Therapist: One way to be easier on yourself is to pick a date to be with your wife. And then you make it happen. #88

Father: (pause) Life doesn't work that way, unfortunately. That's too easy. #89

Therapist: I think that *you* could make it work that way. #90

Father: It could be, I guess . . . but then, again, I know it's hard for you to understand. Sometimes it . . . ah . . . you just can't. #91

Therapist: I've been in a similar position in my work. The change came for me when I made a decision and stuck to it. #92

Father: You can't . . . you're supposed to . . . ah . . . ah . . . keep to the work. I mean, I wanted to just do all the things around the house this week. Things that have waited a long time. It just happened that somebody else had to go on vacation, now, cause they were in the dumps. So I said, "OK" and I stayed and I worked 14 days in a row for him. #93

Therapist: It does not have to be that way. You could say "No" and arrange the way you run the store differently. #94

Father: No, it could cost me.. . . #95

Therapist: Yes; and are you willing to pay for it in the relationship with your wife? #96

Father: I've gotten to a conclusion that the retail business . . . I don't know anybody in business that's happily married or has a happy family relationship with their kids. What I'm trying to do is to work to . . . #97

Therapist: (interrupting) Bob, do you want to go on a weekend with Jean? #98

Father: Oh, I'd love to, so long as she . . . ah . . . ah . . . don't . . . ah . . . ah . . . (long pause) #99

Therapist: My impression is that you don't want to go. #100

Mother: Mine too. #101

Father: No, that's not true. #102

Therapist: You've given excuse after excuse. #103

Father: Not true, not true, no. If you are trying to pin me down and are talking about this summer I won't say yes. I don't know. Probably. We might be able to . . . then again we might not. I have this . . . ah . . . my problem . . . I have . . . ah . . . ah . . . priorities. I always feel the kids first and Jean and I second. You see, and if I have 3 days I really want all of us to go someplace. Which is entirely opposite to what she wants to do. What she wants to do is to get the hell away from them. And I don't blame her, but . . . #104

Therapist: Will you consider that Jean wants to be with *you*? (said very softly) There is a big difference between wanting to be alone with you and getting away from the kids. (Long pause) (To Jean) Say what you are thinking, Jean. #105

Mother: (laughs) I'm thinking that he (laughs) would never think of that (laughs). That's what I'm thinking (laughs). #106

Therapist: Then you need to talk to him so he knows from you. #107

Mother: He knows. I would like to be away with him . . . and without the kids; that would be a second bonus. #108

Therapist: Tell *him*. #109

Roberta: Come on, Mom. Tell him. #110

Mother: (Laughs) Oh, . . . (Bob interrupts Jean and to therapist says) #111

Father: In reality we don't have that many problems. When we take the disagreements about the kids . . . how to raise the kids . . . we don't have any problems together. #112

Roberta: When was the last time you were together, Daddy? #113

Mother: We don't. We don't ever go away together. We are never without the children! It never happens! #114

Father: I don't know . . . we go to the movies occasionally. #115

Therapist: (to Jean) What are you feeling when you say that? #116

Mother: Resentment. I resent it. I resent it (laughs). (Long pause) #117

Therapist: Last week you talked about Karen not talking when she had a problem. My impression is that you also don't talk about what is really significant. #118

Mother: I do . . . but I'm put off so much. I'm usually understanding about being put off, because I know what his priorities are. #119

Therapist: And what are yours? #120

Mother: Mine get mixed. I really can't say to him we should go away for a weekend and spend $500 when I know somebody might need braces or something. So I'm in conflict with myself and I know that. The kids come first. They are more important. However, if it's them going away for a weekend or me going away for a weekend then I would take the priority. I'm not that totally screwed up (said with disgust.) (Long pause) #121

Therapist: (to Jean) I think that you, for a long time, have taken on a pattern of adapting all the time. You don't say clearly what you want. You laugh off your requests. Then I imagine you resent not having your requests fulfilled and the resentment comes out in picky little fights, the content of which is not significant. #122

Father: Hey, let's give that a hand (laughs and claps hands to applaud). #123

Mother: (to Bob) The content is not always insignificant either. That's why I'm angry. I'm a very fair person and if I'm angry and looking for a fight I *will* find something appropriate. I don't do it without cause. #124

Therapist: (to Jean) And is the cause in part from the stored up anger? #125

Mother: Yes (begins to cry).

Therapist: And it seems that you get reasonable to cover up your sadness and anger. #126a (Pause) I suspect that you did the same as a young child. #126b (Jean nods, yes.) My observation of the way you perpetuate the problem is that you are not straight and clear with what you want from Robert—clear all the way to the point of making it happen. The net result is that you are hurt and angry about not getting what you want. You used the term resentment—that resentment will seep into your relationship in lots of other places. #126c

Mother: Yea, it shows up over little arguments that could be quick to solve in other ways—but that's a way to let it out. #127

Therapist: How else? #128

Mother: In our affection—I'm not turned on (long pause). #129

Therapist: (to Jean) What are you thinking? #130

Mother: I'm trying to remember when it started. #131

Therapist: Jean, the starting with Bob is probably so small that there is no place to pinpoint it. And I suspect it's a pattern that you did before—as a child—of adapting to please. #132

Mother: I'm tired of it. #133

Therapist: Do you know what the end of this scenario is like? How it progresses from here? #134

Karen: Yea, I do (sounding scared). #135

Father: Yea. The kids all get married and move away and I'll retire and her and I will go to Europe. #136

Mother: We'll get divorced! #137

Father: Take your pick. #138

Karen: No! What about us kids? #139

Mother: It's a 50-50 chance (laughs). #140

Therapist: (To Roberta, Karen, and Denise, who are cuddled together on the couch between mother and father and are whispering) Say it out loud, girls. #141

Roberta: We didn't say anything. #142

Therapist: I think what you said must be important. Say it out loud. #143

Roberta: What I said was that it (crying) could come a lot sooner than before any of us could get married. That's one thing I don't need. #144

Karen: Where will we go? #145

Therapist: (to Jean) Say it out loud. #146

Mother: (to Bob) What I'm saying is that if we don't have any kind of relationship together, if the kids are here or not, when they go we two have nothing. (Loudly) When they go you and I will have NOTHING! #147

Therapist: (to Jean) And what I want . . . #148

Mother: I want to have something NOW. #149

Father: (to therapist) I love this lady. I've been married to her for 10 years and I'll love her 20 years from now. #150

Mother: If I'm still around. #151

Roberta: Oh, wow! #152

Father: Stop trying to scare me. #153

Therapist: Bob, Jean is telling you she wants a change. She is changing and growing. She wants a relationship with you. #154

Father: If she is changing then she will have to deal with the change, and I will then make up my mind if I will stand for the change or not stand for the change. #155

Therapist: (to Bob) Who is that talking now? #156

Father: It's me. #157

Therapist: Who else would talk that way with those kinds of words and that tone? #158

Father: I suppose my father would. (Pause) Is that my Parent ego state or whatever? #159

Therapist: I think so. I suspect you spend a lot of time relating to Jean the way your father related to you. #160

Mother: (to Bob) For the past 10 years I've been willing not to take the time with you. I've been willing to give up the time. The only thing that's changed is that I'm no longer willing to give up the time because right now the most important thing to me, now, is time with you. (Starts to cry and holds back) #161

Therapist: Let it go, Jean. You don't need to hold back. #162

Karen: Let it out, Mom. (Jean cries for about 1½ minutes) #163

Therapist: Come back and continue talking to Bob. It is important that you carry all the way through on what you want. #164

Mother: No, there is nothing worth saying. #165

Therapist: And what happens when you hold it in? #166

Roberta: She is mad at 3:00 in the afternoon and nobody knows why. #167

Therapist: You do. #168

Roberta: I know it's not us kids. Me, just because I didn't put the vacuum away or left the mayonnaise jar out. But, sometimes I think it's my fault. #169

Mother: Sometimes it is your fault. #170

Roberta: I can tell. If you stop being mad in less than half an hour it was probably my fault. If you're still mad 3 days later, it's not us—it's you and him. #171

Therapist: Are you two willing to look at the dynamics going on between you? #172

Jean's Social Message
Adult to Adult:
"I'd like to go away."

Bob's Social Response
Adult to Adult:
"I have to work at the store."

Jean's Psychological Message
Child to Parent:
"I won't get what I want."

Bob's Psychological Message
Parent to Child:
"Work is more important
than your wants."

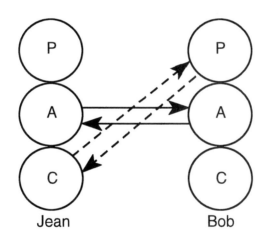

Jean   Bob

Figure 8
Jean's and Bob's Transaction

Father: Yes. #173

Jean: OK; 'cause I've got to figure out what goes wrong. #174

Therapist: Did you begin to read *Born to Win*? Did you understand the basic ideas? #175

Father and Mother: (shake their heads, yes.) #176

Therapist: Both of you transact from what appears on the surface to be Adult—that is, logical communication. (Therapist draws diagram on pad of paper) Jean, you say, "I would like to go away for a weekend," and Bob responds with, "I have to work in the store." I think that the problem in your communication is at the psychological level where your Child ego state sends a message, "I won't get what I want" to Bob's Parent, and Bob responds with a psychological message from his Parent ego state, something like, "Work is more important than your wants." #177a Bob, does that seem right to you? #177b

Father: (Long pause) That's how my father treated me. #178

Therapist: OK, let's assume for now that that is the psychological response you send back to Jean from your Parent whenever she asks for something. Then you (to Jean) use the message to feel . . . #179

Mother: Hurt and angry. #180

Therapist: . . . and then that is your payoff. And then you probably confirm your Child's position, "I won't get what I want," and you wind up feeling victimized again. #181

Mother: Yea, that happens all the time. #182

Therapist: I think it happens because you send a psychological message when you shrug your shoulders or laugh or smile, the few times when you do ask for what you want. #183

In the second session it became apparent that part of Karen's anxiety about not belonging in the family and believing no one likes her is related to the problems between mother and father, which father had been denying and mother had been displaying indirectly in her anger and bossiness with the children. Until this problem is brought into the open and resolved there may not be adequate resolution of Karen's beliefs and fears. The result of this session was that mother decided to join a women's group to gain support for her continued growth, and both parents decided to work on their relationship as a couple before continuing work as a family.

As we attempted to resolve Bob's resistance to spending time with Jean alone it became apparent that Bob was working himself harder and harder, following a script pattern learned from his father to work himself to death. This became evident as Bob talked about his diminishing sexual interest and his concern that if he and Jean went away together for a weekend his decreased sexual interest would be obvious to both of them and could no longer be excused by the children and work.

Further therapy included teaching Bob about ego states and script and how he had incorporated a pattern of working hard and keeping distant from the family that had been his father's. In regressive work with Bob's Child ego state he recalled an early childhood scene where, in order to get father's approval, he decided to be just like father, even if it killed him. In crying out the repressed emotions of his childhood Bob made a redecision to live, not to have to work hard like his father, and made an Adult commitment to spend more time with his wife and children and to hire an assistant to help manage the store.

Jean did more work on her Child being dependent, a pattern that she had learned in her family of origin, and on her beliefs of not belonging and "I won't get what I want." She was encouraged to find more ways to actualize herself outside of the home.

At the current time Bob and Jean are in couples therapy once a week, and Jean is in an ongoing transactional analysis group for women. Plans include working with the entire family again when school starts in September.

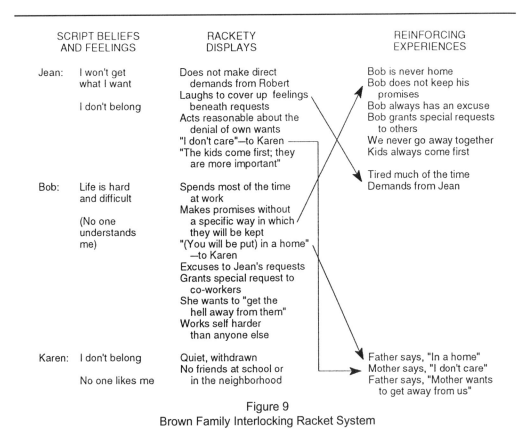

SCRIPT BELIEFS
AND FEELINGS

RACKETY
DISPLAYS

REINFORCING
EXPERIENCES

Jean: I won't get
what I want

I don't belong

Does not make direct
demands from Robert
Laughs to cover up feelings
beneath requests
Acts reasonable about the
denial of own wants
"I don't care"—to Karen
"The kids come first; they
are more important"

Bob is never home
Bob does not keep his
promises
Bob always has an excuse
Bob grants special requests
to others
We never go away together
Kids always come first

Tired much of the time
Demands from Jean

Bob: Life is hard
and difficult

(No one
understands
me)

Spends most of the time
at work
Makes promises without
a specific way in which
they will be kept
"(You will be put) in a home"
—to Karen
Excuses to Jean's requests
Grants special request to
co-workers
She wants to "get the
hell away from them"
Works self harder
than anyone else

Karen: I don't belong

No one likes me

Quiet, withdrawn
No friends at school or
in the neighborhood

Father says, "In a home"
Mother says, "I don't care"
Father says, "Mother wants
to get away from us"

Figure 9
Brown Family Interlocking Racket System

Evaluation

The current literature on transactional analysis consists primarily of case studies wherein clinicians report positive outcomes. Some families have provided self-reports of long-term positive changes in relationships among family members after transactional analysis family therapy (Kadis & McClendon, 1980). Few scientific evaluations have been done on the effectiveness of transactional analysis therapy, and only one study (Bader, 1976) has investigated the effects of a transactional analysis approach to family therapy. Bader investigated both change in the family system and change in each individual and compared five control families with five families who attended a week-long family therapy session.

Both the experimental and control families were white and middle-class and were selected from among those who had expressed a desire for intensive family therapy. A pretest, posttest, and a three-month follow-up test were conducted on both experimental and control families. Bader used the Family Environment Scale to evaluate the family dynamics or system. The California Psychological Inventory and the Personal Orientation Inventory were used to determine change in each individual. At the end of an intensive week of family therapy the five families in the experimental group showed positive gain in cohesiveness and expression of a range of feelings and positive increase in the amount of independence. During this same pre- to posttest period the control group showed no changes on any of the scales.

At the three-month follow-up testing the experimental group had maintained the changes gained in the intensive transactional analysis family therapy session and the control group continued to show no changes. An interesting change also occurred in the follow-up testing where a significant positive change on the California Psychological Inventory in Constructive Dominance for the experimental families indicated that individuals were taking increased responsibility for their own behavior. The control families showed no change.

There are still no studies of family therapy where transactional analysis has been compared with other methods. As with all therapy approaches the effectiveness of the model depends on the skill, personality, and enthusiasm of the therapist in using the model. Effective therapy is an interaction between the method, the person using it, and the readiness of the clients.

Summary

Family therapy can be done effectively using transactional analysis as a model for intervention. Family therapy was illustrated using the basic concepts of strokes, transactions, and script. Demonstrating the use of the interlocking racket system with an actual family, the chapter described both the interpersonal and intrapersonal dynamics of a dysfunctional family.

REFERENCES

Babcock, D., & Keepers, T. (1976). *Raising kids ok: Human growth and development through out the life span*. New York: Grove Press.

Bader, E. (1976). Redecisions in family therapy: A study of change in an intensive family therapy workshop (Doctoral dissertation, California School of Professional Psychology, 1976). *Dissertation Abstracts International, 37B*, 5, 2491. (University Microfilms, No. 76-25, 064)

Bader, E. (1980). A cured family has problems. *Transactional Analysis Journal, 10*, 143-146.

Berne, E. (1949). The nature of intuition. *Psychiatric Quarterly, 23*, 203-226.

Berne, E. (1952). Concerning the nature of diagnosis. *International Record of Medicine, 165*, 283-292.

Berne, E. (1953). Concerning the nature of communication. *Psychiatric Quarterly, 27*, 185-198.

Berne, E. (1955). Intuition IV: Primal images and primal judgment. *Psychiatric Quarterly, 29*, 634-658.

Berne, E. (1957). Intuition V: The ego image. *Psychiatric Quarterly, 31*, 611-627.

Berne, E. (1961). *Transactional analysis in psychotherapy: A systematic individual and social psychiatry*. New York: Grove Press.

Berne, E. (1962). Intuition VI: The psychodynamics of intuition. *Psychiatric Quarterly, 36*, 294-300.

Berne, E. (1964). *Games people play: The psychology of human relationships*. New York: Grove Press.

Berne, E. (1966). *Principles of group treatment*. New York: Grove Press.

Berne, E. (1972). *What do you say after you say hello?: The psychology of human destiny.* New York: Grove Press.

Cassius, J. (1975). *Body scripts: Collected papers on physical aspects of transactional analysis*. Private circulation.

Corsover, H. (1979). Life scripts of asklepieion therapeutic community residents. *Transactional Analysis Journal, 9*, 136-140.

Dusay, J. (1971). Eric Berne's studies of intuition 1949-1962. *Transactional Analysis Journal, 1971, 1*(1), 34-44.

Epstein, S. (1972). The nature of anxiety with emphasis upon its relationship to expectancy. In C. C. Spielberger (Ed.), *Anxiety, current trends in theory and research* (Vol. 2). New York & London: Academic Press.

Erskine, R. (1974). Therapeutic intervention: Disconnecting rubberbands. *Transactional Analysis Journal, 1974, 4*(1), 7-8.

Erskine, R. (1975). The abc's of effective psychotherapy. *Transactional Analysis Journal, 5*(2), 163-165.

Erskine, R. (1980). Script cure: Behavioral, intrapsychic and physiological. *Transactional Analysis Journal, 10*, 102-106.

Erskine, R., & Maisenbacher, J. (1975). The effects of a TA class on socially maladjusted high school students. *Transactional Analysis Journal, 5*(3), 252-254.

Erskine, R., & Zalcman, M. (1979). The racket system: A model for racket analysis. *Transactional Analysis Journal, 9*, 51-59.

Federn, P. (1952). *Ego psychology and the psychoses.* New York: Basic Books.

Goulding, M. M., & Goulding, R. L. (1979). *Changing lives through redecision therapy.* New York: Brunner/Mazel.

Groder, M. (1977). Asklepieion: An integration of psychotherapies. In G. Barnes (Ed.), *Transactional analysis after Eric Berne: Teachings and practices of three TA schools* (pp. 134-137). New York: Harper's College Press.

Harris, R. (1967). *I'm ok, you're ok: A practical guide to transactional analysis.* New York: Harper & Row.

James, M., & Jongeward, D. (1971). *Born to win: Transactional analysis with Gestalt experiments.* Reading, MA: Addison-Wesley.

Kadis, L., & McClendon, R. (1980). Project: Family "cure." *Transactional Analysis Journal, 10*, 147-152).

Karpman, S. B. (1968). Fairy tales and script drama analysis. *Transactional Analysis Bulletin, 7*(26), 39-43.

McClendon, R. (1977). My mother drives a pickup truck. In G. Barnes (Ed.), *Transactional analysis after Eric Berne* (pp. 99-113). New York: Harper's College Press.

Penfield, W. (1952). Memory mechanism. *Archives of Neurology and Psychiatry, 67*, 178-198.

Piaget, J. (1952). *The origin of intelligence in children* (M. Cook, Trans.). New York: International Universities Press.

Schiff, J., with Day, B. (1970). *All my children.* New York: M. Evans.

Steiner, C. (1971). *Games alcoholics play: The analysis of life scripts.* New York: Grove Press.

Steiner, C. (1974). *Scripts people live: Transactional analysis of life scripts.* New York: Grove Press.

Weiss, E. (1950). *Principles of psychodynamics.* New York: Basic Books.

Windes, K. (1953). TA with addicts. *Transactional Analysis Journal, 3*(3), 19-21.

This article was originally published in Arthur M. Horne and Merle M. Ohlsen (Eds.), Family Counseling and Therapy *(pp. 245-275). Itasca, IL: F. E. Peacock Publishers, 1982. Reprinted with permission.*

Open-Ended Scripts:
A Second Chance For Women

Richard G. Erskine and Tehila Selzer

Berne (1972) raised the question, "What do you do after your open-ended script runs out?" In the transactional analysis literature, people with open-ended scripts are seen as non-winners, and people who live them out are said to be waiting for rigor mortis to set in. However, given our culture's role expectations for women, open-ended scripts may be one way in which some women may eventually move out of their scripts. They may provide the means whereby women who were script-bound in their child-rearing years can become self-actualized during middle and old age when children leave home and the women's scripts run out.

Contemporary, youth-oriented American culture provides explicit role scripts for young women (Erskine, 1974) but only minimal role expectations for older women. Traditionally, young women are expected to be wives and mothers and to negate their sense of personhood (Jongeward, 1972). Wyckoff (1974) has pointed out that the female's sex-role scripting permits her to develop strong Little Professor, Pig Parent, and Nurturing Parent. The script does not allow for her to develop Natural Child (own needs) and Adult.

Women who have adopted a stereotypical role might be able to sustain a pseudosense of OKness as long as they follow their script compulsion—to maintain their role of caretaker and/or to fit the media image of youthful beauty. As children leave home and youth diminishes, however, the open-ended scripts start to run out, producing a lack of structure that for some women may result in depression or in a milder sense of loneliness and uselessness. For other women, completion of the script-bound role may open avenues for self-fulfillment.

A review of the literature on personality change with age (Bizzen, 1964; Cameron, 1967; Chown, 1968; Neugarten, 1966) indicates that the direction of personality change for women from young, to middle, to old age is of increased inner orientation and greater unity between real needs and their fulfillment. Older women, for the most part, grow to give themselves the permission to be free of their limited roles.

Several studies compared personality characteristics of young and old women (Brim, 1966; Lehr & Rudinger, 1969; Neugarten, 1968) in terms of interests, general attitudes and values, specific attitudes toward aging, emotional adjustment, and work and work habits. Young women were found to be interested primarily in family and marriage and secondarily in social services, women's magazines, fiction, and biographies (Neugarten, 1968). Older women were less interested in social gathering and more interested in themselves. They were less conforming, had settled, well-defined interests, and enjoyed detective and mystery books (masculine type) (Hardyck, 1964). Young women were found to be more suspicious, rebellious, cynical, concerned with opinions of others, and pessimistic. Older women appeared to have more internalized convictions, were more trusting in others, and more optimistic (Brozck, 1955). Young women tended to view older persons' appearance in more relatively negative terms and looked at aging as an unpleasant process. Older women thought that the most conspicuous characteristic of aging is a sense of increased freedom and a satisfying change in self-concept (Neugarten, 1971).

Young women as a group appeared restless, nervous, and variable in energy and mood. They were less willing to make decisions about their lives than older women. Older women appeared more stable and admitted irrationality only when not feeling well.

In general, young women perceived themselves as having relatively little role outside the family and no great vitality or autonomy. They tended to wait for decisions to be made by others, and they were "nice" and "pleasant." Older women were often found to be key figures in the family. They saw themselves as persons in their own right, aside from their husbands, and were more accepting of their own aggression and dominance. In terms of work and work habits, older women seemed quite settled in contrast to the young women, who reported great changes of heart regarding choice of career. Older women appeared to make their own decisions, to be more whole individuals and less script-bound.

Berne (1972) noted, "The cure for the scriptless aged is permission, but they seldom use it." It is possible that Berne's statement is more relevant to men than women. Men usually run out of their open-ended scripts as provider and hard worker about age 65, while women face the crisis of completing the open-ended scripts at a relatively young age. It is likely that women have greater opportunity than men to solve their end-of-script crisis in a constructive manner by allowing themselves to set new goals that will meet their needs and interests.

As the review of literature points out, young women seem to have a much harder time adjusting to their lives than older women. This is most likely the result of cultural scripting of young women that imposes roles that are alienating to the self. The fact that middle-aged women have completed their open-ended scripts may be a positive rather than negative reality. Most women who experience the "existential vacuum" make new decisions about their roles and needs—decisions that are not shaped by Parental and societal messages. The culture has little concern for the role of older women and allows them to choose their lifestyles more freely than it permits younger women. This may be a major explanation of why older women are more adjusted and satisfied with their lives than younger women.

Much of psychotherapy literature, including literature on script analysis, has been more concerned with women who are caught in the negative binds of their script than with identifying the cause of their despair (Berne, 1961; Steiner, 1974). Literature concerned with treatment has focused on developing ways for women to examine their inner needs, explore new lifestyles, and set constructive "winner" goals for the remaining lifetime (Spence, 1974). The emphasis has been on the destructive aspects of open-ended scripts for women and on specific alternatives for changing their lives. Little attention has been given to the constructive value that the second chance in open-ended scripts may provide for women.

In our clinical work with women who have come to the end of their open-ended scripts, we have found that we get significant change early in therapy when we place little emphasis on the pathology associated with script and focus instead on normal personality development and the associated crisis at each developmental stage (Erikson, 1950; Jongeward, 1972). We give permission to "please yourself." In conjunction with script analysis, the transactional analysis therapist can explain that the crisis need only be momentary; the end of the script means that the woman now has a second chance and may choose to live her own life in ways that are fulfilling to her.

REFERENCES

Berne, E. (1961). *Transactional analysis in psychotherapy: A systematic individual and social psychiatry.* New York: Grove Press.

Berne, E. (1972). *What do you say after you say hello?: The psychology of human destiny.* New York: Grove Press.

Bizzen, J. E. (1964). *The psychology of aging.* Englewood Cliffs, NJ: Prentice-Hall.

Brim, O. G. (1966). Socialization through the life cycle. In O. G. Brim & S. Wheeler (Eds.), *Socialization after childhood.* New York: Wiley.

Brozck, J. (1955). Personality change with age: An item analysis of the MMPI. *Journal of Gerontology, 10,* 194-226.

Cameron, P. (1967). Ego strength and happiness of the aged. *Journal of Gerontology, 22,* 199-202.

Chown, S. (1968). Personality and aging. In K. W. Schave (Ed.), *Theory and methods of research on aging* (pp. 134-157). Morgantown, WV: West Virginia University Library.

Erikson, E. H. (1950). *Childhood and society.* New York: Norton.

Erskine, C. (1974, August). *Six stereotyped women's scripts.* Paper presented at the International Transactional Analysis Association summer conference, San Francisco.

Hardyck, G. D. (1964). Sex differences in personality change with age. *Journal of Gerontology, 19,* 78-82.

Jongeward, D. (1972). What do you do when your script runs out? *Transactional Analysis Journal, 2*(2), 78-81.

Lehr, V., & Rudinger, G. (1969). Consistency and change of social participation in old age. *Human Development, 12,* 255-267.

Neugarten, B. L. (1966). Adult personality: A developmental view. *Human Development, 9,* 61-73.

Neugarten, B. L. (Ed.). (1968). *Middle age and aging.* Chicago: University of Chicago Press.

Neugarten, B. L. (1971). Grow old along with me; the best is yet to be. *Psychology Today, 12,* 45.

Neugarten, B. L., & Gutmann, D. L. (1968). Age sex role and personality in middle age. In B. L. Neugarten (Ed.), *Middle age and aging.* Chicago: University of Chicago Press.

Spence, M. T. (1974). Group work with old people. *Transactional Analysis Journal, 4*(2), 35-37.

Steiner, C. (1974). *Scripts people live: Transactional analysis of life scripts.* New York: Grove Press.

Wyckoff, H. (1974). Banal scripts of women. In C. Steiner, *Scripts people live: Transactional analysis of life scripts* (pp. 176-196). New York: Grove Press.

This article was originally published in the Transactional Analysis Journal, *Volume 7, Number 4, October 1977, pp. 294-297.*

Permissions: A Cure for Sexual Problems

Douglas G. Beattie and Richard G. Erskine

The effective use of permissions is important in the cure of sexual problems. People come to transactional analysis groups to solve a variety of self-identified problems, many of which have related sexual aspects. The therapist's explicit permission to group members to bring up sexual issues in the group is a first step in solving them. The therapist might observe, for instance, "I notice no one has talked about issues related to sexuality, and I want you to know it's OK to discuss sexuality here"; or, "When you stop yourself from talking about an issue in group—such as sexuality—you may be continuing to give that issue power to keep you not-OK." Such an announcement can be followed by discussion of some of the myths about sexuality and consideration of the Parent tapes preventing people from even discussing "it."

Use of Permissions in Group

During a group session the therapist asked one couple, "How does the problem you have identified relate to your sex life?" The man responded with "Our sex life is OK." The therapist queried, "What do you mean by OK?" The woman answered, "We had a good sexual experience when we were on vacation in July but haven't had sex since." (The session was in mid-September.) Her comment paved the way for a more thorough identification of the problems that existed between the couple, several of which were related to Parent ego state messages about sexual behavior.

One man in the group continually spoke of the crossed transactions between himself and "the person I live with." The therapist noted that he had not stated whether the person was a man or woman. The man replied, "It is a man, and we are lovers. I was afraid if I told you, you would all try to change me." The therapist replied, "Your sexual preference is up to you. I am here to work on what you *want* to change." The therapist's response (1) challenged the client's assumption that others would believe "gay is not-OK" and (2) opened the way for others in the group to deal with their sexuality.

A married woman shared her fear of her sexual feelings for her female music teacher, whom she adored. The therapist said, "Isn't it beautiful that you have such loving feelings for a woman you admire so much!" She looked puzzled, paused a moment and with a big smile breaking across her face, she said, "Why, yes, it sure is!" She then began to recognize that there is a difference between having a feeling and choosing to act on the feeling.

Another woman stated, "I'm freer about touching people from watching other people in the group."

Permission, protection, and potency, in addition to coming from the therapist, come from the supportive nature of the group experience itself. Group members have a particular kind of potency to challenge one another's Parent ego state messages, with the therapist present to check out contaminations and misinformation.

Types of Permission

The effective use of permissions in the cure of sexual problems is based on the therapist's awareness of the script messages of the client and the type of protection to offer, data about sexuality, and willingness to get in touch with his or her own sexual self.

Sex role permissions are needed when people have incorporated the idea that there are distinct differences in the role of each partner. Much of the transactional analysis literature on sexuality has focused on sex-role scripting within a social context (Berne, 1972; Erskine, 1974; Hamsher, 1973; Wyckoff, 1971). These writings have served many people as rich resources for permission. In addition, specific permissions may be needed regarding the role one takes when sexually active, such as:

It's OK for men to enjoy being passive sexually.

It's OK for women to enjoy being assertive sexually.

Both of these permissions are based on the concept (applicable for either heterosexual or homosexual relationships) that in sex play there is no necessary "male" or "female" role.

The permissions regarding sex role may also be more general, such as:

It's OK for men to hug and be close to men.

It's OK for women to hug and be close to women.

Sensuality permissions are needed by people who confuse sexuality with sensuality. Many people who lack permission to be sensual report that they are often under a strain to produce sexually whenever they seek bodily contact with a partner. Typical sensuality permissions include:

It's OK to touch and explore your partner's body (Downing, 1972).

It's OK to touch and explore your own body (Dodson, 1974).

It's OK to have minutes or hours of sex play without intercourse or orgasm (Comfort, 1971).

Specific *sex act permissions* may also be needed:

It's OK to have sex in new and different places (closet, kitchen, patio).

It's OK for men not to have an erection every time for sex to be fun.

Adult-to-Adult information can be as effective as a permission if it opens new avenues of awareness, such as: "It is not uncommon for men to occasionally lose erection during sex play."

Steiner (1971) stated that the alcoholic needs permission *not* to drink (p. 143). This kind of *permission to stop* can also be effective with the sexually compulsive behavior of the person who believes, "I gotta get laid every day," "I can't help exposing myself," or "I have to have an orgasm every time."

Some examples of Permission include:
It's OK to stop (the compulsive behavior)!
It's your body and you can say no whenever you choose (Boston Women's Health Collective, 1971).

Often *"no sex" permissions* are needed by people who use sex to achieve early childhood desires for cuddling and affection. Permission is needed to deal with those needs in ways through other than sexual activity. One woman in the group who received permission to be close without having sex reported two weeks later, "Now I know I can take in love without having to worry about sex. I used to think I always had to give sex in return."

Sex preference permissions may be needed by people who because of their script are restricted sexually. Sex preference is a choice that may be either script-bound or free. Heterosexuality as well as homosexuality may be based on script injunctions and early decisions that limit the Natural Child from expressing itself fully in sexual relationships. Permission may be needed to choose heterosexuality, homosexuality, or bisexuality from an "I'm OK" position with awareness, spontaneity, and intimacy.

Conclusion

When the therapist is in tune with his or her sexuality, he or she is more readily able to note absence of discussion of sexuality and can ask, "What's being avoided by me as a therapist or by my clients?"

Adult data about sexuality and a good knowledge of the client's script influences are an important basis for effective permissions. Such permissions can be given verbally ("It's OK to . . .") or by action through role modeling or fantasy techniques.

REFERENCES

Berne, E. (1972). *What do you say after you say hello?: The psychology of human destiny.* New York: Grove Press.
Boston Women's Health Collective. (1971). *Our bodies ourselves.* New York: Simon & Schuster.
Comfort, A. (1971). *The joy of sex.* New York: Grove Press.
Dodson, B. (1974). *Liberating masturbation.* New York: Bodysex Designs.
Downing, G. (1972). *The massage book.* New York: New York, NY and Berkeley, CA: Random House and Bookworks.
Erskine, C. (1974, August). *Six stereotyped women's scripts.* Paper presented at the ITAA Summer Conference, San Francisco.
Hamsher, J. H. (1973). Male sex roles: Banal scripts. *Transactional Analysis Journal, 3*(2), 23-28.
Steiner, C. (1971). *Games alcoholics play: The analysis of life scripts.* New York: Grove Press.
Wyckoff, H. (1971). The stroke economy in women's scripts. *Transactional Analysis Journal,* 1971, *1*(3), 16-20.

This article was originally published in the Transactional Analysis Journal, *Volume 6, Number 4, October 1976, pp. 413-415.*

Part 4

Transactional Analysis in Action

Supervision of Psychotherapy: Models for Professional Development

Richard G. Erskine

The International Transactional Analysis Association has long recognized the integral role that supervision plays in the training of psychotherapists (International Transactional Analysis Association, 1977), but there is little in the literature examining the content, process, and philosophy of supervision. In 1977 Graham Barnes outlined his approach to supervision and provided a model for self-supervision. The need remains for psychotherapy supervisors to have a variety of approaches to assist the therapist in developing professional competence.

This article is designed to provide a framework for supervisors of clinical trainees to organize their approaches to supervision according to the trainee's level of professional skill and acumen. Supervision can be highly effective in promoting competent, ethical psychotherapists when the supervisor varies the supervisory approach to the individual's phase of professional development, which may include such learning tasks as acquiring skills, building confidence, gaining an identity as a therapist, refining treatment planning, resolving countertransference issues, and applying theory in clinical practice.

This outline of supervision models focuses on the content and process of supervision and implies an integration of various philosophical and ethical positions, some of which may seem contradictory at first. Supervisors will have to choose the philosophical stance and methods to which they are best suited and that are most effective for developing competent psychotherapists. Supervisors ultimately face certain philosophical questions that can more readily be answered by having a repertoire of supervisory methods that can be geared to the level of professional development of the trainee. Such questions can include:
- When do I bring out the hidden abilities in a trainee or teach them my skills?
- When do I support mediocre work in order to enhance the therapist's confidence vs. challenging the therapist to reach a new level of competence?
- Is it more beneficial to engage the supervisees in their own psychotherapy to resolve intrapersonal and interpersonal conflicts that may interfere with therapy or to focus on the acquisition of technical knowledge?

Beginning Stage of Training

Skill Development. In the initial stage of training in psychotherapy the aim of supervision is skill development. The trainee who requires this level of training may be either a new therapist or an already skilled psychotherapist who has decided to enhance his or her effectiveness in utilizing a new approach such as parenting, redecision work, bodywork, etc. Therefore, the beginning focus is on the trainee's gaining information, techniques, and the perspective that can be gained from a supervisor's years of experience.

This can be done through a number of different formats, such as the trainee bringing in audio or audiovisual tape-recorded samples of therapy work; describing a client by presenting historical, social, psychological, and the present therapy situations; working as therapist with another trainee who has a personal problem to solve; role playing a client with the supervisor, another trainee, or self as the therapist; or by bringing the supervisor into the therapeutic situation to observe the trainee at work. Each of these supervisory formats can be followed with a discussion of the client's behavior, the interventions used, possible alternative interventions, and the theoretical concepts that apply.

The early stage of training often involves the refining of observational skills and correlating these observations with a theoretical framework such as ego states, racket system, script matrix, or other theoretical models wherein the therapist can organize observations to form a meaningful treatment plan. A sample series of questions is: "What do you perceive your client presenting?" "What do you think this means, for example, in terms of ego states?" (develop thinking on ego state structure and cathexis). "Given that understanding, what kinds of interventions from you are going to be needed to bring the client's awareness to the problem?" (discuss various options for dealing with the problem, possibly including some modeling, role playing of either the therapist or client, sharing experiences from the supervisor's professional past, or asking the trainee to identify with the client and experience the kind of contact needed).

A great deal of technical information may need to be provided by the supervisor. It has often been found necessary to reteach concepts and techniques that have previously been taught but to gear the teaching to the specific case in supervision; in this way the trainee gains a thorough understanding of how the theoretical concepts are useful in clinical practice. Follow-up reading assignments can be particularly helpful to underscore the ideas discussed.

Once this basic foundation has been acquired, many trainees report increased awareness of both the client's and their own psychological functioning when they follow Graham Barnes's (1977) procedure of listening to tape-recorded samples of their therapy several times between sessions, each time listening from a different perspective.

An essential focus of the supervision is on the making of contact—with clients, the supervisor, and other trainees—based on the assumption that full contact is a primary factor in effective psychotherapy. The trainee can be taught to identify areas in which someone is open to contact and where a person is closed to contact, whether it be cognitive, affective, behavioral, or physiological (Erskine, 1982). Some clients may be resistant to behavioral changes until they first receive information that explains the problem or their psychodynamics. Others may need to express pent-up emotions before they can process information about their dynamics, and still others may need to change behavior first and then later cognitively process the meaning of that change.

The skill-building approach is an important first level of supervision since it provides the trainee with a solid foundation for applying theory in clinical practice and provides needed information to the supervisor regarding professional strengths of the trainee and those areas in which further teaching is necessary. A common problem of this skill-development phase of supervision occurs when the supervisor prematurely chooses to support the therapeutic accomplishments of the trainee and focuses on confidence building before the trainee has a thorough foundation in the "how-to's" of psychotherapy. The supervisor observes the responses of the trainee and uses his or her clinical judgment to determine whether inadequate therapy is the result of lack of skill that requires further teaching, simply the lack of confidence that comes through successful experiences, a personal therapy problem, or some combination of these. Since the primary focus at this stage is on increasing the trainee's level of information on how to do psychotherapy, not much emphasis is placed on the resolution of countertransference issues.

Confidence building. Once the trainees have mastered specific psychotherapy skills, the aim of supervision is on the development of a sense of confidence and well-being as a psychotherapist and an ease in using the skills. In this stage the supervisor provides support and strokes for that which has been done well and may even choose temporarily to ignore what is not done well with the purpose of diminishing any sense of inadequacy. The supervisor may have to return to an earlier phase to reteach skills not assimilated, although usually at this level the trainee has acquired information but may lack the confidence to use it, so the supervisor's task is to help bring to awareness what has already been learned.

The advantage of this approach is that it minimizes the therapist's limiting of his or her own potential. In addition, it provides information about the life script of the therapist that can be used in later treatment. When the supervisor has chosen confidence building as a goal, opportunities for doing therapy with the trainee may be postponed. Where these script or countertransference issues interfere with effective therapy for the client, however, the supervisor needs to reorder the supervision priorities so the trainee has those issues resolved.

It is at this stage that Lewis's (1979) concept of developing the "inward eye" is an important consideration in supervision. The therapist needs to be able to make use of what occurs in the therapeutic situation to be in touch with his or her own affect, memories, beliefs, and fantasies and still be able to observe the client's behavior and phenomeno-logical experience and place it within a theoretical context. It is this ability to be in contact with one's own internal experience and the uniqueness of the client's experience that is the basis for empathy.

One way of accomplishing this is through a training exercise that encourages therapists to shuttle back and forth between observations outside themselves and observation internally:
   "Now I am aware that you . . . " (an observation of the external);
   "Now I am aware that I . . . " (a statement of feelings, fantasies, or physical reactions that reflect internal contact).

When a trainee appears to be working confidently and can make therapeutic use of the shuttle between awareness of self and client, supervision can again return to more in-depth organization of observational skills, this time with a focus on the process between therapist and client or between therapist and supervisor or on the parallel process in which the problem between client and therapist is enacted between therapist and supervisor. The sense of confidence can be further developed with probing questions about what the therapist observes in the client, in self, in the supervisor, and the dynamics between them. During this period the modeling of full contact is essential—*healing is in the relationship*.

Intermediate Stage

Treatment Planning and Skill Refinement. After the trainee is confidently using the psychotherapy skills learned previously, supervision is geared to building an identity as a therapist and refining the therapy approach. Here the supervisor focuses on enhancing the knowledge that has been assimilated and stimulating thinking about therapy from new perspectives.

One way may be to ask the trainee for self-evaluation, either directly or through two-chair work in which he or she becomes the supervisor and gives himself or herself feedback. Some of the advantages of this approach are that it stimulates thinking; the supervisor gets further understanding of the trainee's thinking, feeling, and behaving process; it disarms seeing feedback as a game with negative payoffs; and it avoids having the supervisor on a pedestal as the person who knows everything. The disadvantages include the trainee being too harsh in the evaluation or not thorough enough in self-confrontation—both of which provide the supervisor with significant information.

Another important approach at this level of training is to contract with the trainee for what is wanted in the supervision. The advantage of this approach is that the trainee feels in control of the supervisory process and is defining his or her own professional goals; however, it also may carry the disadvantage of leading the supervisor away from other important areas. Contracts for supervision can be made either before or after the supervisor has watched or heard the work. The supervisor needs to avoid too tight a contract so there is the flexibility to comment on other relevant observations for which the trainee may not have asked for feedback.

A question that helps to refine the therapist's approach is, "What would you do differently if you could do this therapy over?" Or alternately, "What will you do next time you work with this client?" Here the aim is in planning treatment and exploring with the trainee options for treatment interventions. The supervisor works with the trainee to learn from his or her mistakes and to develop new treatment plans. This is a time when supervisors can insist that trainees bring tapes of their "worst" therapy sessions for supervision.

Often the problem at this stage is not in the actual intervention used but in the sequence of interventions. A concept borrowed from parametric statistics of "Type A—Type B errors" may be useful in setting priorities for what is said or done therapeutically. When the therapist makes interventions to correct Problem A, he or she may reinforce Problem B. For example, if someone's script beliefs are, "I'm helpless" and "No one understands me" the therapist may temporarily choose potentially to support the helplessness while building the relationship and doing the necessary regressive work to dissolve the belief that "no one understands me." The trainee thus learns how to evaluate which problem can be held in abeyance while another problem receives immediate focus.

The treatment approach can also be expanded by encouraging the discussion of the theoretical basis for interventions used. This can help solidify the frame of reference and develop facility in putting theory into practice. Once the trainee can adequately explain what is being done from a theoretical position, then it may be profitable to have him or her explain how he or she might work with the same client using a different theoretical concept within transactional analysis, leading eventually to the ability to explain the work from multiple frames of reference, either within transactional analysis or from other psychotherapeutic models. In this way the trainee can be stimulated to make use of what was learned in earlier training and supervision and the trainer/supervisor is provided with information as to what areas of theory or practice need further concentration in teaching or reading assignments.

A way to consolidate and help the trainee retain what was learned from the supervisory process is to ask for a summary after a period of feedback and discussion. The advantage of the summary is that it provides immediate clarification of what the trainee has identified as important in the supervisory process and can alert the supervisor as to the feedback that might be avoided; it is an assessment of progress at different stages of professional development. The same approach of consolidating learning may be used at the beginning of the supervisory session with a question such as, "What did you learn from the last supervision?" This question serves to provide continuity from one session to another and may be particularly effective in helping the trainee gain a perspective for ongoing treatment planning and/or case study.

Written assignments may also be used to help maximize the gain in learning. Many trainees report that they have learned significantly from answering the specific questions following a supervision session:
1. What was the problem presented?
2. What did I learn from working with the client and from the supervision?
3. What did I learn about myself?
4. What will I do differently next time?

The advantage of writing a paragraph or two on each of these questions is that it can fix certain points as important in the mind of the trainee and provides an ongoing record of professional growth. As the trainee reads through the file, areas of growth can be identified, as well as areas of resistance to supervision and where there may be an issue requiring personal therapy. The training log increases self-reflection and self-awareness and fosters thinking about alternative perspectives. As a result, it is useful in establishing a sense of confidence and competence.

When the supervisor periodically reads the trainee's log, a written response of appreciative support of strengths or a challenge to take the next step in learning can be added.

Therapy for the Trainee. An integral part of supervision involves the resolution of a therapist's own issues, which may be an interference in working effectively with clients. These issues might be unresolved conflicts from the past or the lack of awareness of that which has been introjected and not thoughtfully rejected or assimilated as one's own.

The aim of this approach in training is to develop the therapist's integrated sense of Self so that the use of self becomes the most powerful tool in psychotherapy. This is accomplished through resolving whatever countertransference issues interfere with full contact between therapist and client. Countertransference is here defined as all the reactions of the therapist to the client that are the result of the unresolved conflicts within the therapist and may include their beliefs, memories, and future hopes and plans. Racker [1968] wrote that countertransference was the "whole of the therapist's images, feelings, and impulses towards the patient insofar as they are determined by the past." The supervisor focuses on the difficulties in the therapist that inhibit optimum effectiveness and then, through contractual arrangement, may proceed therapeutically with the trainee.

While listening to a case presentation the supervisor may question: "What are those words and sentence patterns saying about the trainee, as much as about the client being presented?" For example, one trainee described her client as being "scared to death" to get angry so was hesitant to encourage the expression of anger. With some questioning from the supervisor it was discovered that the therapist had been afraid to be angry with her invalid mother for fear she would die. After identifying this as a personal therapy issue the trainee agreed to work on it immediately, and the supervisor facilitated the trainee dealing with her unexpressed anger with her mother, thus decontaminating her Adult and breaking the unaware collusion with the client that "expressing anger is dangerous."

The supervisor must also be sensitive to what is avoided or not talked about and how this might reflect an aspect of the therapist that is avoided or repressed, such as the therapist who never discusses money or sex.

In the presentation of tape-recorded samples of therapy for supervision, trainees occasionally will select a segment of tape that describes an aspect of their own personal difficulties. This may be evident in script reinforcement of the client, such as not hearing incongruities in the clients' statements, agreeing with script beliefs such as, "There's nothing I can do," or failure to see how the problem the client is describing is occurring in the relationship with the therapist. Personal problems may also be evident in how the therapist designs treatment plans. If, for example, a therapist continually uses one approach with all clients, such as behavioral change contracts or regressive work, the supervisor might question whether that approach is what the therapist needs and is projecting onto the clients or is a way of avoiding something that is needed personally.

Whether doing tape supervision or observing a therapist working with a client, areas to be sensitive to for possible personal issues are:

1. Contact—Is the therapist responding to the client's experience? Does the client seem to feel understood?
2. Introjection—What incorporated aspects of the therapist are not focused on in the client? For example, is the client's father similar to the therapist's father or teacher?
3. Projections—Is the therapist overly empathetic rather than challenging the frame of reference, reflecting the therapist's own limitation?
4. Retroflection—What emotions or behaviors are not encouraged by the therapist, which may indicate areas in which the therapist holds back or is repressed?

5. Symbiosis—What roles does the client play in the therapist's fears, plans, and desires? One therapist who had difficulty with termination discovered that he was relying on his clients to fulfill his needs to feel important.

Even though therapists may be in or have been in personal therapy, some issues may only become apparent through their work with clients and the observation of the supervisor.

Peer Group Supervision. When supervision is done in the presence of other professional therapists the supervisor may choose to invite others to give their perspectives or possible treatment approaches. This often stimulates all the people in the supervision group to think about their potential interventions and the theoretical bases for those interventions. This is most effectively accomplished after the group of trainees has had considerable professional experience; if done too soon the result will be a discussion of techniques or personal preferences rather than keeping the focus on options in treatment planning. Some of the difficulties with the group feedback approach include: the discussion may be sidetracked to the interests of other trainees, the feedback may center on preferential styles, information may become repetitive, the person giving feedback may be more intent on gaining attention than providing information, and the process can be time-consuming. Some ways of drawing on the professional expertise in the group and overcoming these difficulties are to set time limits on discussion, ask trainees not to repeat previous feedback but only add new information, or give each member a specific theoretical area in which to make their observations, such as ego states, parental influence in script formation, or transference with the therapist. Although group participation in supervision may be difficult to manage it is extremely rewarding in that it includes all those present in developing options or treatment plans.

Advanced Stage

Multitheoretical Perspective. The aim of supervision in this stage is the development within the trainee of the ability to integrate multiple theoretical frames of reference and to select various treatment plans based on observations and hypotheses about a particular client. Additional aims include developing acumen in designing and implementing long-term treatment plans while remaining flexible to other ways of perceiving the therapy.

Once trainees have mastered the skills of psychotherapy and have confidence in themselves as psychotherapists, an intensive case-study approach to supervision provides valuable learning in how to plan and carry out in-depth treatment plans for script cure. The case-study method of supervision provides the supervisor and therapist an opportunity to study one client's therapy for several months to a year. Here the emphasis is on thoroughly understanding the psychological functioning of the client over time, how the client is open and closed to contact, and emphasizes in-depth treatment to release Parental introjects and Child fixations that may contaminate the client's ability to perceive, think, feel, and behave in the present moment. A thorough racket analysis and script analysis can be compiled to aid the therapist in selecting therapeutic operations (Berne, 1966) and methods (Erskine, 1974; Goulding & Goulding, 1979; Schiff, 1969). Trainees can be encouraged to use the case-study approach with those clients whom they find difficult to treat. Each verbatim or tape-recorded session provides a check on previous treatment planning as well as the basis for and refinement of future treatment plans.

In the advanced phase of supervision, whether it be the supervision of specific therapy sessions, an ongoing case study, or *in situ* supervision, a primary focus is the development of the supervisee's ability to function from multiple theoretical frameworks. The sequence used for teaching this way of evaluating and planning is:
1. having the trainee describe the problem as a behavioral observation;
2. think of that observation in terms of a theory of human functioning;
3. draw one or more hypotheses from that theory about this particular client; and
4. develop one or more possible interventions that are an outgrowth of the theory and hypotheses.

For example, the therapist may observe that the client encourages people to be close, and when they are, the client uses various means to push them away. The concept of symbiosis could be used to provide the theoretical understanding that when infantile symbiosis is maintained too long or broken too early there will be confusion around closeness and separation in later life. From this theoretical construct the therapist can draw hypotheses based on this observation and other observations of this particular client. Hypothesis A: This client's infantile symbiosis was maintained too long and therefore there is an early childhood need for separation and individuation; Hypothesis B: This client's infantile symbiosis was broken too early and therefore there is a need to reestablish a symbiotic relationship and an expectation of the interruption of that relationship. If the therapist assumed Hypothesis B, the focus of the intervention could include establishing a transferential symbiosis and satisfying previously unmet early childhood needs. If the therapist had assumed Hypothesis A, the focus of intervention could also include establishing a transferential symbiosis followed by support for individuation and separation while still maintaining contact.

When the trainee is competent at developing alternative hypotheses and various interventions from one theoretical perspective, they can then be challenged to examine the same behavior from different theoretical perspectives with concomitant hypotheses and interventions. For example, the same observation can be viewed in terms of script theory with the Hypothesis J, this client has received an injunction not to be close, and/or K, has modeled from someone how not to have close relationships. The supervisor can then discuss various interventions that are an outgrowth of these hypotheses. This multifaceted theoretical look at a client's behavior provides the therapist with the stimulus for thinking about an integrative, in-depth treatment plan for the client and expands the therapist's capacity to be open to new points of view.

Conclusion

The various stages of professional development and objectives of supervision are summarized in Table 1. The therapist's integration of multiple theoretical frames of reference into clinical practice involves acquiring information in the theory, process, and techniques of psychotherapy and assimilating the skills to form a unique way of working

Table 1 — Stages of Professional Development and Objectives of Supervision			
Beginning Stage Skill Development	**Aim** Gain information and techniques. Create a solid theoretical base for clinical interventions. Enhance contact skills.	**Approach** Use of tape supervision, live work, role play of clients, clinical discussion of case, assign specific readings, reteach theory as needed. Focus is on content.	**Conceptual Base** Refine observational skills; begin treatment planning; draw on theoretical models.
Confidence Building	Develop sense of well-being and comfort as therapist.	Provide strokes, support; decide temporarily to ignore what is not done well; draw out trainee's knowledge; focus is on process.	Importance of full contact with self and client.
Intermediate Stage Treatment planning and skill refinement	Build trainee's identity as therapist. Enhance knowledge.	Ask trainee for self-evaluation; use supervision contract; discuss theory used, ask for summary; use training log.	Focus on contractual supervision as growth medium; value of alternative treatment options; setting priorities in treatment plans; trainee's professional growth.
Therapy for the trainee	Develop trainee's integrated sense of self.	Do personal psychotherapy as it surfaces in total context of training involvement.	Focus on contact and interruptions to contact: introjections; projections; retroflection; symbiosis.
Peer group supervision	Stimulate group involvement in training.	Define parameters; give each discussant a focal point; clarify contract for supervision.	Taps value of collective knowledge and experience; provides overview of group process and problem-solving skills.
Advanced Stage Multitheoretical	Develop selection process of alternative and long-term treatment plans; trainee flexibility; integration of multiple theoretical frames of reference.	Use intensive case study, in-depth ego, racket, and script analysis; insightful questioning designed to enhance self-supervision.	Trainee demonstrates mastery of this level by: describing problem as behavioral observation, conceptualizes observation as a theory, postulates several hypotheses for this client as it relates to theory, develops several possible interventions.

with each person. Through the resolution of countertransference and life script issues the therapist's self becomes the most important tool in psychotherapy.

This outline of approaches to supervision, although organized according to stages of professional development, does not have to be followed in a step-wise manner. It may be necessary in some cases to focus on the resolution of countertransference and life script issues early in training or to recycle through earlier stages before following the complete outline sequentially.

The purpose of supervision is to develop competent, ethical psychotherapists— psychotherapists who have the capacity for self-supervision and a commitment to finding the most effective means of promoting the psychological and physical health of their clients.

REFERENCES

Barnes, G. (1977). Techniques of contractual supervision. In M. James and contributors, *Techniques in transactional analysis for psychotherapists and counselors* (pp. 166-175). Reading, MA: Addison-Wesley.

Berne, E. (1966). *Principles of group treatment.* New York: Grove Press.

Erskine, R. (1974). Therapeutic intervention: Disconnecting rubberbands. *Transactional Analysis Journal,* 4(1), 7-8.

Erskine R. (1982). Transactional analysis and family therapy. In A. Horne & M. Ohlsen (Eds.), *Family counseling and therapy* (pp. 498-529). Itasca, IL: F. E. Peacock Publishers.

Goulding, M. M., & Goulding, R. L. (1979). *Changing lives through redecision therapy.* New York: Brunner/Mazel.

International Transactional Analysis Association. (1977). *Training manual.* San Francisco, CA: Author.

Lewis, J. (1979). The inward eye: Monitoring the process of psychotherapy. *Journal of Continuing Education in Psychiatry, 40,* 7.

Racker, M. (1968). *Transference and countertransference.* New York: International Universities Press.

Schiff, J. (1969). Reparenting schizophrenics. *Transactional Analysis Bulletin, 8*(31), 47-63.

_____

This article was originally published in the Transactional Analysis Journal, *Volume 12, Number 4, October 1982, pp. 314-321. The author wishes to thank Bruce Loria, Ed.D., for developing the chart used in Table 1.*

The ABC's of Effective Psychotherapy

Richard G. Erskine

One of the reasons transactional analysis is such an effective psychotherapy is that it incorporates *affective, behavioral,* and *cognitive* approaches to problem solving. (Recent studies suggest that the most effective therapeutic styles are eclectic. See Fielder, 1950; Lieberman, Yalom, & Miles, 1973).

The *cognitive* approach explains; it focuses on the question "Why." It assumes that when the client or patient comes to understand why he or she behaves and thinks in a particular manner, he or she will solve the problem.

The *behavioral* approach describes. It asks "What." The goal of behavioral therapy is to identify (or, where necessary, establish) and reinforce appropriate behaviors. According to this approach, when you can't see the problem behaviorally any more, it ceases to exist.

The *affective* approach must be experienced. It asks "How." The basic problem dealt with in affective therapy is that people are out of touch with their feelings. It is assumed that removing blocks and gaining closure will reduce distortions and provide a fuller range of experiences (see Table 1).

Table 1 Comparisons of the ABC's			
	Affective	*Behavioral*	*Cognitive*
Emphasis	Experiential	Descriptive	Explanatory
Basic question	How?	What?	Why?
Goal of therapy	To facilitate full awareness	To change observable behavior	To understand why we behave as we do
Major theorists	Reich, Perls, Janov	Skinner, Dollard and Miller, Bandura, Wolpe, Lazarus	Freud, Jung, Adler, Sullivan
Criticisms	Just touchy-feely or ventilating	Symptom substitution	Understanding without change

Transactional analysis uses the three approaches in the following manner: the cognitive in teaching transactional analysis theory and in identifying with the client why he or she is having a problem; the behavioral in the negotiation of therapy contracts, which specify what the client wants to change, how he or she will behave differently, and how other people will know he or she has changed; and, finally, the affective in the work done on removing old emotional blocks and establishing new ways of experiencing. The integrative aspects of transactional analysis are shown in Figure 1.

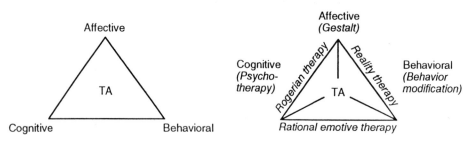

Figure 1
The Integrative Model

Figure 2
Transactional Analysis and Other Therapies

What the integrative model implies is that any transactional analysis concept can be used in any one of the three approaches—that is, to answer why, how, or what. For example, a therapist using the concept of ego state contamination might say to a client:

1. "You are accepting as facts what your Parent ego state (or Child ego state) is telling you" (cognitive).
2. "Are you willing to use your Adult ego state to check out the information?" (behavioral).
3. "Close your eyes and experience how that feels" (affective).

No matter how the client is defended—behaviorally, cognitively, or affectively—the therapist using transactional analysis has optional approaches to solving the problem. By contrast, other schools of psychotherapy tend to confine themselves to one style of analysis or another. For example, psychoanalysis places singular emphasis on cognitive knowledge, behavior modification on behavioral change, and Gestalt on affective growth. Other therapies have combined two of the three approaches. Rogerian therapy, for example, combines the cognitive and affective. It emphasizes insight and the creation of a relationship in which the client is free to express his or her feelings. Rational emotive therapy is cognitive and behavioral, often to the exclusion of the affective sphere. Reality therapy stresses behavioral and affective change and is far less concerned about knowing and explaining. It recognizes that feelings and behavior are interrelated—that by expressing emotions, destructive behavior will change and that behaving differently influences affect. Figure 2 shows the relationship of transactional analysis to other therapies.

Summary

The integrative model establishes the relationship of transactional analysis to other schools of psychotherapy; it also suggests why transactional analysis is effective and provides guidelines for therapeutic interventions and for training therapists.

REFERENCES

Fiedler, F. E. (1950). Comparison of therapeutic relationships in psychoanalytic, non-directive, and Adlerian therapy. *Journal of Consulting Psychology, 14,* 436-445.

Lieberman, M. A., Yalom, I. D., & Miles, M. B. (1973). *Encounter groups: First facts.* New York: Basic Books.

This article was originally published in the Transactional Analysis Journal, *Volume 5, Number 2, April 1975, pp. 163-165. Thanks to Marilyn Zalcman for editorial assistance.*

Six Stages of Treatment

Richard G. Erskine

Berne (1961) and Breen (1970) have considered the assessment of behavior change as an important component in treatment. There are six signposts whereby the therapist can judge the level at which the patient has accepted responsibility for his or her behavior. These six therapeutic stages can serve as a guide in shaping the course of treatment and in making termination decisions (see Table 1).

Stage I—Defensive
The first stage is marked by defensive behavior that is evident during structural analysis when the patient is identifying his or her rackets and their source. Either the Critical Parent or Adapted Child is cathected, and both the patient's rackets and the rackets of his or her parents are defended as authentic feelings.

A typical statement in this treatment stage is, "Doesn't everybody feel this way (my racket)?"

Stage II—Anger
The stage of anger comes when the patient is aware that he or she is repeating rackets in his or her own life that were learned from his or her parents and the realization that many of the desires of his or her childhood were not met. The position taken in this stage is, "I'm OK, parents are not-OK." By offering protection and permission to be aware of feelings, the therapist can deconfuse the angry Adapted Child.

Stage III—Hurt
After anger the patient moves into feeling hurt that his or her needs as a child were not met. He or she takes the position, "I'm not-OK, parents are OK." With the use of rubberbands (Kupfer & Haimowitz, 1971) the Natural Child can now become aware of early life decisions to feel not-OK when hurt.

The patient may equate insight into the cause of problems with the cure and attempt to leave therapy at this point.

Stage IV—Self as Problem
The fourth stage of treatment involves the patient's recognition that his or her parents gave many messages, but that phenomenologically he or she chose to incorporate only selected messages. When the patient says, "I wrote my own script," he or she has begun to recognize the symbiosis with his or her parents.

Through script analysis the therapist can help to decontaminate the Adult.

At this stage the patient becomes aware that he or she is responsible for his or her behavior and may attempt to terminate treatment in order to avoid rewriting the script and to maintain the symbiosis.

Stage V—Taking Responsibility

The fifth stage involves a commitment to change. With permission and protection to change, the patient owns his or her treatment contract with three ego states—Nurturing Parent, Adult, and Natural Child. This Free Child can now exclaim, "I don't have to do script behavior."

Stage VI—Parents are Forgiven

The last stage occurs when the patient has full energy flow between all three ego states and says from each, "My parents did the best job they were capable of doing."

A patient may enter therapy at any of the six stages. Although the stages are linear in their progression toward autonomy, a patient may recycle back through one or more stages before progressing.

Table 1
Six Stages of Treatment

BEHAVIOR	KEY STATEMENT	CATHECTED EGO STATE	CONTRACT	THERAPEUTIC TECHNIQUE	BREEN'S SCALE	BERNE'S TERMS
Defensive	"Doesn't everybody feel this way?" (My racket)	CP AC	Social Control	Structural analysis, source of racket		Ego syntonic
Angry	"My parents messed me up."	AC	Awareness of feelings	Deconfusing the Child, transactional analysis, protection	+1	Ego dystonic
Hurt	"My needs were not met."	NC	Exercising options	Rubberbands, game analysis		
Recognizing self as source of problem	"I wrote my own script."	A	Reversing early decisions	Script analysis, decathecting the Parent	+2	Decontamination
Taking responsibility, decision to change	"I don't have to do script behavior."	NP A NC	Breaking symbiosis	Protection, permission		Reestablishing ego boundaries
Parents are OK	"My parents did the best job they were capable of doing."	NP A NC	Autonomy		+3	Cure

REFERENCES

Berne, E. (1961). *Transactional analysis in psychotherapy: A systematic individual and social psychiatry*. New York: Grove Press.

Breen, M. (1970). An improvement scale. *Transactional Analysis Bulletin, 9*(33), 1-2.

Kupfer, D., & Haimowitz, M. (1971). Therapeutic intervention: Part I, rubberbands now. *Transactional Analysis Journal, 1*(2), 10-16.

This article was originally published in the Transactional Analysis Journal, *Volume 3, Number 3, July 1973, 17-18.*

Counterfeit Strokes

Ted T. Bruce and Richard G. Erskine

Counterfeit strokes are created when people distort what is happening in their transactions with others. Counterfeit strokes are used to reinforce and confirm one's basic life position and to fill a stroke deficit. In our practice we have identified four types of counterfeit strokes, all of which involve discounting (Schiff & Schiff, 1971) as a means of distorting the content of the transaction.

Manufacturing Strokes

Manufacturing strokes is taking factual information and turning it into a feeling that satisfies a stroking need in the Child ego state. For those who feel the need to confirm a basic not-OK life position, the counterfeit stroke takes a negative form. The positive form of the counterfeit stroke is manufactured by the Adapted Child in order to ward off awareness of the not-OK position. In the following exchange, for example, a factual statement is changed into a positive stroke.

Therapist: "I received your script checklist in the mail this week."

Group Member: "Thank you, I'm glad you liked what I wrote."

A factual statement can also be turned into a negative stroke.

Therapist: "It appears you picked up this injunction from your mother."

Group Member: "Well, that's not my fault."

Reversed Strokes

A reversed counterfeit stroke is the result of internally changing the content of the stroke transaction. This can happen in either of two ways. A *Blemish* counterfeit stroke occurs when a person receives a positive stroke and internally changes it into a negative stroke. When several people complimented Betty, she *Blemished* for the way she explained transactions to a new group member; for example, her response was, "I bet you really don't mean that because I forgot to include ulterior transactions." The *Blemish* stroke reinforces a not-OK life position. The internal dialogue with the condemning Parent ego state is, "A not-OK person like you should not get good strokes."

A second variety is the *Polished* counterfeit stroke, in which a negative stroke is polished to provide the person with a positive stroke. For example, Bob was confronted by several group members for discounting his own ability to solve a problem, and when asked to summarize what the group had said to him, he responded that the group felt he was making good progress. *Polished* strokes are used by people who have an investment in trying to feel OK. Their Adapted Child cannot accept negative strokes for fear of being perceived as not-OK and inadequate.

The most viable treatment for counterfeit stroking is to contract with the person to: listen to what is said, repeat verbatim what was said, and summarize the content without distorting the meaning. The contract can also stipulate that the person engage in transactions that will legitimately supply the needed strokes.

REFERENCE

Schiff, A. W., & Schiff, J. L. (1971). Passivity. *Transactional Analysis Journal, 1*(1), 71-78.

This article was originally published in the Transactional Analysis Journal, *Volume 4, Number 2, April 1974, pp. 18-19.*

Graphs as Measures of Cure

Richard G. Erskine, Leroy Clinton, and Anne E. Olmstead

Who has gotten better? How fast? How is the patient different?

Keeping scorecards of the therapeutic work done in treatment groups can be a fun way of turning on the Child in both patient and therapist while providing objective data for research on the effectiveness of transactional analysis treatment. One way we can get a scorecard of therapy progress is by graphing specific behaviors related to the patient's problem.

A simple graphing technique (Campbell & Stanley, 1963) was used in a weekly treatment group to provide feedback to the patient on how well he was meeting his contract. Bill contracted with the group to become aware of and stop using a gallows smile (Steere, 1970). Another person in the group agreed to observe Bill every time he had a transaction with other people and to record whether he used a gallows smile during each minute observed. After each observation period the results were graphed and displayed in a prominent place. In this way Bill got feedback on his use of the gallows smile (while the therapist collected data for writing this article) (see Figure 1).

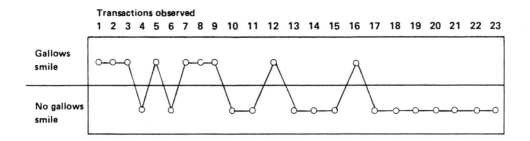

Figure 1
Gallows Transactions

The graph shows several things: first, that Bill has fulfilled his contract. By the end of the two hours he no longer used the gallows smile, and he did not gallows again during the subsequent group sessions. Second, this change in behavior was effected during the group. He was using the gallows smile during the first transactions observed and then gradually used it less and less often. Finally, the new behavior seems to be stable. Seven transactions in a row have no gallows smile.

This type of graphing can be used with any data that can be translated into an observable "yes" or "no" framework, such as whether or not a person is discounting (Schiff & Schiff,

1971), is in a particular miniscript driver (Kahler with Capers, 1974), or is visibly accepting strokes (McKenna, 1974). The graph provides a fast and simple way to transmit information to the Adult, is fun for the Child, and satisfies the Parent that the job is getting done.

REFERENCES

Campbell, D. T., & Stanley, J. C. (1963). *Experimental and quasi-experimental designs for research.* Chicago: Rand McNally.

Kahler, T., with Capers, H. (1974). The miniscript. *Transactional Analysis Journal, 4*(1), 26-42.

McKenna, J. (1974). The stroking profile: Application to script analysis. *Transactional Analysis Journal, 4*(4), 20-24.

Schiff, A. W., & Schiff, J. L. (1971). Passivity. *Transactional Analysis Journal, 1*(1), 71-78.

Steere, D. (1970). Freud on the gallows transaction. *Transactional Analysis Bulletin, 9*(33), 3-5.

This article was originally published in the Transactional Analysis Journal, *Volume 5, Number 3, July 1975, pp. 255-256.*

Time Structuring for "Problem" Students

Jerry Maisenbacher and Richard G. Erskine

"What's it to you?" "I don't care." "Why is everybody always picking on me?" These and other "I'm not-OK" or "You're not-OK" comments were made by a group of socially maladjusted high school students who began a course labeled "Personal Growth." Twelve adolescent students were enrolled who had been identified as maladaptive to the regular high school program. They had a history of antisocial, destructive behavior involving self or others. Chronic truancy, stacks of discipline referrals, drug habits, academic failure, and conflicts with teachers, other students, and parents were characteristic.

The "Personal Growth" class met for one hour each school day for one semester. In order for students to be enrolled they had to be recommended by their counselors and teachers, their parents had to consent, and the students themselves also had to agree to attend the new class.

The course was designed to encourage and facilitate student-initiated social control. The instructor began with the teaching of basic structural analysis and transactional analysis. After the first few class sessions, it became difficult for the teacher to teach because of the constant discounting, game playing, and racketeering (English, 1976) engaged in by class members. Each hour consisted of a smorgasbord of games consistently reinforced by gallows laughs. At times, over half the class would be under the influence of drugs; occasionally their games would get to the tissue-destructive level. The teacher was getting hooked into a "Try hard" driver (Kahler with Capers, 1974) and complained, "I feel I'm bashing my head against a wall."

The first step in changing the situation required the teacher to recognize that his "Be perfect" messages were stopping him from establishing realistic success criteria. The second step was to "do" by reorganizing the class rather than "Try hard" to teach above the disturbances.

The classroom was rearranged. In one area of the room four library tables were grouped (Figure 1). Each table bore a sign that indicated what kind of time structuring was appropriate at that table.

The signs read, "Rituals and Pastimes," "Games," "Withdrawal," or "Activity." In another area of the room a circle of chairs (Figure 2) was grouped. It bore a similar poster, which read "Intimacy" and in smaller letters, "No discounts, no games, no rackets. Sharing and caring only." The students were told that it was OK to sit at any of the tables or in the circle, but that they had to recognize what they were doing there, that is, be aware of how they were spending their time.

Each class started with the whole group sitting in the intimacy circle. When some of the members started "shooting the bull" and were not sharing or caring, they were required

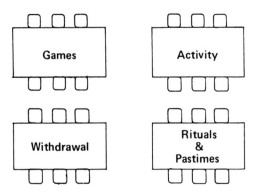

Figure 1
Arrangement of Classroom Tables

to leave the circle and sit at the pastime table until they did something different. If class members came in high on drugs, they had to spend the hour at the withdrawal table. (The students did an excellent job of determining who was high.) When the game players began discounting (Schiff & Schiff, 1971) in the intimacy circle, they were required to move to the game table. When students were asked to read assignments from *Born to Win* (James & Jongeward, 1971) they would go to the activity table to read. They then composed contracts at the activity table before presenting them in the intimacy circle. Within the intimacy circle the students worked on problems they had in school or at home.

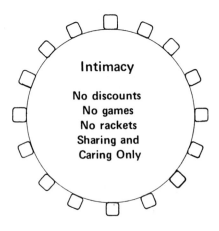

Figure 2
Intimacy Circle

The decision to divide the group members according to the way they structured time changed what was going on in the classroom. Most important, it broke the group into smaller units so that those who wanted to work on personal problems could do so in the intimacy circle without intimidation from the game players. (During the first few weeks, only two or three students were in the circle at a time—the rest were at the other tables.) The trust level went up in the circle as soon as the table plan went into action.

Students soon became aware of how they were spending their time. After several days, and in some cases weeks, they became bored with their behavior. This boredom triggered a desire to change what they were doing. They would then make an attempt to stay in the intimacy circle longer. Early in the semester many students could "survive" for only a few minutes before getting sent to the tables for their destructive behavior. Any discount caused removal.

Gradually, the intimacy circle grew larger. Each week more students could survive the whole period without discounting or indulging in their rackets. It soon became apparent to the members out of the circle that people could and did change.

In addition, the class members began to realize that what they were doing at the pastime, withdrawal, and game table they were doing in their other classes and at home. They, in essence, took their table with them! The members in the intimacy circle soon began sharing and caring when not in class. Losers were becoming winners.

By the end of the semester only two of the 12 members had not changed enough to say in the circle. They were still spending much of their time with either games or withdrawal. The rest of the class had stopped much of their destructive behavior, had become aware of their rackets, and generally were using their Adult ego state to face their problems.

REFERENCES

English, F. (1976). Racketeering. *Transactional Analysis Journal, 6*, 78-81.

James, M., & Jongeward, D. (1971). *Born to win: Transactional analysis with Gestalt experiments.* Reading, MA: Addison-Wesley.

Kahler, T., with Capers, H. (1974). The miniscript. *Transactional Analysis Journal, 4*(1), 26-42.

Schiff, A. W., & Schiff, J. L. (1971). Passivity. *Transactional Analysis Journal, 1*(1), 71-78.

This article was originally published in the Transactional Analysis Journal, *Volume 6, Number 2, April 1976, pp. 196-198.*

The Effects of a Transactional Analysis Class on Socially Maladjusted High School Students

Richard G. Erskine and Jerry Maisenbacher

Teachers trained in transactional analysis can use it to help students who see themselves as losers become winners (Ernst, 1972). Transactional analysis has been used with nursery-school children (H. Capers, personal communication), in the treatment of children with learning disabilities (Ernst, 1971), and with socially maladjusted high school students (Frazier, 1971; Maisenbacher & Erskine, 1974). However, little empirical research has been reported that demonstrates the effectiveness of transactional analysis in school settings.

Traditionally, the position of school authorities toward students with "acting out" or socially maladjusted behaviors is one of "I'm OK—You're not-OK." Often the prevailing pastime in the teacher's lounge is, "If I could only get rid of Duke I could teach the other students! He is such a troublemaker. Why doesn't the principal get rid of him?"

In order to change the atmosphere in a large urban high school from a get-rid-of position to a get-on-with position in regard to socially maladjusted students, the authors offered to organize a class in transactional analysis. School counselors were asked to compile a list of those students who had a history of disciplinary referrals, chronic truancy, or constant conflicts with teachers or other students.

Method

Fifty-three students were recommended by the counselors. From this group 20 students with the worst behavior records were selected. The selection process excluded those with numerous discipline referrals or a high percentage of truancy but who were doing well academically. The selection guidelines were bent somewhat to include two students who were not discipline or truancy problems but whose behavior indicated emotional disturbances.

Twelve of the 20 "worst problem" students agreed to attend the transactional analysis "Personal Growth" class for a semester. Class members met for one hour every day, received one unit of credit toward graduation, and were graded on a pass-fail basis. The academic aspects of the class involved learning the basic concepts of structural, transactional, and game analysis. Discounts, the use of time structuring, and basic life positions were emphasized. The objective of the course was to provide students with Adult awareness of socially acceptable alternatives to their destructive behaviors. Live presentations based on actual problems that individual students were facing with family, teachers, and peers provided a foundation for learning and using the transactional analysis concepts.

To evaluate the effectiveness of the class, before-and-after comparisons were made in the number of discipline referrals, grades, and percent of truancy using the semester previous to the class as a baseline.

Results

The results indicate a significant decrease ($p < .005$) in the total number of discipline referrals from 190 per semester to 40 (Table 1). There was also a significant ($p < .005$) decrease in truancy for the total class from a mean of 34.5 to 14.7 (Table 2) and a significant ($p < .01$) mean increase in grade average from 2.035 to 2.674 for the class (a decrease from 16 to 6 failures) (Table 3). During the semester two students dropped out of school—one joined the Navy and the other became a roofer.

The increase in overall grade average, the 150 fewer discipline referrals for the group, and the marked decrease in truancy for each student led to the conclusion that transactional analysis can be used as an effective educational approach with socially maladjusted high school students. (See page 240 for Tables 2 and 3.)

	Table 1 Discipline Referrals	
	Discipline Referrals	
	1st Semester	2nd Semester
Henny	10	1
Wilma	6	0
Buggs	35	2
Wilber	27	2
Duke	30	0
Jumpy	6	1
Marion	6	3
Bashful	10	4
Elmer	20	7
Ralph	40	20
Mean df = 9; t = 4.21; p<.005	19	4

REFERENCES

Ernst, J. L. (1971). Using transactional analysis in a high school learning disability grouping. *Transactional Analysis Journal, 1*(4), 11-15.

Ernst, K. (1972). *Games students play.* Millbrae, CA: Celestial Arts.

Frazier, T. L. (1971). The application of transactional analysis principles in the classroom of a correctional school. *Transactional Analysis Journal, 1*(4), 16-20.

Maisenbacher, J., & Erskine, R. G. (1974, October). *Time structuring: A therapy approach for socially maladjusted high school students.* Paper presented at the Midwest Transactional Analysis Conference, Chicago.

This article was originally published in the Transactional Analysis Journal, *Volume 5, Number 3, July 1975, pp. 252-254.*

Table 2 Truancy	Times Truant	
	1st Semester	2nd Semester
Henny	40	2
Wilma	10	5
Buggs	50	20
Wilber	55	25
Duke	10	0
Jumpy	0	0
Marion	50	15
Bashful	40	25
Elmer	60	30
Ralph	30	25
Mean df = 9; t = 4.39; p<.005	34.5	14.7

Table 3 Grade Point Average	Grade Point Average	
	1st Semester	2nd Semester
Henny	3.50	3.00
Wilma	2.80	3.50
Buggs	1.80	3.00
Wilber	1.40	2.50
Duke	2.20	3.60
Jumpy	2.40	2.67
Marion	1.50	2.20
Bashful	1.50	2.20
Elmer	1.50	2.67
Ralph	1.75	1.40
Mean df = 9; t = 3.10; p<.01	2.035	2.674

Secondary Stamp Collecting

Richard G. Erskine and Harry D. Corsover

"I'll share my red stamp with you
if you'll share your blue stamp with me."

"It's a deal if you tell me that I'm OK."

The above transaction is an illustration of how people often share their psychological stamps (Berne, 1966) with each other. The process involves each person taking on the other's feelings and calling them his or her own. This results in secondary stamp collections that come from transactional incidents in the lives of others and have not directly affected the new collector. Through secondary stamp collecting each person gets told he or she is OK and multiplies his or her stamp collection without the work of collecting a stamp directly.

The example in Figure 1 illustrates the dual goals of secondary stamp collecting. One goal is reached when each person is indirectly told, "You're OK." His or her not-OK feelings are temporarily warded off by making a third person not-OK. While the social level transaction is, "Tom is unfair," the ulterior transaction is, *"Tell me I'm OK."* (The ulterior transaction in secondary stamp collecting illustrates the Child's motivation for playing "Blemish" [Berne, 1964]). The other goal is reached when each person's stamp collection is multiplied. Now Jane and Bill are both closer to justifying their intended payoffs (see Figure 1).

Although two people can share stamps with each other, the process is often more dramatic when it occurs in groups, where a GROUP GRIPE session or STAMP POOL takes place. If several group members are individually holding onto red stamps against a common person or other "enemy" (such as a school administration, business management, etc.), all members can acquire a stamp collection representing all the red stamps in the group. The stamps can be counterfeited and mass produced, allowing each group member, or the group as a whole, to feel entitled to cash in for a much larger "prize."

Secondary stamp collecting involves the manufacturing of negative strokes (Bruce & Erskine, 1974) from essentially neutral data, the collection and exploitation of racket feelings, and a common enemy.

Secondary stamp collecting is a dynamic involved in playing a wide variety of games. By intervening when secondary stamps are being collected, the therapist can stop a game and offer alternatives early in the course of therapy. When used with a person in the beginning stages of treatment (Erskine, 1973), the therapist can discuss the aims and advantages of secondary stamp collecting, which may be received by the person's Child and Adult more readily than a confrontation of game playing.

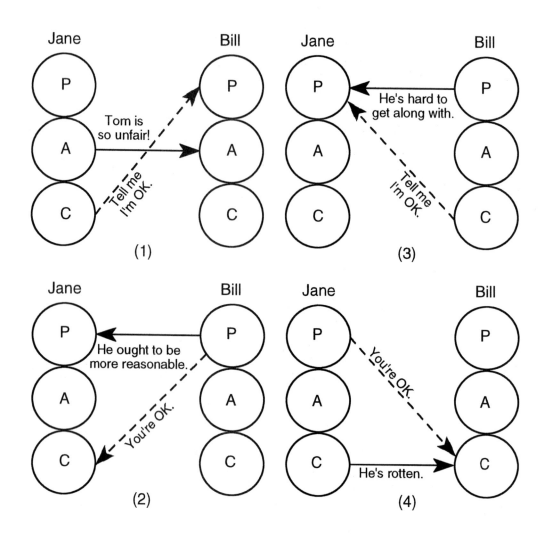

Figure 1
Dual Goals of Secondary Stamp Collecting

REFERENCES
Berne, E. (1964). *Games people play: The psychology of human relationships.* New York: Grove Press.
Berne, E. (1966). *Principles of group treatment.* New York: Grove Press.
Bruce, T., & Erskine, R. G. (1974). Counterfeit strokes. *Transactional Analysis Journal, 4*(2), 18-19.
Erskine, R. G. (1973). Six stages of treatment. *Transactional Analysis Journal, 3*(3), 17-18.

This article was originally published in the British Transactional Analysis Bulletin, *Volume 1, Number 4, Autumn 1975, pp. 4-6.*

About the Author

Richard G. Erskine, Ph.D., is Training Director of the Institute for Integrative Psychotherapy in New York, a postgraduate continuing education institute providing advanced training in psychotherapy. He is a licensed psychologist and a certified Teaching and Supervising Transactional Analyst (clinical).

Dr. Erskine is Visiting Professor of Psychotherapy at the University of Derby, United Kingdom, and has been a professor at the University of Illinois, Urbana-Champaign, Illinois; Purdue University in Lafayette, Indiana; and Chicago City College. He is currently on the faculties of various psychotherapy training institutes in the United States, Europe, and South America.

Dr. Erskine is coauthor with Janet Moursund, Ph.D., of *Integrative Psychotherapy in Action* (now available from the Gestalt Journal Press, 1997, Highland, New York [ISBN 0-989266-32-6]; originally published by Sage Publications, 1988) and is currently writing a book with Janet Moursund and Rebecca Trautmann entitled *Beyond Empathy: A Therapy of Contact-in-Relationship.*

About the Coauthors

Douglas G. Beattie, M.A., is executive director of the Samaritan Counseling Center, Endicott, New York. He received his B.A. from Brown University, his B.D. from Harvard Divinity School, and his M.A. in Marriage and Family Counseling from Syracuse University. He is a Fellow in the American Association of Pastoral Counselors and has led workshops on stress management, spirituality, and leadership for both corporations and nonprofit organizations.

Ted T. Bruce, M.S.W., a Teaching and Supervising Transactional Analyst (clinical), is in private practice in Milwaukee, Wisconsin, and also teaches at the University of Wisconsin Medical School.

Barbara Clark, Ph.D., is a psychologist and consultant with Relational Leadership Systems. Dr. Clark has developed an innovative theory and practice of relational competence based on leading-edge psychological principles. Her programs are designed to permeate both the organizational systems and the personal systems of the people with whom she works. She has over 20 years of experience as a practitioner, consultant, and workshop leader in both organizational and clinical psychology.

Petrūska Clarkson, Ph.D., is a Teaching and Supervising Transactional Analyst (clinical); a 1990 European Association for Transactional Analysis prizewinner for her contribution to transactional analysis theory; and a consultant, psychologist, and supervisor with 25 years of experience and 120 publications. She works internationally in ethics, teaching, supervising, and research at universities and organizations as well as at PHYSIS in London, England. She is the author of *Transactional Analysis—An Integrated Approach* (Routledge, 1992).

Leroy Clinton, Ed.D., received his doctorate from Columbia University. He is currently an associate professor in the School of Education, Boston University. His interests include development, learning, and evaluation.

Harry D. Corsover, Ph.D., a licensed psychologist and a Teaching and Supervising Transactional Analyst (clinical), has served on and chaired various ITAA committees and has been a resource reviewer for the *Transactional Analysis Journal*. He conducted the first published research in the area of life scripts. Harry and his wife, Linda Azzi, are in private practice in Evergreen, Colorado, specializing in co–couple counseling and the integration of psychological and spiritual development.

Kenneth R. Evans, B.Sc., Dip. Soc. Admin., Dip. Fellow Royal Society of Arts, is the director of clinical training at the Sherwood Psychotherapy Training Institute in Nottingham, England. He is also president of the European Association for Integrative Psychotherapy and past president of the European Association for Psychotherapy.

Carl Goldberg, Ph.D., is a writer and lecturer; editor-for-the-Americas, *International Journal of Psychotherapy*; an editor for the *Journal of Adult Development*; book reviewer for *Psychoanalytic Books* and the *American Journal of Psychotherapy*; and the author of 11 books and 150 professional publications.

Robert L. Goulding, M.D. (1917-1992), was the founder, with his wife and partner Mary Goulding, of the redecision school of transactional analysis and the codirector of the Western Institute for Group and Family Therapy. In 1975 the Gouldings were the winners of the Eric Berne Memorial Scientific Award for their work on redecisions. They are the authors of three books: *Changing Lives Through Redecision Therapy, The Power is in the Patient,* and *Not to Worry.*

Martin Groder, M.D., Associate Member of the ITAA, is in the private practice of psychiatry in Chapel Hill, North Carolina, and is assistant professor of psychiatry, Duke University School of Medicine. He is also an organizational consultant and public speaker. He has authored *Games Businessmen Play* and numerous articles in *Bottomline Personal, Boardroom Reports,* the *Transactional Analysis Bulletin,* and the *Transactional Analysis Journal.*

Hanna Hyams, M.A., Teaching and Supervising Transactional Analyst (clinical), is, at age 70, still active teaching, working, helping, and educating people toward a better understanding of the self, which results in better communication with others.

Samuel James, Ed.D., is associate director of the Center for Group Psychotherapy, Massachusetts General Hospital, Boston, Massachusetts, and a Clinical Fellow at Harvard Medical School.

Jerry Maisenbacher, M.A., currently retired, worked for many years as a teacher with emotionally disturbed and socially maladjusted high school students. He now lives in Springfield, Illinois.

Carlo Moiso, M.D., has been a Teaching and Supervising Transactional Analyst (clinical) since 1981 and is in private practice in Rome, Italy. He also leads or participates in training programs in various countries and is involved in activities related to social and political concerns. In 1987 he was awarded the Eric Berne Memorial Scientific Award for his work on ego states and transference.

Anne E. Olmstead, M.S., is a Clinical Member of the ITAA and currently employs her counseling skills in volunteer work in the community and in aspects of her full-time job in computers at Highmark, Inc., formerly Pennsylvania Blue Shield.

Marye O'Reilly-Knapp, D.N.Sc., Certified Transactional Analyst (clinical), has a private psychotherapy training and supervision practice in Philadelphia, Pennsylvania, and is codirector of the Phoenix Centers. She is also an associate of the Institute for Integrative Psychotherapy, New York.

Tehila Selzer, Ph.D., is a licensed clinical psychologist practicing with a private corporation in Richmond, Virginia. Her professional interests include women's issues, group process work, and marital and family therapies.

Rebecca L. Trautmann, R.N., M.S.W., is codirector of the Institute for Integrative Psychotherapy in New York City. She has coauthored several articles with Richard Erskine and is a former editor of the *Transactional Analysis Journal.*

Marilyn J. Zalcman, M.S.W., Certified Teaching Member of the ITAA, maintains a private practice in transactional analysis treatment and training in the Washington, D.C. area, conducts an ongoing PTSTA training program in Italy, and does workshops in other countries. For her updated view of the racket system and racket analysis, please see her article, "Game Analysis and Racket Analysis: Overview, Critique, and Future Developments" in the *Transactional Analysis Journal* (Volume 20, Number 1, January 1990, pp. 4-19).

Additional Works by Richard G. Erskine

Publications

Erskine, R. G. *Developing reading potential: Identification and instruction of disadvantaged high risk readers in kindergarten*. Ann Arbor, Michigan: University Microfilms, 1973. No. 73-15 800.

Erskine, R. G. Diagnostico psicologico de los problemas del aprendizaje. *Programs de la XXX Anniversario Escuela Normal de Especializacion*. Cuidad de Mexico, D.F., 1973.

Erskine, R. G. Tratamineto de los problemas del apprendizaje. *Programa de la XXX Anniversario Escuela Normal de Especializacion*. Cuidad de Mexico, D.F., 1973.

Bruce, T. T., & Erskine, R. G. Manufactured and counterfeit strokes. *Reality*, 5:5, 1973.

Erskine, R. G. Reflexion sabre la evolucion de los problemas de aprendizaje. *Education Especial*. Ano II, No. 9, 1973.

Erskine, R. G. Reaching the hard to teach. *SWAP*, Winter, 1974.

Erskine, R. G., & Texley, R. F. An action structure for solving emotional problems. *Transactional Analysis Journal*, 5:2, 1975.

Erskine, R. G., Cleary, L. E., & Johnson, E. C. *Autism and childhood psychosis*. Urbana, Illinois: University of Illinois, 1975.

Erskine, R. G. An intimate portrait of Fritz Perls and Gestalt therapy. *Journal of Orthopsychiatry*, 46:1, 1976.

Erskine, R. G. Detacher les elastiques. *Actualites en Analyse Transactionelle*, 1:1, 1977. (France)

Erskine, R. G. Une structuration de l'action pour se sentir bien plus vite. *Actualites en Analyse Transactionelle*, 1:1, 1977. (France).

Erskine, R. G. Una estructura de accion para sentirse mejor mas rapido. In C. Camargol (Ed.), *Dinamica de grupos*. Maracay, Venezuela: 1978.

Erskine, R. G. El ABC de la psicoterapia efectiva. In C. Camargol (Ed.), *Dinamica de grupos*. Maracay, Venezuela: 1978.

Erskine, R. Analyse des jeux. In J. Cuveler (Ed.), *French language proceedings of the European Transactional Analysis Association Congress in Elseneur, 1978*. Brussels, Belgium: 1978.

Erskine, R. G. Les caresses contrafaites. *Actualites en Analyse Transactionnelle*, 5, 1978.

Erskine, R. G. Les six etapes du traitement. *Actualites en Analyse Transactionnelle*, 7, 1978.

Erskine, R. G. Les scenarios en suspens: Une seconde chance pour les femmes. *Actualites en Analyse Transactionnelle*, 9, 1979.

Erskine, R. G. Les permissions dans le traitement de problemes sexuels. *Actualites en Analyse Transactionnelle*, 10, 1979.

Erskine, R. G. Le circuit du sentiment-parasite. *Actualites en Analyse Transactionnelle*, 12, 1979.

Erskine, R. G. Les caresses extorquees: Reperage et guerison. *Actualites en Analyse Transactionnelle*, 15, 1980.

Erskine, R. G. Guerir le scenario. *Actualites en Analyse Transactionnelle*, 16, 1980.

Erskine, R. G., & Zalcman, M. J. Favoritkanslor och andra behandlingsfragor. *STAF:s Artikelskritserie I Transaktionsanalys*. Stockholm, 1982.

Erskine, R. G. Modeles et analyse des etats du moi. *Actualites en Analyse Transactionnelle*, 22, 1982.

Erskine, R. G., & Zalcman, M. J. O sistema de disfarces: Um modelo para a analise de disfarces. *Premsio Eric Berne*. Brasilia: UNA-AT. 1983.

Erskine, R. G. Modeles pour la supervision des therapeutes. *Actualites en Analyse Transactionnelle*, 31, 1984.

Erskine, R. G. Review of *TA: The State of the Art*, by E. Stern (Ed). *Transactional Analysis Journal*, 15:2, 1985.

Trautmann, R. L., & Erskine, R. G. Modeles et analyse des etats du moi. *Metamorphose*, Organe Officiel de l'Association Suisse pour l'Analyse Transactionnelle, 5:1, 1985.

Erskine, R. G. Sistema ricatto: Un modello per l'analisi del ricatto. *Neopsiche*, 3:5, 1985. (Milano, Italy).

Erskine, R. G. Beteendemassig, intrapsykisk och fysiologisk. *Svenska TA Foreningen*, 7, 1985. (Stockholm, Sweden).

Erskine, R. G. Guarire il copione: Comportamento, intrapsichico e fisiologico. *Neopsiche*, 3:6, 1985. (Milano, Italy).

Erskine, R. G. A structural analysis of ego. *Keynote Speeches: Delivered at the European Transactional Analysis Association Conference, July 1986.* Geneva: European Transactional Analysis Association, 1987.

Erskine, R. G., & Moursund, J. P. *Integrative psychotherapy in action.* Newbury Park, CA: Sage Publications. 1988.

Erskine, R. G. Cura comportamentale, intrapsichica e fisiologica del copione. *Rivista Italiana Di Analisi Transazionale E Metodologie Psicoterapeutiche,* VIII:14, 1988.

Erskine, R. G. Erkennung und Heilung Erpresserischer Suche nach Zuwendung. *Zeitschrift fur Transaktions-Analyse in Theorie und Praxis,* 6:2/3, 1989.

Erskine, R. G. Structure du moi, fonction intrapsychique et mecanismes de defense: Les concepts originels de Berne. *Actualites en Analyse Transactionnelle,* 14:53, 1990.

Erskine, R. G. Transference or transactions? Psychotherapy for couples. In B. Loria (Ed.), *Couples: Theory, treatment, and enrichment. Conference Proceedings of the Eastern Regional Transactional Analysis Association* (pp. 173-194). Madison, WI: Omnipress, 1990.

Erskine, R. Struttura dell'Io, funzioni intrapsichiche e meccanismi di difesa. *Neopsiche,* 7:11 & 12, 1989.

Trautmann, R., & Erskine, R. Analisi degli stati dell'Io: Una rassegna comparativa. *Neopsiche,* 7:11 & 12, 1989.

Erskine, R. G. Transactional analysis in family therapy. In A.M. Horne & J. L. Passmore (Eds.), *Family counseling and therapy* (2nd ed.). Itasca, Illinois: F.E. Peacock Publishers, 1991.

Erskine, R. G., & Moursund, J. P. *Kontakt, Ich-Zustande, und Lebensplan: Integrative Psychotherapy in Action* (C. Christoph-Lemke, Trans.). Paderborn: Junfermann Verlag, 1991.

Erskine, R. G. The psychotherapy of dissociation: Inquiry, attunement, and involvement. In B. Loria (Ed.), *Stamford papers: Selections from the 29th annual International Transactional Analysis Association Conference.* Madison, WI: Omnipress, 1991.

Erskine, R. G. Transfert et transactions. *Actualites en Analyse Transactionnelle,* 16:64, 1992.

Erskine, R. G., & Moursund, J. P. Tomadodel libro *Integrative Psychotherapy in Action,* Version Libre de Lulula de Quintero, Revisado por: Bernardo Aguilera. *Realat,* 15:7, pp. 71-94.

Erskine, R. G. Shame and self-righteousness. In N. L. James (Ed.), *The Minneapolis papers: Selections from the 31st Annual International Transactional Analysis Association Conference.* Madison, WI: Omnipress, 1993.

Erskine, R. G. A psicoterapia da dissociacao: Inquiricao, sintonia e envolvimento. *Revista Brasileira de Analise Transacional,* Ano II--no 1, 1993.

Erskine, R. G. Indagine, sintonia e coinvolgimento neela psicoterapia delle dissociazioni. *Neopsiche,* 11:19, 1993.

Erskine, R. G. Scham und selbstgerechtigkeit: Transaktionsanalytische sichtweisen und klinishce intervention-en. *Zeitschrift fur Transaktionsanalyse in Theorie un Praxis,* 12:1-2, 1995.

Erskine, R. G. Taxonomies, theories, and therapeutic relationships. *Transactional Analysis Journal,* 25:3, 1995.

Erskine, R. G. La honte et l'attitude 'sans reproche': Perspectives transactionelles et interventions cliniques. *Actualites en Analyse Transactionnelle,* 19:76, 1995.

Erskine, R. G. A Gestalt therapy approach to shame and self-righteousness: Theory and methods. *British Gestalt Journal,* 4:2, 1995.

Erskine, R. G., & Trautmann, R. L. El proceso de la psicoterapia integrativo. *Analisis Transaccional y Psicologia Humanista,* 35:1, 1996.

Erskine, R. G. Nachfragen (inquiry), einstimmung (attunement) und einbindung (involvement) in der psychotherapie von dissoziation. *Zeitschrift fur Transaktions Analyse in Theorie und Praxis,* 13:4, 1996.

Erskine, R. G. Trauma, dissociation and a reparative relationship. *The Australian Gestalt Journal,* 1:1, 1997.

Erskine, R. G. The therapeutic relationship: Integrating motivation and personality theories. (Accepted for publication, *Transactional Analysis Journal, 1998).*

Cassette Recordings

Erskine, R. G. (1979). *Fourth-degree impasse.* (Cassette Recording #17-80-79). New York, NY: Audio Transcripts, Ltd. Workshop given at the 17th Annual International Transactional Analysis Association Conference, Snowmass, CO, August 5-12, 1979.

Erskine, R. G. (1979). *Dynamic approach to script analysis.* (Cassette Recording #35-80-79). New York, NY: Audio Transcripts, Ltd. Workshop given at the 17th Annual International Transactional Analysis Association Conference, Snowmass, CO, August 5-12, 1979.

Erskine, R. G. (1979). *Integrative psychotherapy.* (Cassette Recording #39-80-79). New York, NY: Audio Transcripts, Ltd. Workshop given at the 17th Annual International Transactional Analysis Association Conference, Snowmass, CO, August 5-12, 1979.

Erskine, R. G. (1980). *Treatment of the controlling personality.* (Cassette Recording #6-88-80). New York, NY: Audio Transcripts, Ltd. Workshop given at the 18th Annual International Transactional Analysis Association Conference, San Francisco, CA, August, 1980.

Erskine, R. G., & Trautmann, R. L. (1980). *Life script: An evolutionary and existential perspective.* (Cassette Recording #55-88-80). New York, NY: Audio Transcripts, Ltd. Workshop given at the 18th Annual International Transactional Analysis Association Conference, San Francisco, CA, August, 1980.

Erskine, R. G. (1981). *Challenging the concepts of ego states.* (Cassette Recording #81196-121 - 81196-122). Columbia, MD: Eastern Audio Associates, Inc. (2 tapes). Workshop given at the 19th Annual International Transactional Analysis Association Conference, Boston, MA, August 12-16, 1981.

Erskine, R. G., & Trautmann, R. L. (1981). *An existential view of life scripts.* (Cassette Recording #81196-141 0 81196-142). Columbia, MD: Eastern Audio Associates, Inc. (2 tapes). Workshop given at the 19th Annual International Transactional Analysis Association Conference, Boston, MA, August 12-16, 1981.

Erskine, R. G., & Zalcman, M. (1981). *Clinical applications of the racket system.* (Cassette Recording #81196-322). Columbia, MD: Eastern Audio Associates, Inc. (2 tapes). Workshop given at the 19th Annual International Transactional Analysis Association Conference, Boston, MA, August 12-16, 1981.

Erskine, R. G. (1986). *The introjected ego: Theory and treatment.* (Cassette Recording No. 32). Simi Valley, CA: Convention Seminar Cassettes (2 tapes). Workshop given at the 24th Annual International Transactional Analysis Association Conference, San Francisco, CA, August, 1986.

Erskine, R. G. (1987). *The racket system revisited.* (Cassette Recording No. FB). Hobart, IN: Repeat Performances (2 tapes). Workshop given at the 25th Annual International Transactional Analysis Association Conference, Chicago, IL, August, 1987.

Erskine, R. G., Clarkson, P., Goulding, R., Groder, M., & Moiso, C. (1987). *Transactional analysis theory: Past, present and future.* (Cassette Recording No. RT). Hobart, IN: Repeat Performances (2 tapes). Panel presented at the 25th Annual International Transactional Analysis Association Conference,. Chicago, IL, August, 1987.

Erskine, R. G., & Trautmann, R. L. (1988). *Diagnosis and treatment of adult victims of childhood sexual abuse.* (Cassette Recording No. 86G). Hobart, IN: Repeat Performances (6 tapes). Workshop given at the Eastern Regional Transactional Analysis Conference, White Haven, PA, April, 1988.

Erskine, R. G. (1989). *A relationship therapy: Developmental perspectives.* (Cassette Recording No. C-7AB). Hobart, IN: Repeat Performances (2 tapes). Workshop given at the Eastern Regional Transactional Analysis Conference, White Haven, PA, April, 1989.

Erskine, R. G. (1990). *Transference or transactions? Psychotherapy for couples.* (Cassette Recording Nol 20A-B). Hobart, IN: Repeat Performances (2 tapes). Workshop given at the Eastern Regional Transactional Analysis Conference, White Haven, PA, April, 1990.

Erskine, R. G. (Member). (1991). *Symposium on the treatment of dissociation.* (Cassette Recording No. CE2-AB). With G. Peterson, M.D., Marye O'Reilly-Knapp, D.S.N., Charlotte Christoph-Lemke, Robert S. Mayer, Ph.D., & Shirley Spitz. Hobart, IN: Repeat Performances (2 tapes). Symposium held at the 29th Annual International Transactional Analysis Association Conference, Stamford, CT, October, 1991.

Erskine, R. G., & Trautmann, R. L. (1993). *The process of integrative psychotherapy: 1993 invitational institute.* (Cassette Recording No. 12A-F). Hobart, IN: Repeat Performances (6 tapes). Eastern Regional Transactional Analysis Association Conference, Atlantic City, NJ, May 19-23, 1993.

Erskine, R. G. (1993). *The psychotherapy of shame and self-righteousness.* (Cassette Recording CE-10AB). Hobart, IN: Repeat Performances (2 tapes). Workshop given at the 31st Annual International Transactional Analysis Association Conference, Minneapolis, MN, October 12-17, 1993.

Erskine, R. G. (1993). *Shame: A transactional analysis perspective.* (Panel Moderator). (Cassette Recording CE-8). Hobart, IN: Repeat Performances (1 tape). Panel presented at the 31st Annual International Transactional Analysis Association Conference, Minneapolis, MN, October 12-17, 1993.

Erskine, R. G. (1993). *Shame and self-righteousness in the psychotherapist.* (Cassette Recording BUB-12). Boulder, CO: Sounds True Recordings (4 tapes). 1993 Training Institute and Conference of the American Academy of Psychotherapists, Santa Fe, NM, November 3-7, 1993.

Erskine, R. G. (1993). *Roundtable discussion of Christopher Bollas's work* (Panel Moderator), with Christopher Bollas, Ph.D., Elgan Baker, Ph.D., & Lee Kyser, Ph.D. (Cassette Recording BUB-17). Boulder, CO: Sounds True Recordings (2 tapes). 1993 Training Institute and Conference of the American Academy of Psychotherapists, Santa Fe, NM, November 3-7, 1993.

Erskine, R. G. (1995). *A transactional analysis theory of methods.* (Cassette Recording KN-2). Hobart, IN. Repeat Performances (1 tape). Keynote speech delivered at the First Major International Transactional Analysis Conference, San Francisco, CA, August 7-13, 1995.

Trautmann, R. L., & Erskine, R. G. (1995). *Inquiry, attunement and involvement: The application of TA theory.* (Cassette Recording F-19AB). Hobart, IN. Repeat Performances (2 tapes). Workshop given at the First Major International Transactional Analysis Conference, San Francisco, CA, August 7-13, 1995.

Erskine, R. G. (1995). *Inquiry, attunement and involvement: Methods of Gestalt therapy.* (Cassette Recording SU8 A&B). Sylvia, NC: Goodkind of Sound (2 tapes). The First Annual International Gestalt Therapy Conference, New Orleans, LA, October 12-15, 1995.

Erskine, R. G. (1996). *Inquiry, attunement and involvement: The process of integrative psychotherapy.* (Cassette Recording DIS 26). Mullheim, Germany: BUK-Audio-Planung (2 tapes). 1st Congress of the World Council for Psychotherapy, Vienna, Austria, June 30-July 4, 1996.

Erskine, R. (1996). *Psychotherapy in the USA: A manual of standardized techniques or a therapeutic relationship?* (Cassette Recording DOK 1). Mullheim, Germany: BUK-Audio-Planung (1 tape). 1st Congress of the World Council for Psychotherapy, Vienna, Austria, June 30-July 4, 1996.

Erskine, R. G. (1996). *The psychotherapeutic relationship.* (Cassette Recording F-16 A&B). Hobart, IN. Repeat Performances (2 tapes). Workshop given at the 1996 International Transactional Analysis Association Conference, Calgary, Alberta, Canada, August 14-18, 1996.

Erskine, R. G. (1996). *Contact, relationships, and wholeness.* (Cassette Recording KN-3). Hobart, IN. Repeat Performances. Keynote address given at the 1996 International Transactional Analysis Association Conference, Calgary, Alberta, Canada, August 14-18, 1996.

Erskine, R. G. (1997). *The therapeutic relationship: Inquiry, attunement and involvement.* (Cassette Recording F-23 A&B [2 tapes]). Repeat Performances. The Association for the Advancement of Gestalt Therapy, San Francisco, CA, April 2-6, 1997.

About the International Transactional Analysis Association

Transactional analysis is a psychological and social theory with mutual contracting for growth and change. The International Transactional Analysis Association is a nonprofit organization established to stimulate the growth and development of creative and useful theory and applications of transactional analysis (TA) in psychotherapy, education, business, and other fields of human interaction.

Transactional analysis is a system of both theory and practice. The ITAA is the professional association for those persons who are certified as having demonstrated competence in treatment, counseling, teaching, or consulting using transactional analysis. The ITAA contracts an administratively separate organization, the Transactional Analysts Certification Council, to oversee a rigorous certification process.

The ITAA is dedicated to facilitating international communication among people and groups who use transactional analysis. The ITAA works to build understanding, knowledge, and acceptance of transactional analysis and to provide theoreticians and practitioners with techniques of proven value for enriching life, a forum for evolving new transactional analysis theory and methods and an ethical framework. The values of the ITAA are, in part, that "all individuals shall have the opportunity to live autonomous and socially responsible lives, that respect is given to the individuality and common humanity of all people, and that relationship shall be carried out without discrimination" (ITAA Bylaws).

After many early years of growth and development, the organization is now committed to refining theory and practice. To stimulate original scientific contributions to the development of transactional analysis, the ITAA presents an annual Eric Berne Memorial Award.

There are four levels of membership in the ITAA:
- **Associate Member:** a general interest, nonvoting level membership
- **Regular Member:** a voting-level membership for professionals who have their certification through another source or who are in the process of attaining competency-based certification in transactional analysis. This level requires completion of a TA 101 course.
- **Certified Member:** competency-based membership acquired after passage of written and oral exams. Includes specialties in clinical, educational, organizational, and counseling areas.
- **Teaching Member:** for those who have completed training and examination to become a teaching and/or supervising transactional analyst.

Benefits of membership include:
- The quarterly *Transactional Analysis Journal*
- *The Script* newsletter nine times a year
- *The ITAA International Membership Directory* with alphabetical and geographical listings of members and membership categories
- International conferences and designated (business) meeting discounts
- Many intangibles, such as international networking, committee involvement, group rates on many insurance and travel programs, and much more

For information on membership and upcoming events, please contact the ITAA at 436 14th St., Suite 1301, Oakland, CA 94612-2710, U.S.A.; phone: 510-625-7720; fax: 510-625-7725; email: itaa@itaa-net.org; or visit our web site at http://www.itaa-net.org .

Index

internalized 9, 48, 53, 77, 83, 105, 111, 112, 121, 131, 133, 152, 209

interpersonal 2, 9-11, 13, 14, 21, 22, 24, 26, 28-31, 33, 34, 37, 39, 41, 42, 47, 49, 57, 61, 63, 69, 71, 72, 74, 75, 77, 78, 82, 85, 86, 90, 91, 114, 138, 139, 141, 169, 174, 175, 182, 186, 187, 206, 217

interrelationship 80, 86, 157, 158, 164, 183, 186, 188, 228

interruption 1, 10, 15, 21-24, 26, 32, 34, 38, 40-42, 44, 47, 62, 75, 79, 81, 84, 88-91, 93, 131, 163, 192, 193, 198, 200, 224, 225

intersubjective 9, 69, 70, 82, 130

intervention 1, 3, 7-9, 15, 16, 34, 37, 39, 44, 46, 47, 56, 59, 62, 72, 77, 79, 83, 93, 119, 137, 140, 155, 162, 163, 165, 172, 173, 182, 187, 191-194, 206, 218, 220, 221, 223-225, 228

intimacy 11, 13, 16, 23, 28, 75, 84, 143, 162, 170, 189, 213, 235-237

intrapersonal 157, 174, 186, 193, 206, 217

intrapsychic 3, 7, 9, 12, 15, 16, 21-24, 29, 30, 33, 34, 39, 42, 44, 45, 47, 48, 50, 53-57, 59-62, 64, 70, 72, 76, 80, 83-85, 89, 91-93, 102, 103, 109, 110, 112-114, 129, 130, 132-144, 151-155, 157-161, 174, 183, 188, 190, 193

intrapsychic analysis 3, 57

intrapsychic conflict 23, 34, 45, 47, 53, 54, 84, 93, 132, 137-144

intrapsychic function 3, 21, 59, 60, 109, 112, 133

intrapsychic punishment 44, 92, 93

introjected 8, 51, 53-55, 57, 58, 61, 77, 83, 87, 88, 99, 102, 105, 106, 110-114, 122, 125, 133, 136, 137, 139, 141, 142, 147, 175, 177, 221

introjection 16, 23, 34, 50, 52, 53, 56, 57, 61, 77, 83, 84, 87-89, 93, 100, 106, 107, 109, 111, 112, 117, 121, 124-127, 132-134, 139, 147, 151, 176, 181, 222, 223, 225

intuition 105, 110, 111, 135, 142, 175

involvement 1, 3, 15, 16, 22, 24-26, 29, 31, 33, 34, 37, 38, 42-45, 47, 51, 56, 59, 60, 62, 63-65, 91-93, 133, 167, 190, 191, 225, 235

James 8, 100, 161, 192, 198, 236

Joines 8, 100-102, 141

Jongeward 100, 161, 192, 198, 208, 210, 236

juxtaposition 33, 34, 41, 42, 62, 90, 91

Kahler 8, 56, 102, 103, 234, 235

Karpman 8, 102, 157, 181

kinesthetic 12, 24, 26, 41, 62, 88, 90

Klein, Mavis 75

Klein, Melanie 48, 132

Kohut 9, 21, 28, 29, 50, 64, 82, 84, 109, 131, 142

Kupfer 8, 172, 229

Langs 84, 129, 131

language 12, 27, 44, 57, 63, 93, 122, 126, 137, 154, 188

Lewis, H. 48-50

life plan 14, 56, 151, 174, 181, 182

life positions 29, 48, 102, 170, 173, 211, 213, 229, 231, 235, 238, 241, 242

life script 1, 3, 7, 9, 12, 14-16, 20, 21, 56, 57, 76, 79, 83, 84, 86-89, 143, 151, 153, 166, 174, 181, 182, 219, 226

Loria 52, 77, 83, 133, 136

love 4, 31, 54, 58, 62, 112, 126, 161, 162, 172, 181, 184, 185, 200, 202, 213

Mahler 76, 82, 109, 111

maladjusted 235, 238, 239

manifestation 14, 27, 28, 30, 33, 52-54, 57, 58, 64, 73, 83-85, 99, 101, 102, 109, 110, 113, 114, 121, 124, 131-134, 137-139, 151, 152, 159, 160, 176, 177, 183

manipulation 10, 31, 33, 39, 156, 157, 182, 184

McNeel 88, 124

mechanism 1, 3, 20, 34, 46, 52, 71, 77, 79, 83, 86, 89, 93, 109, 111-114, 125, 132, 133, 136-138, 140, 164, 171, 183

mediation 103, 153, 158, 181

memories 14, 20, 22, 23, 32-34, 37-44, 50, 54, 55, 57-59, 62, 70, 76, 81, 86-93, 112, 113, 120, 126, 136, 138, 141, 151, 158, 160-164, 166, 170, 171, 175, 183, 185, 193, 194, 197, 219, 222

metaphor 24, 41, 90, 118, 123, 129, 134, 144, 192

miniscript 8, 14, 102, 234

misattunements 33, 34, 47

Moiso 116, 133, 134, 139, 141, 142

motivation 3, 7-16, 20, 40, 46, 47, 49, 53, 55, 59, 61, 62, 75, 80, 81, 99, 110, 131, 140, 142, 167, 241

Natural Child 77, 101, 102, 107, 113, 135, 147, 148, 208, 213, 229, 230

neopsyche 99, 100, 110, 118, 121, 134

neopsychic 20, 38, 40, 89, 110, 111, 113, 114, 121-124, 133, 138-141

neurological 20, 81, 124, 158

neurophysiological 122, 123

nightmares 32, 43, 44, 92

nonconscious 10, 152

nontransference 23, 84, 131, 133, 136, 137, 139

nonverbal 13, 26, 27, 29, 32, 43, 63, 64, 91, 92, 161, 180, 184

normalization 15, 16, 25, 27, 29-33, 37, 42-44, 61, 63, 64, 88, 91, 92

not-OK 48, 102, 103, 170, 172, 173, 211, 229, 231, 235, 238, 241

Novellino 133, 143

nuclear war 3, 166, 167

nurturing 9, 34, 38, 40, 45, 54, 75, 93, 102, 112, 120, 121, 126, 127, 142, 176

Nurturing Parent 101-103, 107, 126, 127, 135, 208, 230

obsessive 14, 55, 56, 166

Oedipal 75, 109

OK 14, 27, 29, 48, 58, 59, 72, 102, 103, 170, 172,